Neva Dunn

LIBRARY OF LATIN AMERICAN
HISTORY AND CULTURE
GENERAL EDITOR:
DR. A. CURTIS WILGUS

INDIANS OF THE ANDES

INDIANS OF THE ANDES

AYMARAS AND QUECHUAS

by

HAROLD OSBORNE

New York
COOPER SQUARE PUBLISHERS, INC.
1973

Copyright 1952 by Harold Osborne
Reprinted by permission of Harold Osborne
Published 1973 by Cooper Square Publishers, Inc.
59 Fourth Avenue, New York, New York 10003
International Standard Book Number 0-8154-0448-4
Library of Congress Catalog Card Number 72-92122

Printed in the United States of America

*To friends
in Bolivia and Peru*

CONTENTS

INTRODUCTION	*page* xi
I. DARKEST ORIGINS	1
II. VANDALS OF HISTORY	15
III. MYTH AND ARCHAEOLOGY	42
IV. THE INCA IN LEGEND AND HISTORY	80
V. UNDER INCA RULE	115
VI. UNDER SPANISH RULE	157
VII. THE INDIAN TODAY AND TOMORROW	201
BIBLIOGRAPHY	252
INDEX	260

ILLUSTRATIONS
(at the End of the Book)

1. Portrait vase from Tihuanacu (black on red). Height 4¼ inches. (The bulge in the right cheek represents the coca quid)
2. Whistling jar, Chimu (black). Height 7¼ inches
3. Portrait jar from Chancay (red and black on white). Height 12 inches
4. Whistling jar, Chimu (black). Height 7¼ inches
5. Zoomorphic jar, Chimu (black monochrome), representing head of the Badaño, a local deer. Height 7 inches
6. Terracotta figure, Chimu (red and black on white). Height 9½ inches
7. Water jar, Chicama Valley (Mochica) (red on white). Height 10 inches
8. Terracotta figure, Chancay (black on white). Height 8¼ inches
9. Modern Indian terracotta from Southern Peru. Height 4¼ inches
10. Modern Indian terracotta from Southern Peru. Height 4½ inches
    (The above are all from the author's collection)
11. Stone of Worship in the Temple to the Sun near the top of the Fortress of Ollantaytambo. The five monoliths of red porphyry from which this altar is constructed were quarried high in the hills across the valley and measure from 3.10 metres to 4.27 metres in height, 1.35 metres to 2.28 metres in width and 1.30 to 1.88 metres in depth
12. Prehistoric Perron at Tihuanacu. The seven steps are each cut from a single block of stone, except the top two, which are from one block
13. Quechua Indians in the Plaza at Pisac near Cuzco

14. A part of the Ruins of Machu Picchu
15. An Encampment of the Fabulosa Mines, Ltd, at the foot of Huaynu Potosi
16. Over life-size carving from the Early Period of Tihuanacu. Now in the Open-air Museum at Miraflores, La Paz
17 (*a*) and 17 (*b*). A curiously cut stone in an embrasure at Machu Picchu
18. Altiplano Landscape. Indians with Llamas
19. Plaza of the modern village of Tihuanacu
20. Coca Plantations in the Yungas
21. Cachi or drying-floor for coca
22. Indian Quarter of La Paz
23. Llamas in La Paz
24. Aymara types
25. Aymara Chola
26. Cholo Children
27. Chola Street-vendor in La Paz
28. Bolivian Cholo
29. Aymara Indian showing hair-style and Aguayo
30. Urubamba Valley. The Sacred Valley of the Incas

MAPS

Peru   *page* ix
Bolivia   x

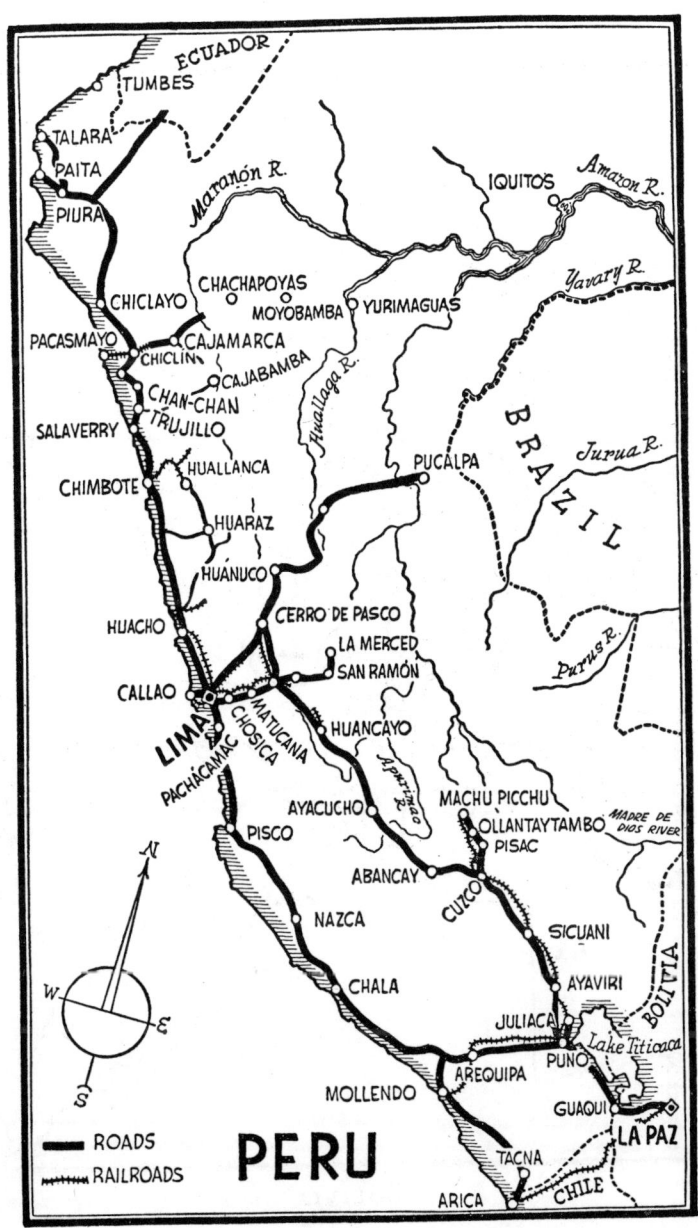

BOLIVIA

INTRODUCTION

THE very name 'Indians' had no other justification than the famous blunder of Columbus. Its continued use had a twofold disadvantage. It encouraged the tendency to lump all the peoples of the New World together as 'backward' races and favoured the tendency of the Conquistadores to adopt the same attitude of superiority towards the peoples who had built the great civilizations of Mexico and Peru as they took up to the savage tribes of the jungle. And it has encouraged the quite false supposition that all the peoples of the Americas are united by links of conscious kinship.

This book is written about the highland peoples of the Central Andes, who formed the nucleus of that great Inca Empire which extended for two thousand miles along the Pacific coast over the mountains to the fringes of the tropical interior.

When Pizarro's small band of adventurers crashed in upon them, the peoples of the Central Andes were living through a Bronze Age culture and enjoyed a civilization which, although less advanced in technology than Europe, was in human quality equal and perhaps superior to any civilization, except the Chinese, which had been developed in the Old World up to that time.

They had had no cultural contacts with the Old World for twenty millenia and were without the knowledge of iron, glass, the plough, the wheel, writing, money, and those domestic animals and plants, with the exception of cotton, which had achieved the greatest economic importance in the Old World. They had already passed independently through stages of development usually associated in the Old World with the Neolithic Age. Before discovering bronze metallurgy they had used polished knapped flint weapons and tools; they had learnt to domesticate their own plants, in particular maize, quinoa, cañahua, coca, cotton and the potato; they had learnt to domesticate animals, in particular the llama, the alpaca and the guinea pig; they had passed through a stage of megalithic construction; they had discovered how to make pottery and to weave cloth and in both they had achieved a degree of technical and artistic excellence which could not be anywhere surpassed in the Old World; they had a long history of religious beliefs and funerary cults. Finally, in their Bronze Age they evolved in perhaps the most perfect form which is known to have existed anywhere in the world the institution of divine Kingship combined with the worship of the Sun, which since W. J. Perry's *The Children of the Sun* has been regarded as typical for the emergence of a settled 'food producing' community after having left behind the 'food gathering' stage.

Since the influx of European civilization with the Spanish conquest, the native peoples have isolated themselves so far as has been permitted to them from this civilization. They were living in their Bronze Age when Pizarro burst disastrously upon them and today they are still living to all intents and purposes in an Age of Bronze. For by 'Bronze Age' anthropologists mean a specific way of life and culture which has usually characterized periods of human history which coincided with the use of bronze. It is this way of life which has survived in the midst of a civilization alien and unfavourable to it. The higher levels of the social organization moulded by the Incas were destroyed, but the lower levels have been kept. The native peoples have been taught to worship in the creed of Christ, but they have made of Christianity a religion to suit their own temperament and traditions. They have appropriated much from the European—among domesticated plants many of the commoner cereals, fruits and vegetables, but maize, quinoa and the potato remain their staples; among domesticated animals, the horse, donkey and mule, cattle and sheep, pigs, goats, poultry, but they are still most at home with the llama. They have found little use for the wheel and to this day do not make for themselves wheeled carts. Except where they are in enforced contact with the whites, in the immediate vicinity of the towns, they have retained their Bronze Age culture essentially unchanged. And this is not for lack of ability. The Indian of the Andean uplands can understand the internal combustion engine, can operate and service mining machinery and can learn the principles of Trade Unionism. They have retained their ancient way of life by positive opposition to the 'higher' way that was offered. There is nowhere else in the world where a Bronze Age culture has survived so pertinaciously side by side with a more advanced civilization, with such firm repudiation of weakening influences and so few signs of racial perdition.

INTRODUCTION

In four centuries of contact there has of course been appreciable acculturation and osmosis. But except in the vicinity of the large centres of population it has had little effect on essentials. And through the creation of a virile and growing *mestizo* class, the influence of the Indians upon their countries has been greater than the influence of the white man's civilization upon them.

It is the purpose of the following pages to trace the history and ecology of these peoples, the Aymaras and the Quechuas, so far as can be known or conjectured from the scanty evidences which survive.

INDIANS OF THE ANDES

Chapter One

DARKEST ORIGINS

SPECULATION about the origin of human beings in America has been ebullient ever since America was discovered, and has hardly yet sobered into science.

In an age for which the legends of the Old Testament were inspired history, and deviation from them condemned as heresy, the discovery of races of men in the New World raised a theological rather than a scientific problem—or at any rate a scientific problem which had to be settled within an established theological framework. The naive speculations of the early years were inevitably committed to the traditional Biblical world-picture and had to find a place for the native peoples of America within that picture. Thus within a few years of the discovery Arias Montanus of the *Biblia Poliglota* (1569-73) propounded the theory that the American populations were descended from Shem, son of Noah, after the Biblical deluge. Early in the seventeenth century appeared an alternative view that some of the tribes of Israel, dispersed by the Assyrians, had found a refuge and a new home in the New World. Many other speculations followed, involving the Phoenicians, the Chinese and the people of the lost continent of Atlantis. While these wild and groping guesses are today no more than a curiosity of history, the attitude of mind which they represent was antipathetic to the preservation of the native legends and memories. For the Indians had their own legends of their origins and their own stories of a flood. But in so much as these were necessarily in conflict with Biblical 'truth', they were contemptuously rejected by the chroniclers as pernicious follies of the infidel and wicked deceits of the devil. Thus a wealth of material which might have been of inestimable value to the modern student was irretrievably lost. After solemnly showing that Peru was originally peopled from Plato's Island of Atlantis—which itself had been populated by descendants of the eight persons who were saved from the Flood in Noah's ark—Sarmiento dismisses the local legends with lofty and righteous contempt. 'As these barbarous nations of Indians were always without letters, they had not the means of preserving the monuments and memorials of their times, and those of their predecessors, with accuracy and method. As the devil, who is always striving to injure the human race, found these unfortunates to be easy of belief and timid in obedience, he introduced many illusions, lies and frauds, giving them to understand that he had created them from the first, and afterwards, owing to their sins and evil deeds, he had destroyed them with a flood, again creating them and giving them food and the way to preserve it. By chance, they formerly had some notice, passed down to them from mouth to mouth, which had reached them from their ancestors, respecting the truth of what happened in former times. Mixing this with the stories told them by the devil, and with other things which they changed, invented, or added, which may happen in all nations, they made up a pleasing salad, and in some things worthy of the attention of the curious who are accustomed to consider and discuss human ideas. One thing must be noted among many others. It is that the stories which are here treated as fables, which they are, are held by the natives to be as true as we hold the articles of our faith, and as such they affirm and confirm them with unanimity, and swear by them.' And Sarmiento was more broadminded and more curious than most.

While the stories of the Creation and the Flood were dogmatically believed, and their dates had been calculated for the years 4004 B.C. and 1990 B.C., the site of the Garden of Eden was not considered to have been finally established in orthodox belief. Therefore it is not surprising that some early speculators, regarded as cranks in their age but not technically heretical, should have hit on the idea of placing the Creation and the Garden of Eden in the New World and of maintaining that mankind had spread to the Old World from the New. The first to formulate a 'nativist' view of this type was Antonio de Leon Pinelo, a Spaniard who settled in the Province of Charcas, which is now Bolivia. His book, *El Paraiso en el Nuevo Mundo*, was recently published in Lima after remaining three centuries in manuscript. In it he asserts that the Earthly Paradise and the Creation according to *Genesis* were situated in the then little known east of Bolivia and that the rest of the world was populated by migrations from there. A similar view was put forward a century ago by the Bolivian enthusiast and polymath, Emeterio Villamil de Rada, who in a book entitled *La Lengua de Adan* tried to prove on etymological grounds that Aymara was the original language of mankind from which all other tongues derived. He thought that the human race had originated in Sorata, a canton at the foot of Mount Illampu in the eastern Cordillera of the Bolivian Andes. The first scientific defence of the view that mankind originated in South America came from the Argentine paleontologist Florentino Ameghino in 1880, who published his conclusions in *La Antigüedad del Hombre en el Plata*, utilizing observations of the Danish scientist P. W. Lund in Brazil and his own explorations in the Argentine pampas. The belief that human beings were autochthonous in South America, without going so far as to claim that they were the original progenitors of all mankind, has found considerable support among modern South American archaeologists, not uninfluenced by a nascent nationalism. It has been recently claimed by the Bolivian writers Leo Pucher, Frederico Avila and others that human remains and cave drawings found at Tarija in southern Bolivia in conjunction with remains of the mastodon, the megatherium and the glyptodont prove the existence of men in the Tertiary epoch. While these extreme claims have not yet been confirmed, it is generally agreed that humanity existed in South America before the extinction of the mastodon, the giant sloth, the horse and other animals characteristic of the Tertiary epoch. But it is now thought that such essentially Tertiary species survived in South America, as in Australia, much later than in the rest of the world, so that the discovery of archaeological remains in association with them is not regarded as evidence of the great antiquity of man in South America.

Therefore the majority of anthropologists have inevitably inclined to an immigration theory of human origins in South America, since it would be surprising to say the least if it were proved that *homo sapiens* evolved twice in the world's history. But there has been little consistency among immigration theories. The peoples of South America have been held to have come from Europe, Africa or Asia, from the lost continents of Atlantis or Oceania, down from the north after crossing the Behring Straits or over the sea from the Pacific Islands.

The Bolivian scholar Belisario Diaz Romero has built up a fanciful picture of a composite immigration type. He holds that the first men on the South American continent were of negroid type, who arrived from Senegambia in the Quaternary epoch when South America and Africa were linked by the lost continent of

Brasilia. Some 120 centuries later a blancoid race of the Cromagnonian type reached the east coasts, spread along the west coast by the Isthmus of Panama, occupied the Altiplano, which was then a temperate and fertile plain some 300 metres above sea level, and built an empire with its centre at Tihuanacu. These blancoid immigrants originated in the lost continent of Atlantis, baptizing the Andes with their own name, *Antis*, and brought with them the first germs of civilization to the continent. Their civilization was destroyed by extensive floods at the end of the Glacial epoch some 6,000 years ago, and new immigrants of Arian Asiatic type forced them from the Altiplano into the jungles of eastern Bolivia and Brazil, where they mingled with the descendants of the original negroid immigrants to form the Guarani and Camba races. The new immigrants, called Kollas, built in their turn a civilization with its centre also Tihuanacu, until some three thousand years later they were ousted by a mongoloid immigration, from whose mingling with them originated the modern Aymaran and Quechuan peoples. While such pretty schematizations have a certain charm to the imagination, they lack scientific basis, and our knowledge of human origins in South America is far too indefinite to warrant anything so elaborate. The tendency of modern research is, however, to regard the multitude of racial and linguistic groups scattered throughout South America as variations from one main racial type rather than the result of minglings of several racial stocks.

The view that has become orthodox among contemporary anthropologists supposes that the present peoples of America all originated from the immigration of a predominantly mongoloid stock in a series of waves, but not in great numbers, across the Behring Straits from Siberia into Alaska towards the end of the Ice Age. In the *Geographical Review*, vol. 25 (1935), E. Antevs concludes: 'The first man to arrive in North America was of modern type and probably at the Neolithic stage of culture. He came from north-eastern Asia to Alaska and probably spread along the eastern foot of the Rocky Mountains where an ice-free corridor had formed some 20,000 to 15,000 years ago. He seems to have reached the south-west at the age of transition between the Pluvial and the post-Pluvial epochs, or roughly 12,000 years ago.' Jacobs and Stern say somewhat more definitely in their *Outline of Anthropology* (1947): 'The American Indians are therefore only the numerous and slightly specialized descendants of an

DARKEST ORIGINS 5

original handful of Paleasiatic Mongoloid immigrants, mixed perhaps with some Ainu and Caucasoid, who crossed from Siberia into western Alaska by way of the Behring Straits over twenty thousand years ago and migrated throughout the New World after about 18000 B.C. No other peoples migrated to America by trans-oceanic canoes or other means of entry until the recent coming of the Europeans.' This view has several surprising features. It necessitates a very rapid spread of human beings over the whole of North and South America, adaptation to widely different conditions of climate and environment ranging from the arctic to the tropical, the rapid differentiation of very many distinct local types and cultures and makes very difficult an explanation of the large number of apparently unrelated linguistic groups. It also seems surprising that once immigration across the Behring Straits had taken place in sufficient bulk and variety to account for all the many different racial and linguistic groups of North and South America, contact between the Old and the New Worlds should so completely have ceased.

While it is accepted that, for whatever reasons, after the main immigration across the Behring Straits had taken place, there was no further extensive racial infiltration from the Old World, most authorities agree that there were contacts by sea from very early times between the Pacific Islands, probably Melanesia, and America. In *Origin of the Indian Civilizations in South America* (1931) Erland Nordenskiöld gives a list of some fifty striking similarities between Oceanic and South American ethnological characteristics and N. C. Nelson says, 'It is a demonstrable fact that more than two hundred varieties of implements and ornaments found in the New World are duplicates of Old World forms.' These contacts seem, however, to have been sporadic and not to have involved the movement of great numbers of people. While they brought technological, cultural and social influences, there was apparently no interchange of basic agricultural products and the Oceanic Islanders did not influence the South American physical or linguistic types. The view that the Chinese reached South America directly is numbered among the very early immigration theories and is stated by Diego Andres Rocha in *Tratado Unico y Singular del Origen de los Indios del Perú* (1681) and Fray Gregorio Garcia in *Origen de los Indios del Nuevo Mundo* (1729). It has been revived recently by Francisco A. Loayza in *Chinos Llegaron antes que Colon* (1948), who undertakes a detailed examination of supposed Chinese influences in early Peruvian decorative designs, place names and social institutions. His arguments have not, however, been accorded general acceptance. Arturo Poznansky, known for his investigations at Tihuanacu, has stated his belief that small immigrations from the Chinese Empire took place by sea in the distant past, and mentions an Indian village named Aten in the Bolivian northern Province of Caupolican, whose inhabitants are said to speak a language comprehensible by the Chinese. He also suggests, as has been suggested before, that the Inca dynasty may have originated from such an immigration of a few persons from China, who in virtue of their more advanced civilization were able to impose themselves as rulers upon the rank and file of the undeveloped natives of Peru. While this speculation cannot be ruled out as impossible, the main argument advanced in its support is removed when it is realized that the Inca regime represented a great advance in political and military organization but no notable advance on the technical and cultural civilization which had already been reached in Peru. There is also a curious tradition surviving in Inca history that one of the Incas made a great naval expedition westwards to unidentified territory in the Pacific. It seems highly unlikely that the Incas, who were not a seagoing people, could have realized such a feat, but the existence of the tradition may be contributory evidence that some knowledge of the Pacific Islands existed among the pre-Columban peoples of Peru.[1]

Civilization, with a settled agricultural subsistence pattern, was developed in South America first on the Central Andean highlands, which now fall within the territories of Bolivia and Peru. It is thought that this region was first visited by nomadic hunters of the Palaeo-American type such as are known to have occupied southern Patagonia, but positive evidence of their passing is still to be found. Our present archaeological material in the Central Andean region, which seems to go back to a period roughly

[1] Sarmiento tells the curious story that in his expedition against the coast of Manta, the island of Puna and Tumbez, Topa Inca Yupanqui encountered certain merchants who had come over the western sea in boats and who told of two wealthy and populous islands, Ayachumbi and Ninachumbi, whence they came. After verifying their story by means of a magician, Topa Inca manned a large expedition of 20,000 men, sailed to the islands and returned with black people, much gold, a chair of brass, and the skin and jawbone of a horse. The horse's skin and jawbone were said to be still in the possession of the Inca noble who told Sarmiento the story.

DARKEST ORIGINS

coinciding with the beginning of the Christian era, indicates that an advanced stage of culture had already been attained throughout the highland region and the coastal area of Peru. Agriculture had long passed the exploitation stage. Domestication of plants and animals lay well in the past. Complicated agricultural techniques had been perfected. The protection of soil from erosion, irrigation, the use of fertilizers and crop rotation were practised. Pottery, weaving, stone carving and building, metallurgy and a number of minor crafts had reached a high level of technical and artistic achievement. There is evidence of developed religious and burial practices, of political organization and trade. All the domesticated plants and animals and all the basic techniques of craftsmanship were already used at the dawn of the period of which we have archaeological knowledge and no important additions were made until the Spanish invasion brought with it the influences of European civilization. There is no archaeological material from a pre-horticultural or pre-ceramic period in the Central Andes. Archaeologically we begin with a culture fully grown.

These facts support the view that the transition from a food-gathering to a food-producing culture occurred first in Central Mexico and that the peoples who carried the banner of civilization in South America may have come down to the region of the Central Andes from Central America after agricultural culture had already been developed there. But of course this supposition does not preclude the likelihood that many characteristic plants and animals were first domesticated, and many techniques first evolved, in the Central Andean highlands. It is thought that maize, the great American staple, may have been first domesticated in the Central Andes, though some authorities think Central America is a more probable region of origin. It is almost certain that the potato and oca were first cultivated in the highlands of the Central Andes and mandioca possibly in the warmer valleys of the same region.

About as many plants were domesticated in the New World as in the Old, although the lists are very different. From the beginning of the period of which we have direct archaeological evidence in the Central Andes the following cereals, vegetables and fruits were known and no important additions were made before the European conquest: maize, quinoa, cañahua, potatoes, oca, mandioca, sweet potatoes, beans, pumpkin, groundnuts, aji (chilli peppers), lupines, yacon, mashua, ulluco, jiquima, achira, cacao, tomato; pineapple, melon, alligator-pear, papaw, tumbo, cucumber, lucuma, tuma (opuntia), algarrobo (carob), chirimoya (custard apple), and guanaba (sour-sop). Cotton was cultivated in the coastal valleys. Coca was cultivated as a stimulant and tobacco for use medicinally and perhaps as snuff. Of domesticated animals the dog had been introduced from the Old World with the Neolithic migration across the Behring Straits; the guinea pig and two types of the guanaco, an animal autochthonous to the Andes between sheep and camel, were domesticated locally. The latter were the alpaca and the llama, which remain the most important of domestic animals to the native peoples of the region to this day.

The length of time which was necessary to develop so elaborate an agricultural civilization is very difficult to estimate comparatively, particularly as the New World culture seems to have been in the main oriental and conservative in type rather than progressive. But when it is considered that of the potato alone 240 different types had been evolved on the Altiplano together with complicated techniques for their preservation by dehydration, and that advances in several other fields were hardly less complex, the development period must have lasted many centuries and perhaps some millenia before the Christian era. The fact that with the exception of cotton and the bean no important Old World crops were produced in the New World, together with the fact that such important inventions as glass, the plough and the wheel were unknown in the New World, is a striking proof that there can have been no important cultural contacts between the Old World and the New during the whole of this long period of development with the possible exception of sporadic visits of small bodies of immigrants from the Pacific Islands by outrigger canoe.

It is a very remarkable thing that without direct contacts the development of the human race in the Old World and the New ran so remarkably parallel in agricultural discoveries, inventions and techniques of craftsmanship and industry and even in social organization and religious and funerary practices. The importance of these striking similarities in the development of the two branches of the human race from Neolithic times onwards, without major contacts for some twenty millenia, and their significance for comparative anthropology and the understanding of

DARKEST ORIGINS

the emergence of culture and the development of civilization among mankind, has seldom been adequately recognized.

Of the many closely related racial groups which populated the Central Andean highlands and the coastal valleys of Peru during the millenium or so before the Conquest, the Quechuas and the Aymaras are the most important. These two peoples are racially distinct; neither was an off-shoot from the other and there are strong reasons for believing that they did not originate by variation from a common stock inhabiting the Altiplano. There is no very satisfactory evidence that either one or the other was of greater antiquity in the Central Andes. Archaeological evidence shows such continuity of development from the time when it starts about the beginning of the era until the fall of the Inca Empire as would seem to preclude any massive invasion from outside the region during this period.

The theory of a *Kolla* civilization on the Altiplano before the Aymaras and Quechuas is of recent origin and has been interpreted according to nationalistic prejudices, in Bolivia with the hope to establish the greater antiquity of the Aymaras and in Peru consistently with the greater importance there assigned to the Quechuas. The word 'Kolla' first appears in history as the name of one of the topographical sections into which the Aymara people was divided when the Incas first pushed their military conquests south of Vilcanota on to what is now the Bolivian Altiplano. For reasons which are not known the Incas gave the name *Kollasuyu* to the whole of the Altiplano under their dominion, the southern of the four areas or *suyus* into which their empire was divided. The Spanish followed their example, abbreviating *Kollasuyu* to *Kollao*. The word *Kolla* has been adopted into South American Spanish as a local idiom and is today used quite generally of people who live on the heights in distinction from those who live on the plains. In eastern Bolivia the inhabitants of La Paz and the other towns of the Altiplano, whites and natives alike, are referred to somewhat disparagingly as 'Kollas'.

Indeed any theory that the Aymaras and Quechuas had a common origin from a stock originally inhabiting the Altiplano has to confront very serious difficulties. Although their way of life is in many respects very similar, as both are agricultural peoples inhabiting the lofty plateaux and high valleys of the Andes, the really remarkable thing is the extent to which the two races have remained distinct through many centuries of close contact with each other and of subjection to the same conditions of economic depression under the Spanish rule. The Quechuas and Aymaras have been united under one political organization since the Incas pushed their conquests on to the Bolivian Altiplano, and even before then there was ancient limitrophe contact around Lake Titicaca. Yet they have retained their racial distinctness, their distinct physical and psychological characteristics, their differences of language, dress and agriculture. In the *pueblo* of Mocomoco, in the Bolivian province of Camacho, east and north of the lake, to take only one example of many, one half of the village is Aymara and the other half Quechua with a sharp division between the two. Admixture of the two races with the Spanish to produce a new mestizo race seems to have gone very much further than any racial admixture between the Aymaras and the Quechuas. They have kept surprisingly distinct from each other. The two languages are not mutually comprehensible and when the two peoples are living in close contact the Quechuas, who tend to be mentally quicker and more adaptable, generally learn Aymara in addition to their own language, while the Aymaras seldom speak or understand Quechua. Although both languages are agglutinous in type, they differ profoundly in grammatical structure and vocabulary. Their phonetic is similar but not identical. About 30 per cent of the vocabulary is now common to Aymara and Quechua and some fundamental words are common to both languages, but in general the fundamental vocabulary is quite distinct. They are distinct languages of a common linguistic group, not dialects of one language. In general the Quechuas inhabit the northern plateaux, those which form part of what is now the territory of Peru, and the Aymaras the bleaker and more arid Bolivian plateau, with considerable interpenetration round the lake. There are pockets of Quechuas in the south of the Bolivian plateau in the Department of Oruro and around Cochabamba, Potosi and Sucre, which almost certainly owe their origin to the Inca policy, similar to that of the ancient Assyrians, of establishing artificial settlements of the milder and 'civilizing' race amidst the territory of the rougher and more bellicose newly conquered peoples, in order that the former might help in the peaceful administration of the latter.

The view that the Aymaras were of very great antiquity on the Andean highlands, the founders of the primordial civilization of

DARKEST ORIGINS

Tihuanacu, and the Quechuas more recent arrivals, has been supported mainly in Bolivia for patriotic reasons. It will be found in most Bolivian writers of the last fifty years. The present tendency in scientific archaeology, however, is to date Tihuanacu very much later than used to be supposed and there also seems to be some reason for doubting whether the people we know as the Aymaras were identical with those responsible for the Tihuanacu culture. While it is beyond doubt that the Aymaras formerly extended over much wider territory than they now occupy, it is less than certain that they were ever a 'dominant' race in the Central Andean region in the same sense that the Quechuas became a dominant race under the Incas. Besides the very debatable argument from their supposed association with Tihuanacu, belief in the great antiquity of the Aymaras depends partly on the alleged negative evidence that there are no signs of an earlier race on the Altiplano and partly on the fact that when the Spanish first came into contact with them the Aymaras appeared to have no recollection of an earlier race and when questioned about their origins spoke of the origins of the world.

There are, however, still surviving in remote regions of the Altiplano the last remnants of an earlier people, the Urus and the Chipayas, now reduced to a few small groups of families. Their language, Puquina, has nothing in common with Aymara or Quechua but is thought by some authorities to be akin to Arawak. They live by the lakes and rivers, devote themselves primarily to hunting and fishing, and are little given to agriculture. It is often thought that they migrated to the Altiplano in the remote past from the tropical Amazon basin, perhaps owing to widespread flooding of that region, and were later dispossessed by the Aymaras. At one time they occupied a far more extensive area of the Altiplano and may have extended to the coastal regions. They refused to amalgamate with the invading Aymaras and retired under pressure to remote and out-of-the-way regions. At the dawn of written history they bear all the marks of a primitive and oppressed people, and are said to be 'looked down upon by everyone and of very low intelligence,' although Puquina was still called a '*lengua general*' of Peru by sixteenth-century writers. In his *Historia natural y moral de las Indias*, Father José Acosta says of them: 'These Urus be such dull and brutish people, as they esteeme not themselves men. It is reported of them, that being demanded of what nation they were, they answered, they were not men, but Uros, as it were some kinde of Beastes. (They were more probably, however—*pace* Father Acosta—distinguishing themselves from the Aymaras, who never called themselves "Aymaras," but *haqe* or "men.") There are whole villages of these Uros inhabiting in the Lake in their boates of *totora*, the which are tied together and fastened to some rocke, and often times the whole village changeth from place to place. So, as hee that would seeke them now whereas they were yesterday, shall finde no shew nor remainder of them, or of their village.' In a curious report written in 1688 to the Viceroy by the Chief Justice of Challacollo, he says that the shores and islands of Lake Poopo were inhabited by 'many Uru Indians, an unruly race and mightily given to idleness and ever shunning contact with the Spanish.' Modern writers have described them as being of low intelligence, suspicious, brutal and avaricious and the ethnologist Weston La Barre characterizes them as 'an inhospitable, apathetic and hate-filled group which has been condemned and harassed throughout its history.' I found in them a stolid reserve extremely difficult to pierce or interest. Once perhaps the lords of the land, they are now reduced to a very few groups of families, the Urus around the southern shores of Lake Titicaca and the upper reaches of the river Desaguadero and the Chipayas in the Bolivian Province of Carangas around Lake Poopo, both doomed to rapid extinction. Their name survives in the mining town of Oruro, a corruption of 'Uru-Uru'—as it were, 'Much Uru.' And many place-names on the Altiplano—such as Llacsa, where La Paz was first founded —derived from the Puquina language bear witness to the time when the Urus were once widely disseminated on the highlands. Such tradition as survives agrees with the evidence of their culture that they were earlier on the Altiplano than the Aymaras. Whereas other Indian groups claim to be the children of the Sun, the Uru tradition says that they are the oldest people in the world, ante-dating the sun. What they were in their prime it is possible only to guess. They now bear all the signs of degeneration characteristic of a dispossessed and despised relic, refusing to amalgamate or adapt and incapable to resist. A stubborn insistence on independence without the ferocity to support it has left a sorry and pathetic picture of human degradation. Nor is it entirely fanciful to trace some analogy between the history of the Urus under the Aymaras and the history of the Aymaras under the Europeans.

DARKEST ORIGINS

The Aymaras are a people without a history. Their very name does not belong to them but was applied to them in error. We now use the name of Aymara for the whole group of peoples who inhabit the lacustrine basin and the Bolivian Altiplano, speaking a common language. These people have never called themselves Aymaras but either collectively *Haqe*, or 'men', or by the names of the various territorial groups into which they were organized. The *Aymaraes* were originally a people of the Quechua group established about a hundred miles north of Cuzco; at some time after their incorporation into the Inca empire a colony, or *mitmac*, of these Aymaras was settled by the southern shores of the lake. Much later, when the Jesuits began their missionary work at Juli, they came across some of these old colonists of the Aymaraes and quite mistakenly transferred their name to all the peoples of the southern shores of the lake and the Altiplano whom we now call Aymaras.

Aymara mythology knows no other origin than their creation by the supreme god Virajocha at the time of the creation of the Sun from Lake Titicaca and they have no legendary memory of a migration from elsewhere to the Altiplano. If they were the builders of Tihuanacu and the founders of the Tihuanacan culture which spread widely over Peru and south into the northern Argentine, they have no memory of this past greatness. When Cieza de León visited Tihuanacu in 1548 the Aymaras living there did not know by whom the ruins had been constructed but regarded their origin as miraculous and the modern Aymaras do not associate Tihuanacu with the past history of their race.

The Quechuas seem to have a more definite history as identified with that of the Inca Empire. But their origin is equally obscure. We do not know whether they immigrated with the Incas and dominated the earlier inhabitants of the land, and if so whence they came, or whether they were themselves prior to the Incas who as a small dominating race imposed themselves as their rulers. The Aymaras and the Quechuas are, however, closely akin, not identical and not divergent from a common stock within the Andean highlands. It therefore seems probable that they belong to closely related immigrant groups and that they probably reached the Andean highlands at roughly the same period. The continuity of the archaeological evidence in Peru renders it unlikely that either Aymaras or Quechuas immigrated in large numbers after the maturing of civilization on the Altiplano. The

Urus and related types preceded them. They were men of the lakes and rivers; not nomads, though they subsisted mainly by fishing and hunting. They probably represent a stage of development between the 'food gathering' and the 'food producing' stage. The origin of agricultural civilization in the Central Andean region is probably due to the Aymaras and the Quechuas, although the people now known as Quechuas are an intermingling of a number of related racial and linguistic groups which were distinct in Peru until the unification due to the expansion of the Inca Empire. It seems probable that before Inca times the Quechuas were only one of a large number of racial groups inhabiting the Peruvian highlands. If so, the stimulus to the sudden creation of the greatest empire which had been known in the New World may have come to them from outside, although there is still no positive evidence that this was so.

Chapter Two

VANDALS OF HISTORY

THE Spanish occupation of the New World brought with it a violent opposition between principle and practice. The first conquerors of Peru were led by the lure of gold through hardship and endurance beyond measure into the unknown, where dangers awaited them which only that ranting, adventurous, religious age could have surmounted with success. Their goal achieved, a riot of wanton destructiveness was followed by a long period of wasteful exploitation. These men understood no duty to preserve the achievements of an alien people. Wonders of wrought silver and gold aroused their admiration and were melted down for the value of the metal. Buildings whose grandeur aroused the astonishment of the crudest soldier were used as quarries for stone. Then as the first thrust of conquest gave way to the business of colonial organization, it was judged wise to remove from the minds of the subjected natives the cherished memories of their past greatness by destroying everything which might serve as a reminder of the glories of Inca days. Destruction became more systematic. Soon followed the serious crusade to carry the cross to the infidel and in the name of Christianity all that seemed symbolic of an alien religion was destroyed. And in an empire organized on the principle of divine kingship there was very little of artistic or historical value which had not some religious significance. Destruction now became a purposeful crusade. In his record of the *Extirpación de la Idolatría del Perú*, printed in Lima in 1621, Father José de Arriaga says: 'Whatever can be burned is burned immediately, the rest is broken.'

The Conquistadores, with the qualities and the limitations of militant adventurers, smashed what they feared and seized what they desired. But the riot of destructiveness, in which the lust for gold and domination caused the economic enslavement of peoples previously organized in a stable social structure and the glory of proselytism the rape of an alien culture, did not proceed without searchings of the national conscience. The Spanish of the sixteenth century derived from their own historical background an eminent addiction to legalism and religiosity. From the beginning of their adventure in the New World the rights of the conquered natives to their liberty and their possessions were debated and the question of their natural right to be considered as human beings was decided in their favour by the Congregation of Valladolid under the combined influences of Francisco Vitoria and Bartolomé de Las Casas. On this basis, and because the Spanish Crown saw that a too ruthless exploitation was in danger of becoming wasteful and uneconomic for the future value of the Colony, a legal system of colonial administration was drawn up which has been rightly pointed to as both enlightened and moderate. The interests of the men on the spot were, however, not by any means on all fours with the interests of the Crown and the get-rich-quick policy of the former had more practical influence than the wiser policy of long-term exploitation which governed the Council of the Indies. As is not uncommon in the history of human affairs, principle and practice remained at variance and despite repeated royal ordinances designed to prevent the enslavement and subsequent annihilation of the native races, their exploitation followed as ruthlessly from economic convenience as though their rights had not been ventilated in principle. This is why a good case can be put up both by historians like Salvador de Madariaga who defend the enlightened moderation of the Spanish colonial system and by those who condemn the destructive oppressiveness of their regime.

But the national, and indeed the European, conscience was awakened. And when conscience has become sensitive and practice is persistently in opposition to the principles approved of conscience, it is found necessary to justify practice by distortion. And in this case a contemporary legend was built up representing the peoples of Peru as barbarous, bestial, uncivilized, idolatrous and inherently vicious; the Inca regime was pictured as unrelieved and oppressive tyranny without legal justification and the Spanish colonial rule in contrast as benign, enlightened and legal, bringing to the ignorant and distressed natives the inestimable benefits of freedom and the advantages of European civilization, manners and religion. Modern studies of mass persuasion and the psychology of propaganda have taught us how easy it is for such a legend to be created and having been created to influence even observers who are normally unbiased and historians who regard themselves as objective. In this case the legend was the easier to create because the first discoveries of the New World had brought Europeans into contact with races which, if not vicious and debased, were at a primitive level of civilization. The sixteenth century was not in any case an age favourable to the objective comprehension of a foreign culture of the sort to which the modern ethnologist aspires and the natural obtuseness which the early chroniclers share with their age was exaggerated by their tendency, honestly unconscious or—as in the case of Sarmiento de Gamboa—consciously dishonest, to defend the havoc which had been wrought by denigrating what had been destroyed. So the historical report of the Incas suffered no less from the conscience of their conquerors than their civilization had suffered from the lack of it. Soon too it became necessary to defend the Colonial regime from attacks both in Spain and in European countries which were hostile to Spain and not unwilling to make profit out of the alleged abuses of the Spanish in the New World. In 1542 Bartolomé de Las Casas, Bishop of Chiapa, who won fame throughout Europe as the protagonist of the Indians, presented to the King a pamphlet entitled *Brevísima Relación de la destruyción de las Indias*, which was published in 1552 and in which he idealized the Indians as the innocent martyrs of oppression. Las Casas had never been to Peru and his work is characterized by exaggerations and inaccuracies equal though opposite to those of the chroniclers who wrote within the ideology of the orthodox legend. The nature of criticism outside Spain may be gathered from the titles given to translations of this pamphlet in France and England. In France it was published under the title *Tyrannies et cruautés des Espagnols perpetrées es Indes occidentales qu'on dit le Nouveau Monde* (1579), and in English *The tears of the Indians: being an historical and true account of the cruel massacres and slaughters of above twenty millions of innocent people* (1656). The history of Sarmiento de Gamboa was commissioned by the Viceroy Toledo for the express purpose of counteracting the effects of Las Casas.

The foundations of the legend were laid by the first generation of chroniclers and it was perpetuated by their successors, who copied largely from those who had gone before, usually without the courtesy of acknowledgment. The Inquisition provided an instrument of literary censorship hardly less efficient than that of Soviet Russia and because of it few of the writers who gave the opposite side of the picture were published. Thus many valuable documents were lost, many were first published in the second half of the nineteenth century and some have been but recently rediscovered and brought to the light of day. The modern historian has therefore fuller material available to him than at any previous time since the first years of the Conquest. Yet apart from a brief period of romantic idealization in the Rider Haggard style during the eighteenth century, and apart from modern tendencious histories for or against the Inca Empire as an experiment in state socialism, the historical legend created at the beginning of the colonial period has persisted up to our own day. The belittlement of the Inca civilization, which thus had its origin in sixteenth century obtuseness, half conscious feelings of guilt and the need to combat adverse criticism of the colonial system, is perpetuated in one modern school of South American history. Thus C. H. Haring, Robert Wood Bliss Professor of Latin-American History and Economics in Harvard University, writes in *The Spanish Empire in America*: 'Here was a virgin continent occupied only by tribes of native savages, or by the easily subdued semi-barbarous native states of Mexico and Peru.' Even Madariaga, who certainly writes if any without conscious bias, finds the chief keys to the Indian character in cannibalism, drunkenness and apathy. He does not even allow him to be a liar from conviction but from inertia. 'Throughout the pages left by eye-witnesses, earlier or later, one feels this kind of *listlessness*; a forlorn, passive, silent, sullen state, relieved only by bouts of drunkenness, or, if provoked, by the excitement of war'. Yet there is ample evidence from the earlier Spanish conquerors that the Indian was at first naively and instinctively truthful even to his own disadvantage, until he soon learnt to lie in self-protection. And Madariaga himself admits 'In the long run, his inertia will win.' It is perhaps inevitable that the attempt to show the Spanish conquest and colonial policy in its best light will easily fall into the temptation to do less than justice to the Indian. Just as the anti-Spanish writer will be apt to idealize and romanticize the Indians beyond recognition. What is seldom realized is that the Indian, with all his faults and latent possibilities, with the passive stubborn obstinacy which all have recognized, has never accepted that the benefits offered him by European civilization are worth the change in his traditional habits which their enjoyment demands.

Following the early chroniclers who stood outside the orthodox legend and attempted to glorify the greatness of the Inca culture —and so for the most part escaped publication until a recent date—is a school of modern historians, mainly South American, such as Jorge Basadre, Luis E. Valcarcel, José Maria Camacho and Luis Alberto Sanchez, who in reaction from the predominant tradition have sometimes gone too far in the opposite direction. An objective history of the Incas remains still to be written.

The written sources for such a history may be classified as those on the one hand who supported the orthodox legend of the debased Indian and the tyrannical Inca, either from motives of conscious propaganda or because they accepted uncritically and unconsciously the contemporary fiction, and those on the other who opposed the legend and tried to do justice to the greatness of the Inca achievement before it was destroyed by the Spanish conquest. The former observed the Inca organization in degeneration and their interest in what had existed before its destruction was secondary or tendencious. They tended to plagiarize both verbally and factually without acknowledgement, so that statements which seem to be supported by strong independent evidence of a number of chroniclers are very often no more than repetitions of one original observation. Those who wrote to record the greatness of Inca civilization, most of whom have become accessible only in modern times, were for obvious reasons much more interested to gather memories and traditions of the past which preceded the arrival of the Spaniards. They are therefore in general far richer sources for pre-Columban history of Peru. But they are not necessarily more reliable; as the one school tended to belittle and denigrate, the other tended to exaggerate. It is a well-known fact that in the minds of a people conquered, persecuted and oppressed, memories of the past tend to take on more glowing colours and past greatness is exaggerated by contrast with present abjection. Whether their purpose was, like that of Las Casas, to arouse the indignation of men against the physical abuses to which the Indian peoples were subjected, or like Garcilaso, Guaman Poma or Salkamaywa, to protest against the moral depreciation of the Indian people by the orthodox chroniclers, they are no less liable to exaggeration and inaccuracy than the others. Every writer must be approached critically and read with caution; none can afford to be neglected. Original observations are to be found in the most unlikely places and assertions which seem to be the most strongly supported are sometimes no more than plagiarisms from one doubtful source. There can be no absolute estimate of the reliability of any one writer and the value of each must be judged differently according to whether he is to be used as a source for Colonial or for pre-Columban history. Whether a writer is or is not tendencious in either direction has little to do with his reliability as a source. Sarmiento, although outstandingly tendencious, is a most useful historical source.

I shall now give a brief description of a few of the more interesting of the chroniclers for the benefit of those who care to browse at first hand among them.

1. Several short accounts of the Conquest were written by eye-witnesses who accompanied Pizarro's expedition. Whatever they have to say is important on grounds of priority and because they *were* eye-witnesses of the facts they relate. But in the main they are concerned with military events and they have little information about earlier Inca history. They are obviously without value for later colonial developments.

Francisco de Xéres left Spain at the age of fifteen, entered Peru as the secretary of Pizarro and was present at the capture of Atahuallpa at Cajamarca. He returned to Spain in 1534 and published the *Verdadera relación de la conquista del Perú y provincia del Cuzco, llamada la Nueva Castilla, conquistada por Francisco Pizarro*. English translation by C. R. Markham in *Reports on the Discovery of Peru*, published by the Hakluyt Society in 1871. A soldier's memoirs.

Pedro Sancho de la Hoz followed Xéres as secretary of Pizarro and official chronicler of the conquest. His work was a continuation of the preceding and was completed in Jauja in 1534. Sancho returned to Spain in 1535, in 1539 returned again to Peru, took part in the Chilean expedition, joined the revolt against Valdivia and was beheaded in 1547. His work was first published in Italian in 1556. The Spanish text was first published in Lima in 1917 in the *Colección de Libros y Documentos Referentes a la Historia del Perú*, edited by H. H. Urteaga and C. A. Romero. An English translation by P. A. Means entitled *An account of the Conquest of Peru* was published in New York in 1917.

Cristóbal de Molina followed Pizarro to Peru and Almagro to Chile, lived in Cuzco and Lima and in 1551 became lay clerk to the cathedral in Santiago de Chile. About 1552 he wrote a

VANDALS OF HISTORY

Relación de muchas cosas acaescidas en el Perú, en suma, para entender a la letra la manera que se tuvo en la conquista y poblazon destos reinos, first published in Lima, in 1916, in the same collection as the foregoing. It contains nothing of interest for pre-Columban history.

2. *Juan de Betanzos* was a Spanish soldier who came to America with Francisco Pizarro, married a sister of the Inca Atahuallpa, knew Quechua, and wrote a *Suma y narración de los Incas*. He had excellent opportunities for acquainting himself with Inca history and antiquities, his account is sympathetic and owing to its early date and the information available to Betanzos it is one of the most valuable sources for pre-Columban history. The book is unfortunately unfinished. It is dated 1551, but probably owing to the fact that it did not conform with the orthodox picture of pre-Spanish Peru it remained unpublished until 1880.

3. *Pedro de Cieza de León* was born in Seville in 1518, left Spain at the age of thirteen, served under Jorge de Robledo and Benalcazar and was befriended by Pedro de la Gasca. He spent seventeen years travelling through the length and breadth of what had formerly been the Inca Empire and left the first complete account of what was found by the Spaniards. His *Crónica del Perú* was in three parts. The first, an account of his travels, contains his geographical, ethnological and general observations; the second was an account of the Inca Empire; and the third was the story of the civil wars. This work was written in 1551 after Cieza's return to Spain and the first part was published in 1553. The third part was not published until 1877 and the *History of the Incas* remained unpublished until 1880. An English translation of the first part was published in 1864 by the Hakluyt Society under the title *The Travels of Pedro de Cieza de León*. An English translation of the second part appeared in 1883.

Pedro de Cieza de León was a straightforward, honest and observant soldier and traveller, without imagination but considerably interested in what he saw around him. What he saw was the Inca Empire in disintegration and ruins, smashed and bleeding after twenty years of occupation. His work is the Baedeker of its time and our earliest and best authority for the outlying parts of the Inca Empire. He is meticulous and writes without conscious bias, but he had completely because unconsciously absorbed the orthodox legend of the barbarous, uncivilized and uncivilizable savage. At times he is moved to wonder despite himself, but he has no imaginative power to realize the organization and the culture which must have contributed to the ruins and relics which he saw. He speaks of the Indians always with a kind of pitying contempt as a race whose natural inferiority it never enters his mind to question. After accusing them individually of cannibalism, human sacrifice, sodomy and idolatry, his natural honesty compels him to say towards the end of the first part (chap. CXVII): 'Since some people speak great ill of the Indians, comparing them to beasts, saying that their customs and manner of life are nearer those of brutes than of men, and that they are so evil that they not only practise the abominable sin but that they eat each other, and whereas in my history I have written something of this and of some other of their foulnesses and abuses, I wish it to be known that it is not my intention to say that this is to be understood of all; rather is it to be known that if in one province they eat human flesh and sacrifice the blood of men, in many others they abhor this sin. And if, similarly, in one they sin against nature, in many they consider it great foulness and do not practise it, but rather abhor it. And thus are their customs; so that it would be unjust to condemn them in general.' Time and again he instinctively accepts the contemporary legend and speaks of the Inca regime as a sombre and malevolent tyranny. In his use by later chroniclers he has become the corner stone of the orthodox legend of denigration. Yet when he is writing specifically of the Inca achievements, particularly in the second part of his work, he is roused to genuine and generous admiration and preserves much which, because of its relatively early date, is invaluable to the modern historian.

4. *Agustín de Zárate* went to Peru in 1543 as 'Treasurer of the Crown', returned to Spain in 1549 and published in 1555 a *Historia del descubrimiento y conquista de la Provincia del Perú*. His work is superficial but vigorously carries on the idea that the Inca monarchy was an unrelieved tyranny in which force and violence were the only laws of succession and whose right depended solely upon arms.

5. We may notice three works which have gained considerable reputation although their authors were not in Peru and do not therefore write from first hand researches.

Bartolomé de Las Casas wrote several works in defence of the Indians and in protest against their despoliation by the Spanish. He became known as the 'Apostle of the Indians' and has been alternately praised and attacked as the originator of the Black

VANDALS OF HISTORY

Legend of the Spanish colonial system.[1] His works are of more value as illustrating contemporary controversy than as a source for pre-Columban Peruvian history.

Francisco López de Gómara accompanied Hernán Cortés as chaplain in the conquest of Mexico and published in 1552 a *Historia general de las Indias*. He agrees with Cieza de León in representing the Peruvian Indians as cruel, bestial and given to human sacrifice and the monarchy of the Incas as a tyranny.

Gonzalo Fernández de Oviedo y Valdés lived in Santo Domingo and between 1526 and 1547 published a voluminous *Historia general y natural de las Indias*. He had no first hand knowledge of Peru and is insufficiently critical of what he heard at second hand.

6. *Juan Polo de Ondegardo* was a lawyer and government official at La Plata and subsequently at Cuzco, who lived in Peru between 1545 and 1575 and wrote a number of reports on Inca religion and government between 1561 and 1571. These were used in manuscript by Cobo and Acosta and some have since been published, including an English translation *Report by Polo de Ondegardo. The rites and laws of the Incas*, published by the Hakluyt Society in 1873. He was a great admirer of the Inca system of administration and undertook honest and productive research. His style is, however, extremely obscure and he is excessively difficult to read.

7. *Pedro Sarmiento de Gamboa* was a typical Spanish adventurer, gifted, reckless, cruel, swashbuckler, inventor and charlatan. He discovered the Solomon Islands in 1567 and pursued Drake beyond the Magellan Straits. He was the inventor of several nautical instruments and took active part in the extirpation of the surviving members of the Inca family. He was a favourite of Francisco de Toledo, Viceroy of Peru from 1569 to 1582, who saved him on two occasions from the Inquisition and by whom he was employed to write a history of the Indians which should counteract the unfortunate effect which the works of Las Casas had had in Europe. He travelled largely over Peru and wrote a *Historia de los Incas* purporting to be based upon narratives of prominent Indians. This work is more obviously partial than any which had preceded and ranks as purposeful propaganda against the Incas, who are represented throughout as tyrannical in the worst sense, cruel and oppressive, and their reign a highly coloured rule of terror, ignorance and shame. In order that this production

[1] *e.g.* Romulo D. Carbia, *Historia de la Leyenda Negra Hispano-Americana* (Buenos Aires, 1943).

should have the value of authenticity it was read before forty Cuzco Indians who were compelled to guarantee its truth. On the way to Spain it was lost, was rediscovered, in 1893 at Göttingen and published in 1906 under the title *Geschichte des Inkareichs*. An English version was published by the Hakluyt Society in 1907. Despite and beneath its tendenciousness this work contains some genuine investigation of facts.

Sarmiento combined a frank tendenciousness with considerable care in collecting and compiling his facts, travelling about Peru and recording the legends of the past which were still remembered by the ancients and wise men of the Indians. As he says: 'Examining the most prudent and the ancients of every estate, I pursued and compiled this history, comparing what one group said of their enemies with the version of the opposite band and confronting the two, comparing all those records and memories which I obtained and comparing them with opposing versions and rectifying them in the presence of the opposing sources brought together with myself as Judge, using men skilled in the general tongues and trusty interpreters and in this way what is here written has been polished and sifted, all this to justify the authority of the King of Castile and to justify the Conquest and by mandate of His Excellency the Viceroy Toledo and of which none needs doubt that it is sufficiently well proved.'

Sarmiento also sent back a number of *Informaciones* direct to the King, which remained in the Library of the Escorial until the end of the nineteenth century when selections were published. Here he took a very different view of the Inca rule, going so far as to say 'With all his power the Emperor Charles could not effect a part of what the prudently ordered authority of the Incas achieved.'

8. *José de Acosta*, a Jesuit who lived in Peru from 1570 to 1586, published in 1590 a *Historia Natural y Moral de las Indias*, which contains some useful material about Inca history and much keen naturalistic observation which is still of interest.

9. *Garcilaso Inca de la Vega* was born in Cuzco in 1540, of mixed blood. His father, Garcilaso de la Vega came to Peru in the suite of Pedro de Alvarado soon after the Conquest. His mother was a niece of the Inca Huayna Capac. He passed his early years in Cuzco among the surviving members of the Inca royal family and at the age of twenty left Peru for good. In his old age he settled down in Cordoba and wrote his *Comentarios Reales*, the first

VANDALS OF HISTORY 25

volume dealing with Inca history and the second with the story of the Conquest. He wrote for the purpose of commending the past glories of his country, of which he was serenely proud, to an educated European audience. To the scholar his work suffers from the fact that it was written by an enthusiast in his old age, relying upon the memories of his youth supplemented by correspondence with the friends of his youth. The *Comentarios Reales* have been the most widely read and highly estimated of all the chronicles of Inca history. They are now suffering under a reaction and often receive less credit than is their due. In his article 'Inca Culture at the Time of the Spanish Conquest', in the *Handbook of South American Indians*, published by the Bureau of American Ethnology, R. J. H. Rowe says 'his accounts of Inca history and religion are entirely fanciful.' Prescott, who was by no means blind to his unreliabilities, says of Garcilaso 'The difference between reading his Commentaries and the accounts of European writers is the difference that exists between reading a work in the original and in a bald translation. Garcilaso's writings are an emanation from the Indian mind.' It is still, I believe, true that for the non-specialized reader, who desires to obtain a general picture of the state of pre-Columban Peru rather than exact accuracy in every detail, Garcilaso will give a more interesting and perhaps a more truthful, though highly coloured, general impression than most other chronicles.

Licence for the publication of the first part of the Commentaries was refused in Spain and it was published in Lisbon in 1609, being subsequently prohibited in Spanish America. The second part was published in Cordoba in 1617. An English translation appeared in 1688 by Sir Paul Rycaut, Knight, of which Prescott has said, 'No one who reads the book will doubt his limited acquaintance with his own tongue, and no one who compares it with the original will deny his ignorance of the Castilian.'

10. *Joan de Santacruz Pachacuti Yamqui Salkamaywa* was an Indian who in 1620 wrote a *Relación de antigüedades deste reyno del Perú*. This work was first published in Madrid in 1879 and again in 1927 in the *Colección de Libros y Documentos Referentes a la Historia del Perú*. It contains useful material on Inca history and customs and preserves some old Quechua texts. But its Spanish is bad and its composition confused. It is a work for the specialist.

11. Another Indian writer of about the same date is *Felipe Guaman Poma de Ayala*, whose voluminous work of some thousand

INDIANS OF THE ANDES

pages profusely illustrated with pen drawings, entitled *Nueva Corónica y buen gobierno*, was first published in 1936. Like the preceding it is difficult to read, but it is very valuable as a source for Inca religion, customs, daily life and artistic achievements. The lively and unsophisticated pen drawings are so expressive that they are a document in themselves.

12. *Martín de Morúa* lived for a long time in Cuzco and on the shores of Lake Titicaca. Beyond the fact that he belonged to the Order of La Merced, little is known of his personal history. In 1590, he concluded a *Historia del orígen y genealogía real de los Reyes Incas del Perú, de sus hechos, costumbres, trajes y manera de gobierno*. Like Guaman Poma he gives some account of the Inca queens, and also of the great captains. His work is useful for social and economic aspects of the Inca Empire and contains much incidental information about customs. It is written sympathetically, and was not published until the twenties of the present century.

13. *Fernando Montesinos*, a Jesuit, spent fifteen years in Peru. He was a great traveller, who boasted that he had crossed the Andes sixty times, an adventurer, a converter of the Indians by force. His *Memorias antiguas historiales y politicas del Perú* was written in 1652 and first published in Madrid in 1840. Although written late, it was probably based upon early documents some of which have been lost. It is one of the most controversial of all the sources of pre-Columban history. Montesinos has been called 'the Münchausen of Peru' and 'one of the greatest liars of history'. A reaction in his favour caused him to be described about the beginning of the present century as one of the most honest and well informed historians of Peru. The present tendency is to use him with caution, but without ridicule. In fact, he made undistinguished—and unacknowledged—use of a valuable early source.

14. The Jesuit Father *Bernabé Cobo* wrote a two volume *Historia del Nuevo Mundo* in 1653, which is described by J. H. Rowe as 'the best and the most complete description of Inca culture in existence.' It is based partly upon personal researches in Cuzco and Lima and partly upon Ondegardo and Cristóbal de Molina of Cuzco and government records. Louis Baudin describes him as lacking originality and purloining conscientiously from his predecessors. It is a well written, balanced and scientific survey. As Baudin says, 'his main fault is that he came a century too late.' It is the most useful source for those who do not wish to go to the

VANDALS OF HISTORY

trouble of perusing the earlier authorities. The work was published in four volumes between 1890 and 1895 at Seville.

Of the above, Cieza de León, Gómara, Agustín de Zárate and Sarmiento de Gamboa were the four corner-stones of the anti-Inca legend. Garcilaso, Las Casas, Betanzos, Salkamaywa, Morúa and Guaman Poma were the chief writers who tried to do justice, albeit with exaggerations, to Inca history and achievement.

Having now said something about the written sources available for the reconstruction of pre-Columban history of Peru, about the motives from which they wrote and the way in which their motives influenced their works, we must consider also what sources were available to them for recovering the history of the times preceding the Spanish Conquest. For while the history of the Colonial epoch was written by men who, though often partial and biased, were contemporaries and eye-witnesses, written history begins with the Spanish and we have no contemporary written records of pre-Spanish times.

While all other writers agree that the Indians of the Andes were without the knowledge of writing, Montesinos alone states (Chap. XV) that writing was known before the Incas and was forbidden under penalty of death. Montesinos is defended by Francisco A. Loayza, *Chinos Llegaron antes que Colon* (p. 98), who argues from the fact that the word *kellka* in Quechua, *kellkata* in Aymara and *kilka* in Araucanian, means 'writing', that writing must once have been known. But *kellka* means 'painting' or 'drawing' primarily and was applied by natural association to writing after writing was introduced by the Spanish. Thus according to Mossi's *Diccionario Quichua* (1860) *qqellccani* means 'write', 'draw', 'paint', *qqellccascca ppachha* means 'embroidered or worked garment', etc. It is unlikely that among so conservative a people the art of writing once known could have been lost and there is no good reason for thinking that it was ever known. All other writers are quite specific on the point and no inscriptions exist.

It is certain that writing was unknown at the arrival of Pizarro. All our sources agree upon this. Like most pre-literate peoples, they had excellent powers of memory, which they cultivated systematically and professionally. Their knowledge of past history was embodied in epic poems and genealogical traditions, which were composed, memorized and handed down by experts. Cieza de León says (Part 1, Chap. CI), 'they use a kind of folk-poems and romances (*romances o cantares*) by means of which they retain a memory of events, without forgetting them.' There were local historians with local historical traditions and a centralized history, since the Inca Pachacuti (according to Sarmiento and Cobo) caused the history of his ancestors to be painted and started central depositories or archives of national history.

Sarmiento says: 'Pachacuti made a general convocation of all the historians of the country he governed, united them in the city of Cuzco, examining them much time on the antiquities and the notable deeds of their forebears of these kingdoms, and after having explored all things well, he had it painted in chronological order on boards and kept it in the House of the Sun, in a chamber bedecked with gold, in such sort that they were as it were a library, and then he appointed doctors who would know how to understand and to interpret them. Into this room no one could enter except the monarch and the historians with express permission.' The reign of Pachacuti is dated about 1438–71.

Although they lacked writing, the Quechuas used a mnemonic device called the *quipu*, which consists of a string from which hang down groups of pendant cords. By means of knots at various intervals the *quipu* could be used as a numerical and statistical record. By means of different coloured cords, differences in the method of twisting and, according to Morua, differences in the size and form of the knots, the *quipu* could express concrete ideas and could be used in conjunction with memorized verses as a record of history and events. Louis Baudin (*L'Empire socialiste des Inka*) quotes a description by Antonio de la Calancha, an Augustinian who was born in Sucre and in 1638 wrote a *Crónica moralizada* of the Augustinian Order in Peru, how it was possible to express by means of a *quipu* the following complicated set of ideas: 'Suppose that a functionary wishes to express that before Manco-Capac, the first Inca, there was neither king, chief, cult nor religion; that in the fourth year of his reign this emperor subdued ten provinces, whose conquest cost him a certain number of men; that in one of them he took a thousand units of gold and three thousand units of silver and that in thanksgiving for the victory he had celebrated a festival in honour of the god Sun.' Follows a description how this may be expressed in a *quipu* by means of different coloured cords knotted at the proper intervals. Many writers speak of the *quipus* almost as though they were a form of written history. Garcilaso, who, however, is clear that the

VANDALS OF HISTORY

quipu was not a true form of writing, states on the authority of Blas Valera that after incorporating a province the Inca caused to be inscribed in coloured knots 'the grazing lands, the cultivated lands, the estates, the mines, the salt deposits, the springs, lakes and rivers, the cotton plantations, the fruit trees and the greater and less livestock, with and without wool.' Guaman Poma speaks of them at length, using such language as one would use of written records. Martín de Morúa says that they understood their *quipus* with as much ease as we in our language understand from paper and ink, and goes on, 'for the things which they wish to tell they differentiated, made the knots larger or smaller and in different colours, in such manner that for one thing they had a red knot and for another green or yellow and so with the rest; but what surprises me most is that by these same cords and knots they related the successions of times and when each Inca reigned and if he was good or bad, if he was brave or a coward, everything, in a word, which could be obtained from books was obtained from them; how this could be I do not know or understand, but this is certain that there are *quipus* to this day and the ancients use them, from which source has come the greater part of what is written in this book.' Sarmiento again says 'Before entering upon the body of this history I wish to notice in case of future difficulties which may be made how the barbarians of this land had not letters but supplied the lack by transmitting one to another, from fathers to sons, all the ancient happenings until their own days; repeating them many times as one who reads a lesson in the pulpit; and persisting in the repetition until it was fixed in the memory; thus each generation used to communicate their annals in order, their history, exploits, antiquities, the number of the tribes, towns, and provinces, days, months, years, deaths, destructions, fortresses and leaders; the numbers they noted on cords, which they called *quipus*, which have certain knots and the differences in colour distinguishes them, and they record everything as with letters. Wonderful how they preserve even petty details in these little cords, of which there are professionals as among us professionals of the art of writing; besides this they had historians of these nations, which was a profession which was handed down from father to son.'

Yet it is clear that the *quipus* were not a true form of writing. They could not be read by one who had learnt the interpretation of the idiom, as a pictogram can be read. In each case they need an interpreter who has *memorized* the key. As a mnemonic aid they were an ingenious and effective device, without being a true form of script. They were most useful for statistical material, for which purpose they were originally devised, but were by no means limited to this use. The many enormous archives of *quipus* were destroyed and burnt by the Spanish in their campaign against relics and reminders of the Inca regime and we now possess only those which have been recovered from graves. Some of these have been compared with the instructions of the chroniclers for their interpretation and the numerical method of recording, at any rate, has been discovered. They are of course quite valueless as an addition to our knowledge of Inca history. The best accounts of the *quipus* are by L. Leland Locke, *The ancient quipu, a Peruvian knot-record* (1923), and Erland Nordenskiöld, *The secret of the Peruvian quipus* (1925).[1]

While some *quipus* escaped destruction in the outlying areas, the annihilation of the main body of archives was a rude blow to a historical record which depended entirely upon aided memory. It throws an altogether unwieldy burden upon pure archaeology. But the trained memory of the Peruvian Indians and their long training in handing down memorized history explains why a much better showing could be made by the chroniclers, despite their inadequacies and double tendenciousness, than would be made by chroniclers of British history fifty or a hundred years hence if all written records were destroyed today. It is an irreparable loss that instead of systematically recording the immense historical wealth which was stored in the great archives of *quipus* and in the memories of the *quipucamayuj*, these should have been wantonly and senselessly destroyed.

The historians who are now our sources had, then, themselves exceptionally good opportunities for recovering pre-Columban history, which they used indifferently well, and these opportunities can now never recur. But even before the Spanish disrupted the historical tradition, it appears probable that it had been subjected to a sort of editing and selective distortion not entirely unlike the tendencious distortion to which the Spanish themselves subjected it in their turn. When the great Inca monarch Pachacuti centralized historical records and created as it were an official Inca history, he appears to have selected among

[1] A further account of pre-Spanish Peruvian historical methods is contained in the appendix to this chapter.

the many various local historical traditions and eliminated most that was not directly concerned with the Inca dynasty. The histories of the many centres of civilization which had preceded the Inca Empire were allowed to lapse and thus there was created a great gap between the legendary time when men were living without organized polity and with a rudimentary culture until the foundation of the Inca dynasty. The result, if not the purpose, of this selective manipulation of remembered history was to represent the Incas as the bearers of civilization to mankind on the Andes and to cast into oblivion all those peoples who had come before them in the long growth of civilization. That this was done can of course be only inferred; but it seems to be an inevitable inference from the difference between recorded history from the traditions surviving at the time of the Spaniards and the story given by archaeology. Archaeological material may be badly interpreted but it does not lie. And the story archaeology tells is of a long succession with the Incas coming last into the field as great organizers and inheritors rather than creators of culture, rather as the Roman Empire inherited and engulfed the cultures of the Greeks and the Hebrews.

For the period before the Spanish Conquest we have a historical tradition which has suffered a double disruption and a twofold distortion. For the history of the Aymara and Quechua peoples since the Conquest we must reckon with the fact that their nature is peculiarly difficult for the European and the modern mentality to understand. While the Spanish conquerors were not adapted by the atmosphere of the age in which they lived to be understanding of an alien mentality, the American Indian has a nature which is as difficult for the European to comprehend as the nature of the Chinese is traditionally supposed to be and in the four centuries which have elapsed since the Conquest little progress in mutual understanding has been achieved between the white and the native races who now possess the Andes. Salvador de Madariaga quotes Humboldt's description in 1800 of Mexican native families 'who under the appearance of extreme poverty, hide considerable wealth.' I have myself known Indians living in the Yungas of Bolivia who have become fairly prosperous from the cultivation of coca but are without ambition to deviate from the sordid and empoverished conditions of life which they share with their fellows. Nor is this disuse of wealth solely due to the fear, ingrained from bitter experience, that wealth displayed will be lost. For the American Indian happiness does not consist in the extension and multiplication of desires nor in the lust for power and domination or in material benefits beyond his reasonable needs. He has the more 'oriental' nature which moderates its desires to the comforts proper to a way of life and a culture which is his own and which he does not wish to change for another.

Nor did the Indian himself help towards an understanding. Perhaps more than the material exploitation the disruption of those social and political bonds which had sustained the Inca Empire, and the sacrilege to all he held sacred, caused him to retire into himself and hold aloof. The Indian was not averse from being ruled nor unwilling to adopt another worship in conjunction with his own. But whereas the rule of the Incas seems to have been on the whole beneficial and his religion tolerant, the intolerance, the greed and the lack of honourableness of the Spaniard towards the native did not induce respect. From the white man he has known only oppression without fairness or justice. The Inca gave him a hard life but a fair one.

Despite the rapid and complete collapse of their political organization before the inroad of the Spaniards, the Quechuas and Aymaras have shown a remarkable tenacity for survival. While mestization has not proceeded so far as in Mexico, a mixed 'cholo' class has grown up which is an important social element in both Peru and Bolivia. The Indians are considered conservative and incapable of improvement. They have been quite remarkably tenacious of such elements of their ancient culture as have been allowed to survive and have no desire to change their traditional way of life for the 'better' civilization of the whites. Against all attempts to break up what is left of their way of life they oppose a passive but stubborn resistance and are not tempted by the allurements of prosperity or comfort. Inherently conservative they are not, as is shown by their power to adapt what is suitable to their inherited culture, to amalgamate the Christian religion of their conquerers with their own, to make their own innovations of dress, music and so on. Madariaga claims that Spain gave freely to her colonies the best of what she had to offer; this is almost certainly true—though what she gave was not always or for the most part given to the Indian peoples. But the majority of what Europe has had to offer to the American Indian has not seemed to him worth having in comparison with what his own inheritance gave. And the Quechua and Aymara remain that historic anomaly, a people unconverted to the superior merits of the 'economic man' and the 'industrial state'. Thus up to our own time very little progress has been made towards an understanding of these peoples.

Appendix

PRE-SPANISH HISTORICAL RECORDS IN THE ANDES

The myths and legends of the Indian peoples were handed down in folk poems or romances, repeated from generation to generation by memory, and were not written down until the Spanish brought the art of writing to Peru. Not that these traditional poems were spontaneous music of the people. They were composed and handed down by a special class of *amautas*, or wise men, who were also the professional historians, the teachers, and consultants in matters of national policy. The careful preservation of legend and history was treated as a serious and important matter, particularly under the Incas who endeavoured to impose a single uniform tradition of artificial and tendencious history, suppressing all that had gone before the emergence of the Inca dynasty and representing the Incas, to the greater glory of that regime, as the first to bring the benefits of civilization and the first to introduce law and order to peoples who before their time had lived in barbarism and ignorance. But they were only very partially successful in imposing this arbitrary distortion of history and many local traditions survived tenaciously alongside and in conflict with the 'official' version. An amusing example of a retaliatory anti-Inca tradition of Inca origins is preserved by Montesinos. We may see too the influence of independent and rival traditions in the stories that have been preserved of the foundation of Cuzco, the capital of the Inca Empire. Cieza de León, who had a great admiration for the Inca rule and institutions and obtained his information from survivors of the Inca royal family, says 'It is held for certain that, at the time when Manco Inca Capac built this house, there were Indians in large numbers in the district, but as he did them no harm and did not in any wise molest them, they did not object to his remaining in their land, but rather rejoiced at his coming.' Sarmiento, on the other hand, whose purpose was to represent the Inca monarchy as a tyranny imposed by force and arbitrary violence, found another tradition telling how when the Incas first established themselves in the valley of Cuzco the Indian tribes were suppressed and partially annihilated with great ferocity; Mama Guaco, one of the founder-sisters, is represented as a veritable virago of terror, cutting out the heart and lungs of her enemies, blowing up the lungs and advancing with them between her teeth, whirling a sling in her hand.

As is always the case when traditions are handed down by memory, very great attention was given to strict verbal accuracy so that the core of the tradition was maintained from generation to generation unchanged. Often one may recognize interpolations of the individual narrator, explaining his own understanding or conjecture of the motives which influenced the events recorded in the verbal tradition he repeats. Cieza de León, for example, says that Ayar Cachi was immured in a cave by his brothers because they were envious of his superior prowess. Others relate that the brothers caused him to be immured because his fierce and warlike disposition set against them the peoples through whom they passed and were causing dissatisfaction among their own followers. Such discrepancies of interpretation are only evidence of the permanence of the main outline of the traditional stories.

In addition to verbally memorized poems the Andean Indians used a system of mnemonic recording by means of bundles of various coloured cords knotted at intervals, which they called *quipus*. This method was developed to a quite surprising degree of complicated perfection and although primarily adapted for statistical records was also used as a supplementary means of recording historical events. As it has often been a matter of astonishment how these peoples preserved so long and so well the memory of their past without any knowledge of writing, I shall quote the accounts given by some of the Spaniards who studied and took advantage of the methods they used.

Here is the account of Cieza de León in the second part of his *Chronicle of Peru*.[1] 'I understood, when I was in Cuzco, that it was the custom among the king Incas, that the king, as soon as he died, should be mourned for with much lamentation, and that great sacrifices should be offered up in accordance with their religion. When these ceremonies were over, the oldest people of the country discussed the life and acts of the recently deceased king, considering whether he had done good to the country and what battles he had gained over the country's enemies. Having

[1] In this and other excerpts from the second part of Cieza's *Crónica del Perú* I use the translation of Clements R. Markham, issued by the Hakluyt Society in 1883.

settled these questions, and others which we do not entirely understand, they decided whether the deceased king had been so fortunate as to merit praise and fame, and to deserve that his memory should be for ever preserved. They then called for the great *quiposcamayos*, who preserve the records and understand how to give an account of the events that occur in the kingdom. Next they communicated with those who were most expert and who were selected for their skill in rhetoric and the use of words. These knew how to narrate the events in regular order, like ballad singers and romance writers. These compose the songs, so that they shall be heard by all at marriage ceremonies and other festivities. Thus they were instructed what to say concerning the deceased lord, and, if they treated of wars, they sang, in proper order, of the many battles he had fought in different parts of the empire. And for other events there were songs and romances to celebrate them on suitable occasions, so that the people might be animated by the recital of what had passed in other times.

'These Indians who by order of the kings had learnt the romances were honoured and favoured and great care was taken to teach their sons and other men in their provinces who were most able and intelligent. By this plan from the mouths of one generation the succeeding one was taught, and they can relate what took place five hundred years ago as if only ten years had passed.

'This was the order that was taken to prevent the great events of the empire from passing into oblivion. When a king died, if he had been a valiant and a good ruler, without having lost any province inherited from his father, nor been guilty of mean or paltry actions, it was permitted and ordained that songs in his honour should be composed, in which he should be praised in such wise as that all the people should be astonished to hear of deeds so mighty. These songs were not to be recited always and in all places, but only on occasions when there was a great and solemn assembly of people from all parts of the empire, or when the principal lords met together before the king on special occasions, or when they held their *taquis*, or drinking bouts. Then those who knew the romances, standing before the Inca, sang with loud voices of the mighty deeds of his ancestors. If any of his predecessors had been negligent, cowardly or vicious, or preferred pleasure to the labour of extending the bounds of the empire, it was ordered that such a king should receive little or no mention.

VANDALS OF HISTORY

If the name was preserved, it was merely to complete the line of succession. On other points there was silence concerning him, and the good and valiant alone were kept in memory. . . .

'And it is to be noted that besides this, it was the custom among them, and a law much kept and observed, for each king, during his reign to select three or four old men, known for their intelligence and ability, who were instructed to retain in their memory all the events that happened in the provinces, whether they were prosperous or whether they were the reverse, and to compose songs to be handed down, so that the history of the reign might be had in remembrance in after times. But these songs could not be recited or made public except in the presence of the lord and those who were charged with this duty, in the reign of the king, were not allowed to say anything which referred to him. But after his death they spoke to his successor in the empire, almost in these very words: "Oh! great and powerful Inca, the Sun, the Moon, the Earth, the hills and the trees, the stones and thine ancestors, may they all preserve thee from misfortune and make thee prosperous, happy and successful over all that are born! Know that the events which occurred in the days of thy fathers are these." Then, in the narration they stood in great humility, with eyes cast down on the ground and hands lowered. They could well do this, for there were among them some men with very good memories, sound judgments, and subtle genius, and full of reasoning power, as we can bear witness, who have heard them even in these our days.

'As soon as the king understood what was related to him, he caused other aged men to be called and charged them with the duty of learning the songs which were handed down from memory and to prepare others touching the events which might occur in his own reign. The expenditure and the account of contributions from the provinces were recorded in the *quipus*, that it might be known how much was paid in the former reign, and also during that of the new lord. No one was allowed to treat of historical events except only on days of great rejoicing or on days of mourning and sadness for the death of some brother or child of the king. If the histories were recited on other occasions, those who did so were severely punished.

'They had another method of knowing and understanding what had been received from the contributions in the provinces, what provisions were stored on the routes that the king would take with his army or when he was visiting the provinces, how much was in each place of deposit, how much was delivered out. And this method exceeded in artifice the *carastes* used by the Mexicans for their calculations. The system of the Peruvians was by *quipus*. These were long ropes made of knotted cords, and those who were accountants and understood the arrangements of these knots could by their means give an account of the expenditure and of other things during a long course of years. On these knots they counted from one to ten, and from ten to a hundred, and from a hundred to a thousand. On one of the ropes are the units, on another the tens, and so on. Each ruler of a province was provided with accountants who were called *quipucamayos*, and by these knots they kept account of what tribute was to be paid in the district, with respect to silver, gold, cloth, flocks, down to firewood and other minute details. By the same *quipus* they could report to those who were commissioned to take the account at the end of a year, or of ten or twenty years, with such accuracy that so much as a pair of *alpargatas*[1] would not be missing.

'I was incredulous concerning this system of counting, and although I heard it described I held the greater part of the story to be fabulous. But when I was at Marcavilla in the province of Xauxa, I asked the lord Guacarapora to explain it in such a way as that my mind might be satisfied and that I might be assured that it was true and accurate. He ordered his servants to bring the *quipus* and as this lord as a native, and a man of good understanding, he proceeded to make the thing clear to me. He told me to observe that all that he, for his part, had delivered to the Spaniards from the time that the Governor Don Francisco Pizarro arrived in the valley was duly noted down without any fault or omission. Thus I saw the accounts for the gold, the silver, the clothes, the corn, the sheep and other things; so that in truth I was quite astonished.

'There is another thing that should be known, for I take it to be very certain. The long wars, cruelties, robberies and tyrannical treatment which these people have suffered from the Spaniards would have led to their complete destruction, if it had not been for the excellent order and concert of their regulations. But they, having been trained in the intelligent system of accounts which was established by their wise princes, made an agreement among themselves that if an army of Spaniards passed through any of the

[1] Sandals.

VANDALS OF HISTORY

provinces and did such damage as would be caused by the destruction of growing crops, sacking of houses and other mischief of still worse kinds, all the accountants should make the best provision possible in the districts through which our people passed, in order that all might not be devastated. So it was arranged and as soon as the Spaniards were gone the chiefs assembled, the *quipus* were examined and checked and if one province had lost more than another, that which had suffered less made up the difference: so that the burden was shared equally by all.

'To this day accounts are kept in each valley and there are always as many accountants as there are lords and every four months the accounts are made up and balanced. Through their former orderly government they have been able to endure such great oppression and if God should be served by all ending with the good treatment that the people now receive, and with the decent order and justice that has been introduced, this kingdom might again be, to some extent, what it once was. But I believe that such a result will come tardily or never.'

So wrote Cieza de León fifteen years after the conquest of Peru. And for some two generations the ancient traditions continued to be handed down and the *quipus* were kept. Thirty years later Father José de Acosta gave the following account. 'Before the Spaniards came to the Indies, they of Peru had no kinds of writing, either letters, characters, ciphers, or figures, like to those of China and Mexico: yet preserved they the memory of their Antiquities, and maintained an order in all their affairs of peace, warre, and pollicie, for that they were carefull observers of traditions one to another, and the young ones learned, and carefully kept, as a holy thing, what their superiors had told them, and taught it with the like care to their posteritie. Besides this diligence, they supplied the want of letters and writings, partely by painting, as those of Mexico (although they of Peru were very grosse and blockish), and partely, and most commonly by Quippos. These Quippos are memorialls or registers, made of bowes, in the which there are diverse knottes and colours, which do signify diverse things, and it is strange to see what they have expressed and represented by this meanes: for their Quippos serve them insteede of Bookes of histories, of lawes, ceremonies, and accounts of their affaires. There were officers appointed to keepe these Quippos, the which were bound to give an account of everything, as

Notaries and Registers doe heere. Therefore they fully believed them in all things, for, according to the varietie of business, as warres, pollicie, tributes, ceremonies and landes, there were sundry Quippos or braunches, in every one of which there were so many knottes, little and great, and strings tied unto them, some red, some greene, some blew, some white; and finally, such diversitie, that even as wee derive an infinite number of woordes from foure and twenty letters, applying them in diverse sortes, so doe they draw innumerable woordes from their knottes and diversitie of colours. Which thing they doe in such a manner that if at this day in Peru, any Commissory come at the end of two or three years to take information uppon the life of any officer, the Indians come with their small reckonings verified saying, that in in such a village they have given him so many egges which he hath not payed for, in such a house a henne, in another two burdens of grasse for his horse, and that he hath paied but so much mony, and remaineth debtor so much. The proofe being presently made with these numbers of knottes and handfulls of cords, it remaines for a certaine testimony and register. I did see a handfull of these strings, wherein an Indian woman carried written a generall confession of all her life, and thereby confessed herselfe as well as I could have done it in written paper. I asked her what those strings meant that differed from the rest: she answered mee they were certaine circumstaunces which the sin required to be fully confessed . . . and they sooner submitte themselves to reason by these Quippos what everyone ought to pay, than we can do with the penne. Hereby we may judge if they have any understanding or be brutish: for my parte, I think they passe us in those things whereunto they do apply themselves.'

During the Colonial period of Spanish occupation there was no place among a harried and depressed people for the learned *amautas* and after the first two or three generations the old poems were forgotten and the legends disappeared or survive in a shadowy and distorted form, often amalgamated with stories of the Christian saints. But for fifty years or more after the Conquest, such a rich depository of material was available for research upon the history, the legends and the beliefs of the Indians of the Andes as has seldom been available in any country or age. Unfortunately the use made of this material was pathetically amateurish and inept, and the opportunity is now lost. Many of the early chroniclers have recorded legends and myths which they heard from the wise men of the Indian communities or from surviving members of the Inca nobility. But they had not the knowledge to investigate them scientifically as the modern ethnologist would desire and in their patronizing superiority towards people they regarded as an inferior race, and their complacent condemnation of all non-biblical notions, they had not even the interest to record fully or accurately what was told them. To them the wealth of myth and legend which lay outside the book of Genesis was as the idle foolishness of children or the lure and lies of the Devil.

In his *Suma y narración de los Incas, que los indios llamaron Copaccuna, que fueron señores de la ciudad del Cuzco y de todo lo a ella objeto*, Juan de Betanzos, who was married to an Inca princess, daughter of the last Inca king Atahuallpa, concludes a confused account of the Aymara cosmogonical myth with one of those typical statements which are so irritating now that there is no means of recovering what he was too little interested to include: 'Many other things more would I have written here about this Viracocha according to what those Indians have told me about him, but to avoid prolixity and great idolatry and bestiality, I have not included them.' And Pedro Cieza de León, after briefly mentioning the mythical birth of the sun from the lake, goes on: 'and as they are so superstitious they will have invented this story and the illusions of the devil will also have helped them to it, God permitting it on account of their sins.' In our attempts at reconstruction we are frustrated by poverty in the midst of a plenty which has perished.

Chapter Three

MYTH AND ARCHAEOLOGY

1. MYTH

GUAMAN POMA DE AYALA records an Indian tradition that there were four epochs before the Incas: the first or most ancient, called *Auca Runa*, probably 'warrior people', lasted for 2100 years; the second, called *Purun Runa*, or 'savage, lawless people', lasted 1100 years; the third, called *Wari Runa*, lasted 1300 years; and the fourth, called *Wari Huiracocha Runa*, or the people of Viracocha, lasted 800 years. Fray Buenaventura Salinas gives the same tradition in his *Memorial de las Historias del Nuevo Mundo* (1630) with the following periods of time for the four epochs: first epoch 1100 years; second epoch 1000 years; third epoch more than 500 years; fourth epoch more than 1000 years.

In the present state of our knowledge it is impossible to equate this tradition of four pre-Inca epochs with the evidences of archaeology, although were our knowledge more complete it might well be possible to show that the four epochs of the tradition have some relation to remembered facts. It does, however, seem almost beyond doubt that during the relatively short period covered by our present archaeological evidence, from about the beginning of the Christian era to the European Conquest, the Andean region comprised by the modern countries of Peru and Bolivia was able either to resist or to absorb any large-scale migration of populations from outside and that there was in consequence no total disruption of development over the whole area. There is no reason to question the judgment of Wendell C. Bennett.[1] 'This unity of achievement in Peru and Bolivia, regardless of geographical and time differences, implies that the total development was relatively independent of the rest of the Americas. This does not deny the possibility of external influences from Colombia, Central America, and the Amazon, but rather suggests that the region was sufficiently advanced and organized to resist any wholesale migration or influence from the outside.'

[1] *Handbook of South American Indians*, vol. 2, p. 64.

MYTH AND ARCHAEOLOGY

When we look at the Indian mythology, it seems to contain a rather curious inconsistency. As mythology it is rather unusually practical, matter-of-fact and lacking in the more fanciful picturesque elements of story. There is what appears to be a very clear mythological recollection of an earlier race of men living in the region at the hunting and food-gathering stage of development, without settled agriculture, stable social organization or the crafts of civilized men. On the other hand the Indian, who regards himself as the bearer of civilization in the region, also regards himself as aboriginal. The mythology retains no memory that the present inhabitants have ever migrated into the region from outside.

The Jesuit Father José de Acosta[1] dismisses the Indian legends with the contempt usual in his day, saying 'It is no matter of any great importance to know what the Indians themselves report of their beginning, being more like unto dreams, than to true Histories.' But Father Acosta, besides being wise and of balanced judgment in the learning of his time, was an intelligent and indefatigable observer and a very diligent collector of information, for which he had exceptionally good opportunities. When he says, therefore 'Instructing my selfe carefully of them, to know from what land and what nation they passed, to that where they now live, I have found them so farre unable to give any reason thereof, as they believe confidently, that they were created at their first beginning at this new world, where they now dwell,' we must regard this downright statement as very strong confirmatory evidence that Indian legend did not in fact retain any memory of their migrations on to the highlands of the Andes.

The Aymaras connected their many small scattered tribal settlements, or *ayllus*, with natural features, such as rivers and rocks and mountains, from which they were believed to have sprung. Cieza de León says of the peoples of the Collao 'They give us to understand that their ancestors are of great antiquity, of whose origin they recount so many stories and fables that I am unwilling to pause and repeat them, for some say that they came from a spring, others from a mountain crag, others from lakes.' Upon this primitive layer of topological mythology was grafted a cosmological myth, which connected the origin of the world and the human race with Lake Titicaca and with which was usually

[1] Acosta, *Historia natural y moral de Las Indias* (1590), English translation by E(dward) G(rimston), 1604, re-issued by the Hakluyt Society in 1880.

amalgamated an aetiological myth explaining the origin of the monolithic sculptures of Tihuanacu.

At the beginning of time, Virajocha rose out of the lake and created a world in which there was no sun, no light and no warmth. And in this first age of the world, *chamajpacha*, the limbo of darkness before the birth of the sun, he created large strong men of more than normal size (the word used by Sarmiento is *Jayaneo*, which was the name given to giants in the early Spanish books of chivalry), who lived but a half-life of unreality like animals. This first race of men angered Virajocha and he destroyed them by the flood *una pachacuti*, the world overturned by water. Then after the flood, appearing again from the Island Titicaca which is in the Lake, he created the sun to shine by day and the moon and stars by night and brought into being a new race of men of his own stature, which was the average height of men. 'The flood being passed and the land dry, Virajocha determined to people it a second time, and, to make it more perfect, he decided upon creating luminaries to give it light. With this object he went, with his servants, to a great lake in the Collao, in which there is an island called Titicaca. . . . Virajocha went to this island, and presently ordered that the sun, moon and stars should come forth, and be set in the heavens to give light to the world, and it was so. They say that the moon was created brighter than the sun, which made the sun jealous at the time when they rose into the sky. So the sun threw over the moon's face a handful of ashes, which gave it the shaded colour it now presents.'

This is the simple kernel of the creation-myth of the Aymaras, which explains their origin on the Altiplano itself and expresses their rooted belief that they were autochthonous in the land. But it was combined with another myth invented later to explain the origin of the great stone statues of Tihuanacu, which seemed miraculous to later generations. Sometimes it is said that the race of giants who lived in the first age of the world, the times of *chamajpacha*, angered Virajocha and when he appeared again to create the sun, he turned those first men into stone. Another version says that when he created the present races of men he first fashioned stone prototypes of all the peoples at Tihuanacu and after this model he instructed his assistants to call into being the various peoples from rocks and caverns, lakes, streams and fountains, each in its appointed district, 'Leaving the island,' Sarmiento goes on, 'he passed by the lake to the main land, taking

MYTH AND ARCHAEOLOGY

with him the two servants who survived. He went to a place now called Tihuacanu in the province of Colla-suyu, and in this place he sculptured and designed on a great piece of stone, all the nations that he intended to create. This done, he ordered his two servants to charge their memories with the names of all tribes that he had depicted, and of the valleys and provinces where they were to come forth, which were those of the whole land. He ordered that each one should go by a different road, naming the tribes, and ordering them all to go forth and people the country. His servants, obeying the command of Virajocha, set out on their journey and work. . . . Virajocha himself did the same along the road between those taken by his two servants, naming all the tribes and places by which he passed. At the sound of his voice, every place obeyed, and people came forth, some from lakes, others from fountains, valleys, caves, trees, rocks and hills, spreading over the land and multiplying to form the nations which are today in Peru.' Which accords too with what Cieza de León tells us of the belief among Aymara peoples that each community or *ayllu* was sprung from some natural feature of the district in which they lived.

The version of Juan de Betanzos, which is one of the earliest and the fullest which has survived, deserves to be read in full. 'In ancient times, they say, the land and province of Peru was dark and there was no light nor day in it. That there was at this time a certain race in it, which race had a certain Lord who commanded them and to whom they were subject. The name of the race and of the Lord who commanded them they do not remember. And in those times when this land was all night they say that there came out of a lake which is in this land of Peru in the province which they call Collasuyo, a Lord whom they called Con Ticci Viracocha, who they say had brought out with him a certain number of peoples, how many they do not remember. And when he had come out of this lake he went to a place close to the lake, where today is a town which they call Tihuanacu in this province already mentioned of Collao; and when he had come there with his people, then they say he suddenly made there the sun and the day, and commanded the sun to traverse the course which it traverses; and then they say he made the stars and the moon. The which Con Ticci Viracocha they say had once before come out of that lake and on this first occasion he came out he made the sky and the earth and left it all dark; and that he made that race which existed in the time of darkness already mentioned, and that that race did a certain ill service to this Viracocha, and as he was angered with them he returned this second time and came out as before he had done and then in punishment for the wrath which they had caused him he made that race and their Lord to be turned into stone.

'As he so came out and in that self-same hour, as we have already said, they say that he made the sun and the day and the moon and stars; and this done, in that place of Tihuanacu he made of stone certain people and a kind of pattern of the people which were hereafter to be produced, doing it in the following manner: he made of stone a certain number of people and a chief who governed them and was their lord, and many pregnant women and others recently delivered and the children they had in cradles as was their usage; all which made in stone he set apart in a certain place; and he then made another province there in Tihuanacu, fashioning them of stone in the manner afore said, and when he had finished making them he commanded all his people that all those whom he had there with him should depart, leaving two only in his company, whom he told to look at those statues and the names which had been given to each species, pointing to them and saying: "These shall be called such and shall proceed from such a spring in such a province and shall people it and there they shall increase; and these shall issue from such a cavern and shall be called such and such, and such a district shall they populate; and as I have so made and fashioned them here of stone, so shall they issue from the springs, rivers, caves and peaks, in the provinces which I have spoken and named to you; and all of you shall go in that direction (pointing to them where rises the sun), dividing them each one his separate direction and showing to them the course each was to take."

'And thus set forth those viracochas of whom you have heard, and went through the provinces which Viracocha had said unto them, calling in each province as they arrived, each one of them in the province to which they were to go, those whom the Viracocha in Tihuanacu had shown to them in stone that they were to issue forth in such and such a province; each one of those viracochas placing himself there close to the site where it had been told them that such a people was to issue forth; and being so, there that Viracocha spoke in a loud voice "Such a one, come forth and populate this land which is deserted because thus was the com-

MYTH AND ARCHAEOLOGY

mand of the Con Ticci Viracocha who made the world." And as they thus called, then came forth such peoples in those parts and places as had been told them by the Viracocha. And so, they say, they went calling forth the peoples from the caves, rivers, fountains and high mountain crests and peopling the land in the direction where rises the sun....'

It is clear that we have here a fusion of three mythological stages: (1) a very primitive topological level connecting the various local groups with natural features; (2) a cosmological myth; and (3) an aetiological myth expressing the wonder of a later age at the stonework of Tihuacanu and finding for it a supernatural origin. It is curious that this whole cycle of mythology contains no hint of a racial memory of tribal migration from outside the Andean region. It may be that the story of the men of *chamac pacha*, who lived the life of beasts without light or sun and who were destroyed by the Creator to give place to new races, embodies a racial memory of a people, perhaps the Urus, who preceded the Aymaras on the Altiplano. If so, we should expect the myth to contain at the same time some memory of the provenance of the Aymaras rather than to connect their origin also with the Altiplano. But always Aymara mythology claims that they were created in the land around the lake.

Even the Creator was unnamed. He was called Ticci Virajocha, which means 'Creator Lord' and is a title not a name. When the Spanish first appeared in the land they were addressed as 'Virajocha' as a term of respect and today the word 'virajocha' is the equivalent in Aymara of 'caballero' in Spanish. I was always addressed as 'Virajocha' by the Indians if they were speaking Aymara or 'caballero' if they were speaking Spanish. Other epithets were added to the divine name to describe the attributes he was believed to possess. Montesinos tells us that the god of the Pirua dynasty of Tihuanacu was called Illatici Huira Cocha. To this name was sometimes added the epithet Yachachic (Teacher), or, according to Sarmiento and other writers, Pachayachachi (Teacher of the World). The word 'Illa' means 'light' or 'glory' (Illapu is the god of storm and lightning). 'Tici' or 'Ticci' means 'original cause' or 'foundation.' According to Montesinos 'Huira' is a corruption of 'Pirua' (the name also of the founder of the first Megalithic Dynasty), which means 'granary' or 'storehouse of all things.' Finally, 'Kocha' ordinarily means 'Lake', though Montesinos says, on what authority is not clear, that it here means 'abyss and profundity.' Thus the divine name of the god worshipped by the founders of Tihuanacu may be interpreted: 'The light and glory, the creator and originator, he from the Lake in whom all things have their being, the teacher of the world'—certainly no mean conception of deity.

Legend and tradition have telescoped the long line of civilized development which preceded the Incas, while retaining some memory of primitive inhabitants on the verge of civilization and little removed from the hunting and 'food gathering' stage. Garcilaso says, repeating the story current in the Inca royal family 'In bygone centuries all these regions which you see were covered with mountains and brush, and the people in those times lived like brutes and wild animals, without religion or polity, without houses or towns, without cultivating or sowing the land, without covering or clothing themselves, for they did not know how to work cotton or wool to make garments; they lived in twos and threes, as they happened to join together in the hollows and crevices and caves of the earth. Like beasts they ate herbs of the field and roots and uncultivated fruits which the trees bore of their own accord and human flesh. They covered themselves with leaves or the bark of trees and the skins of animals; others went naked. In a word they lived like wild beasts or animals that are hunted and even their women they possessed like brutes, for they did not know to own and recognize wives of their own.' (I, xv) Garcilaso wrote, of course, to the great glory of the Incas and is here repeating the Inca version—which he accepted—making them responsible for bringing the benefits of civilization and culture and social organization to the people. But he is not alone in this. The almost complete absence in the early chroniclers of any reference to a civilization before the Incas would give the impression, if we depended on them alone, that agricultural civilization and political organization had first been brought to this region by the Incas, although this is obviously impossible if the dynasty originated about A.D. 1200. Probably, as has been suggested, when the Incas began to systematize the memorized history of the past, they excluded the contributions made by their predecessors to the development of civilization while retaining the picture of a race of hunters and food-gatherers, living the life of animals, who had occupied the Andean region before the immigration of the bearers of agricultural lore and culture. The very curious thing once more is that no memory should have survived

MYTH AND ARCHAEOLOGY

of this immigration, but that instead mythology should consistently represent the agricultural invaders as indigenous sons of the region in which they had settled.

It is the archaeological discoveries of the last fifty years which have shown quite conclusively that far from starting with the Incas—with Tihuanacu as a mysterious and almost supernatural heritage from a remote and unconnected people and age —there had been a steady growth of civilization to a high level before the Inca monarchy was founded. Some historians now even go so far as to say with Ricardo Rojas of the University of Buenos Aires 'The dynasty of the fourteen kings which ended with Atahuallpa corresponds to an epoch of decadence. The Incas, inheritors of archaic cultures superior to their own, were politicians and warriors in the Roman manner; by war they founded a communist empire, which was still expanding when the Spanish arrived.'

We shall now summarize the present conclusions of archaeology up to the Inca period.

2. ARCHAEOLOGY

With regard to the important matter of chronology Peruvian archaeology is unusually adamant. In the absence of written records, of dated stones or datable contacts with external cultures, with no fixed points of time derived from calculable astronomical events or in any other way, the dating of the various archaeological epochs according to centuries is little better than guesswork. Without some known date as a starting point and a source of comparison it is difficult to gauge the antiquity of archaeological finds absolutely in time from the state of their preservation when found. And the preservative properties of the special conditions of soil and climate in the coastal regions and the mountain regions of the Andes are so different from each other and from conditions elsewhere, that it is difficult to make an absolute estimate of age by comparing the state of the archaeological material here with that of datable material elsewhere in the world. Even comparative dating within Peruvian history itself presents serious difficulties, since conditions are widely different in different parts of the country, material is very irregularly available, and the best material from the archaeological point of view is not stratified in 'layers' to anything like the same extent as is often found elsewhere. Wendell C. Bennett says in the *Handbook of South American Indians* 'At the present time, there is no absolute chronology in Andean archaeology. The only concrete date is 1532, the year of the arrival of the Spaniards in their historic conquest of the area. Otherwise, calendrical dates are guesses and, furthermore, prospects of obtaining dates on the basis of internal evidence are meagre.' It is to be remembered, too, that South American archaeology as a science is in its infancy. Research has been sporadic and interpretation has often been influenced by extraneous motives. Since the time when the Spanish first began to loot and destroy in the search for gold, archaeological material has suffered abuse and distortion; it is still being continually frittered away by illicit diggings and sales. Serious work still remains to be begun on many of the most interesting areas, such as the sites at Escoma and elsewhere on the east shores of Lake Titicaca, and future discoveries may do much to modify or revolutionize the conclusions which are at present tentatively held. The abundance and wealth of the material recovered from the sites which have been searched is unbelievable in its value and variety; its historical interpretation remains doubtful until research has covered a wider area more evenly.

The archaeological history of Peru must therefore continue to be constrained by the sporadic nature of research and discovery. It must also be interpreted in close relation to the geography of the country, which intimately affected both the actual development of populations and culture and also the survival of archaeological material.

From Vilcanota in southern Peru the Andes run southwards in two chains or Cordilleras which spreading in a vast oval enclose the Lake Titicaca basin and the Altiplano of Bolivia, an enormous tableland at about 12,000 feet above sea level. Northwards from Vilcanota run three chains, to meet again at the node of Pasco in central Peru and enclosing the two high valleys of the Urubamba and the Apurimac, which run roughly parallel in a northwesterly direction. North again of Pasco run three chains enclosing the high valleys of Huallaga and Marañon. To the east of the most easterly chains begin the wet tropical jungle territories of the Amazon basin. West of the westernmost chains a series of short horizontal spurs run down to the coast, dividing the coastal region into a large number of small valleys often watered by short rivers which flow down from the western chains to the Pacific.

MYTH AND ARCHAEOLOGY 51

Climatically the coastal region is hot and dry, with no regular rainy season and often for long periods without rainfall. Except where watered by the rivers, the land is desert and barren. Population groups were formed in the valleys, where extensive irrigation works increased the areas of fertility produced by the natural watercourses. The high plateaux enclosed by the various mountain chains are frigid, with temperate high valleys in their midst. They have an annual wet season on which agriculture depends with the aid of artificial irrigation and the area of cultivable land was increased by artificial terracing. The high mountain regions were called *puna*, the temperate highland valleys *keshuas* and the low valleys of the coastal region and the eastern jungle were called *yungas*. Travel and communication, particularly through the whole extent of the high plateaux, appear to have been frequent. But the geographical nature of the country inevitably favoured the growth of a large number of population centres which, although in communication with each other, developed their individual cultures with a relative degree of independence. Archaeological research has discovered a large number of such population centres and has traced the sequence of the various stages of development in each and the influences of one upon the other. There is an enormous amount of material available, particularly from the coastal region where the dry sandy soil and the absence of rain has preserved mummies, textiles, feathers and other delicate structures as well as ceramics, stone, metal and bone implements.

Archaeologists distinguish three main coastal groups. (1) The valleys in the north around the modern towns of Trujillo and Chimbote. The general style of this region is called 'Mochica' or 'Chimu' and is particularly notable for its fine realistic pottery, which is like a picture book of the life of the people. An extraordinarily detailed and vivid impression of the life and culture of these peoples can be reconstructed imaginatively from the ceramics contained in the Magdalena Museum at Lima. There are groups of war scenes, domestic scenes, hunting, a large number of portrait vessels depicting various diseases and physical deformities, the characteristic occupations for example of the blind as musicians, etc., sexual and phantastic themes—in a word a pictured record which is difficult to equal from anywhere else in the world. This region at some early date became politically unified under the rich and resplendent Chimu kingdom, with its centre at Chan-Chan near Trujillo, which persisted until it was conquered by Topa Inca about 1475 and incorporated into the Inca Empire. (2) There was a central group around Lima, with centres at Ancon, Rimac and Pachacamac, where early remains ante-dating abundant examples of Tihuanacu influence have recently been discovered. (3) Finally the southern group was centered round the valleys of Nazca, Ica, Paracas and Chincha. Here enormous burial grounds have been discovered, with great abundance of pottery, textiles in an excellent state of preservation, and general utensils and tools. There are in this region signs of very extensive irrigation works, which were maintained until the effects of the Spanish invasion led to their destruction or abandonment and over some ninety kilometres near Nazca are curious geometrical markings on the surface of the soil, which are still very prominently visible from the air, and whose purpose is not known.

As one drives along the coastal road from Arequipa to Lima, passing occasional fertile valleys amid oceans of barren desert, as one sees the signs of ancient irrigation systems and ancient remains showing how much more extensive were the habitable areas in prehistoric times, the extent to which neglect has depopulated a once prosperous and fertile land becomes impressively obvious. Water is the key of life in this region. When irrigation is abandoned the country dies. It died with the Spanish invasion and its resurrection has been but indifferently successful to this day.

The frequent representation of tropical animals such as monkeys, parrots, snakes, toucans, and the ubiquity of the jaguar and puma motifs, often in combination with the snake, in the ceramic and sculptured decoration of the coastal region has caused much surprise. The Pacific coast of Peru owes its extreme dryness and hence its barren desolation to the cold Humboldt current, which sweeps up from the Antarctic until it meets and checks a warm southward-flowing current off the coast of Ecuador. In 1925 and 1926 the Humboldt current for some reason failed, the warm current came further south and torrential rains fell on the coast of Peru. If this condition were maintained for some years, the whole coastal region would be turned into tropical jungle. It is, therefore, not beyond the bounds of possibility that in prehistoric times or somewhere about the beginning of the Christian era the climate was very different from what it now is and fauna and flora not known in historical times to have been acclimatized in the coastal belt may have been common at an earlier date. But

MYTH AND ARCHAEOLOGY

against this assumption the state of preservation in which the mummies and other archaeological remains have been found could only be accounted for by extreme dryness of climate and soil, so that it seems more probable that the familiarity of the early peoples with tropical animals must be explained by intercommunication with the eastern jungles of the Amazonian region.

Little is known about the racial type to which the bearers of this early civilization belonged. They have now disappeared or become merged with the conquering Quechua and the many racial immigrants since the Conquest. The coastal population of Peru is today a racial cocktail into which are stirred Quechua, Spanish, Negro, Chinese, Japanese and perhaps some surviving influence of the pre-Quechua peoples whose life and work is now known only from their archaeological remains. The Quechua element now predominates and the costume and language are mainly Quechua, although the temperament of the coastal peoples is more lively and mercurial than that of the highland Quechuas. The bodies which are found in the vast burial grounds of the coast show a peculiarly elongated skull deformation due to manipulation of the skull in infancy, which is not characteristic of the Incas. Together with this type are tens of thousands of Quechuas without skull deformation, evidencing the bulk colonization of the coastal region under Inca times.

As has been said, it has not been possible to trace the gradual emergence of civilization in the Andean region. Our archaeological evidence starts with civilizations already well developed and presuming long centuries of agricultural experience. Archaeologists divide the time covered by the known evidence into three periods, Early, Middle and Late, up to the time of the Incas. It is now customary to date the beginning of the Early period, before which we have no knowledge of what was happening, about A.D. 300, although it is admitted that this date is little more than a guess and that it may be as many centuries *before* the Christian era. Within this period, from perhaps about A.D. 300 until the founding of the Inca Empire about A.D. 1200, two *general* cultures have been distinguished which seem to have exercised a strong influence upon the small individual centres of population without destroying their individuality or wholly distorting their independent development.

At the beginning of the period is the Chavin culture, marked by a distinctive style in architecture, stonework and decoration, named after the principle site at which it has been discovered, Chavin de Huantar in the north of the central highlands of Peru on a small tributary of the river Marañon. The style spread along the coastal population groups as far south as Paracas and the Pisco peninsula; its extent in the highlands cannot yet be gauged from existing discovery. Extensive construction in stone always implies some unification of population with a political centralization which will free the necessary manpower for non-productive labour, and in a country like ancient Peru, where population groups were geographically scattered in a large number of relatively independent centres, such unification is the more necessary for works which are beyond the capacity of any one group on its own. Chavin must have been produced as the result of such political unification. And the prevalence of the feline motif in sculpture and decoration seems to imply that the political organization was religious in character or involved the propagation of a unified religious form. Indeed the site of Chavin itself appears to be a religious centre rather than an important population metropolis. Wendell C. Bennett writes as follows of Chavin in the *Handbook of South American Indians*: 'The chronological position of the Chavin period as the earliest yet discovered in Peru does little to solve the problem of the ultimate origin of the higher civilization in this area. Chavin is a sophisticated and complete culture with a good knowledge of stone masonry, architecture, goldwork, weaving, stone carving, ceramics, and agriculture. There is some evidence of a reasonably well organized political organization, at least to the extent of being able to erect large buildings. A dominant religion, plus perhaps a religious organization, is implied by the conventionalization of design, altars, religious centres, and the ubiquitous feline concept' (pp. 91-2).

The Tihuanacu culture, called after the site at which it is found, has two periods, Early and Classical, and the Classical Tihuanacu style had great influence on the coastal sites towards the end of the Early Coastal period and formed the basis of the Middle Coastal period. In the *Handbook of South American Indians* the Early Tihuanacu period is dated about A.D. 700, Classical Tihuanacu about A.D. 900, and the influence of the Classical Tihuanacu style in the coastal regions and elsewhere in Peru is dated between A.D. 800 and A.D. 900 and onwards. My own view tends to make the Early Tihuanacu style contemporary with Chavin and to date both rather considerably earlier than A.D. 300

MYTH AND ARCHAEOLOGY

and I would put the Classical Tihuanacu style earlier than A.D. 900. It seems to me that the dating on purely archaeological evidences has not taken into consideration the length of time necessary to give rise to the widespread political organizations which alone could make possible the large volume of non-productive manpower needed for great megalithic works in an agricultural community and a country whose soil does not easily favour the support of surplus labour.

3. TIHUANACU

The modern hamlet of Tihuanacu is situated at 16° 33' latitude south and 68° 42' longitude west, in the Province of Ingavi of the Department of La Paz of Bolivia, about eighteen kilometres due east of Guaqui, the port of the Bolivian-Peruvian railway on Lake Titicaca, in a level plain between two ranges of hills, Kimsa-Chata to the south and Achata to the north. It is on the present road from La Paz to Guaqui and lay just off the old Inca highroad from Cuzco to Sucre. Its height above sea level is 3,845 metres, 35 metres above the present level of the lake. It is a *pueblo* of the Aymara Indians, with houses built of adobe and stones removed from the ancient ruins, a fine stone church, an important cemetery and a large public square paved with beautiful tiles from the ruins. The prehistoric remains are on the outskirts of the present village. They are generally thought to mark the site of the metropolis of the earliest civilizations of South America and are in many ways the most interesting survivals on the continent.

The origin of Tihuanacu was a mystery to the natives who were encountered in its vicinity by the earliest Spaniards to penetrate and remains a mystery to this day. Its purpose has been variously represented as a religious centre and as a political metropolis. The view of Philip Means that it was an important market has much to recommend it and would not preclude a religious and political significance as well. It seems not to have been a large city with a heavy concentration of population. As to the antiquity of the remains estimates are vastly discordant. The early chroniclers such as Ondegardo and Acosta, relying on the verbal memories of the Indians, ascribed to the remains an age of some few centuries only. Max Uhle ascribes to them some fifteen centuries, José Maria Camacho about four thousand years and Arturo Posnansky ten or twelve thousand years.

Federico Diez de Medina defends the Indian tradition that Tihuanacu had its origin in the time of the *chamacpacha* (the age of obscurity) or the last Glacial epoch. Official archaeology has recently tended in the opposite direction and places the earliest Tihuanacu period after Chavin and some four or five centuries before the Incas.

The etymology of the name 'Tihuanacu' has been the subject of controversy from the earliest Colonial period and remains obscure. It is not even agreed whether the name is Aymara or Quechua, if either. There is a legend that the Inca monarch Tupac Yupanqui despatched a courier, or *chasqui*, who arrived with unusual speed at Tihuanacu, whereupon the Inca exclaimed 'Tiay huanacu', which in Aymara means 'Sit and rest, guanaco!' This legend was rationalized by the Conde Francis de Castelnau in *Historia del Viaje* (1850), who supposed that Tihuanacu was a stopping place for caravans of llamas and guanacos on the long Cuzco road (which of course makes the origin of the name later than that of Cuzco). Attempted derivations from both Quechua and Aymara are almost as many as there are writers and are so far-fetched and various that they must be wide of the mark. It is certain, however, that the word retains no natural and obvious significance for those who now speak either Aymara or Quechua as their mother tongue. This I have verified personally. Although students of Aymara declare that it has a distinctively Aymara phonology, that would be inevitably the case as it has been handed down for centuries in the Aymara language, and is not evidence that it was of Aymaran origin. It seems, therefore, most reasonable to suppose that it belongs to a language other than Aymara and Quechua, rather than that it has a recondite significance in either of those languages which is obscure to those who speak them. Equally obscure is another old name for the site, 'Chucahua', which has come down through the clouds of history. Cobo says that until the Inca conquest it was called in Aymara *Paypicala*, which means 'stone in the middle', because this stone city was believed to be the centre of the world. If Cobo is right, and if the name 'Tihuanacu' was due to the Incas, it cannot be Quechua for the Incas would not have re-named it meaninglessly. I have not seen this suggested elsewhere, but if Cobo is to be believed and the name 'Tihuanacu' is due to the Incas, it may be a word from the esoteric language which according to Garcilaso the Inca royal family spoke. The use of a name from this esoteric language could be accounted for by the special religious sanctity of the place.

Owing to the extensive depredations which have taken place and to the fact that the ruins are set in the midst of a vast expanse of the Altiplano which would dwarf the most impressive structures into puny insignificance, the first sight of Tihuanacu is apt to be disappointing to the prosaic visitor. An effort of imagination is necessary to reconstruct the imposing reality which was once there. Perhaps wonder is first aroused by the size of the individual stones, some of which weigh a hundred tons and must have weighed twice as much when transported before shaping. When you consider that these immense blocks were transported over difficult country without the use of the wheel and that they were carved to razor sharp edges and polished to the smoothness of glass by people who did not know the use of iron, you are inclined to disbelieve the visible reality before your eyes. I shall not here attempt to describe in detail the remains still to be seen or the various reconstructions which have been advanced. I shall first summarize the views of Arturo Posnansky, who spent the greater part of a lifetime in the study of Tihuanacu and is recognized to be the most prolific of all students of these remains, although the theories he reaches from his facts are too often both fanciful and inconsistent.

Posnansky claims to distinguish five periods in the pre-history of Tihuanacu.[1]

First Period

In the earliest times of which any trace can be recovered the Altiplano was inhabited by primitive groups of people, possibly racially akin to the Arawaks, with little political cohesion and a low degree of culture. They lived in caves hollowed out of the ground, roofed with stone tiles or straw in the form of a 'false arch', and so small that inside them it was necessary to adopt a crouched position with the knees beneath the chin. (This type of dwelling can still be seen at Kollana, a purely Indian settlement which has kept its identity a few leagues to the south of La Paz and dwellings consisting of caves hollowed out in the sides of mountains are still inhabited in the region of Huayna Potosi near the mine La Union. Today too the crouching posture with the knees drawn up beneath the chin is much used by the Aymara Indians for

[1] *Tihuanacu: The Cradle of American Man.*

sleeping, protected against the cold by their ponchos.) Posnansky thinks that at this early period the Altiplano was considerably lower than at present, the climate was warm and beneficent, the soil fertile, life was easy and the region densely populated.

The first or primitive period of Tihuanacu was the result of predominance of one of these local tribes, superior in intelligence and resource, which chose the margins of Lake Titicaca and Tihuanacu as the centre for the empire they established. The constructions of the primitive period are sunk into the ground but walled inside and were probably roofed. The walls are constructed of large blocks of stones roughly shaped into pillars and set up without foundations at intervals of about two metres. The spaces between the pillars were filled with smaller square-cut stones polished on the inside face. Peculiar to this period are the carved stone heads, rough but realistic in style and cut in the round, utterly different from the stylised geometrical carving in low relief which is characteristic of later periods. There were also more than life-size three-dimensional sculptures, crude but vigorous and full of power. Two stand on either side of the entrance to the village church. Two more and a number of heads and smaller figures have been placed in an enclosure outside the stadium of Miraflores, a suburb of La Paz, and a number of heads are to be seen in the Archaeological Museum of La Paz.

Bronze was unknown to these early stone carvers and the material in which they worked was the relatively soft calcareous sedimentary sandstone, red and grey Grauwake, which is plentiful in the region and around Quinachata, Quimsachata and Andamarca. (The more easily manageable limestones, although they exist—as does marble—in the vicinity of La Paz, were never used by the prehistoric stoneworkers of the Altiplano, perhaps because they lacked the means of quarrying them.)

Second Period

The building of the first period was not completed but seems to have been violently interrupted either by some natural catastrophe—Posnansky suggests a volcanic eruption (although there are no signs of volcanic larva deposits), a short glacial period (although of this too there are no signs in the surviving stones) and the overflow of the lake (though there are no mud deposits)— or by invasion and conquest by a new race of immigrants to the

MYTH AND ARCHAEOLOGY

Altiplano. The difference in style and still more in the technique of the later constructions is so great and so obviously not the result of a continuous development, that Posnansky rightly says, 'it is manifestly impossible that the constructors of the works of the primitive period can have been the same as those of the later period without having received a strong impulse from outside.' This outside impulse he attributes to the immigration of a new race, the Kollas.[1]

The sandstone used in the primitive period gives place to the harder, volcanic Andesite. Although the same constructional principle of columns intercalated in the walls is used, the blocks of stone are carved with fine exactness and fitted together with sharp accuracy by means of 'keys' cut in the stone and held by wedges of wood or metal. In place of the old realistic carving in the round is an entirely different system of stylised semi-geometrical carving in low relief of fine craftsmanship.

Third Period

About his third period Posnansky is even more incoherent than usual, which is saying much. In Chapter VII of his first volume he describes the third period as a gradual development from the second, distinguished from it by signs of greater technical skill and heavier and stronger construction within the same style—'one period keeps flowing gradually from the other.' In Chapter IV of the same volume, and elsewhere, he describes the third period as 'the period of "enchased" or polygonal stone.' Posnansky held that this polygonal style was introduced by a new immigration of the Quechuas after work upon Tihuanacu in its second period had been abruptly brought to a close by a large inundation of the lake. This polygonal style is characteristic of the buildings in Peru, and is best known to tourists from the examples in and around Cuzco. The most significant fact of all is that this style is *nowhere found at Tihuanacu*. It is found in the Island of the Sun, in Huanakaure, in and around Cuzco, in the fortress cities of the Urubamba valley and further north. But as Posnansky himself says 'The architectural style of the period of enchased stone is completely distinct from that of Tihuanacu.' It can hardly, therefore, have been carried from Tihuanacu into Peru, for, although it reached the lake, it did not reach Tihuanacu.

[1] See above on the Kollas, p. 9.

Fourth Period

Posnansky's fourth period is that of building in adobe and drystone, the periods of the *huacas*, and he holds that it was due to an emigration from the Altiplano towards the coastal regions and a more temperate climate when the Altiplano began to cool.

Fifth Period

Posnansky's fifth period is that of the Incas.

If we take the more solid factual side of Posnansky's work, which contains some of the most thorough description of Tihuanacu that has been published, and neglect his more extravagant theories, there seem to be two clearly defined periods, his first and second periods, corresponding to the Early and Classical Tihuanacu styles of contemporary archaeologists. The first period is characterized by realistic sculpture in the round and the latter by more geometrical and formalized figures and stylized pattern carving in low relief. It is probable that the two periods are also characterized by differences in architectural style and structural conventions, although the site has been so disrupted by treasure hunters, vandalistic pilferers of stone who have used it as a readymade quarry for building material and by incompetent archaeological digging, that it is not now easy to discriminate the early from the late by position at the site. Posnansky states that the early period used mainly the softer sandstone and the later period basalt, but even this cannot be entirely proved. Some of the statues which seem to approximate to the Classical style are in sandstone. Yet the two styles and the techniques which go with them are so distinct that it is flying in the face of reason and probability to suppose that they are not the outcome of two periods widely separated in time, if not the products of different peoples. Stonework, whether sculpture and carving or stone construction, is the job of experts. And the stonemason, like other expert craftsmen, is conservative. Style and technique go closely together and both are the result of long experience and tradition handed down through many generations. The old stonemason, unlike the modern, did not work in any of a number of styles to suit the taste of his customer; the tradition in which he had been brought up and trained was binding and right. And the excellence of the work at both periods of Tihuanacu bespeaks a long tradition for both. It is unthinkable that both styles should have been produced at the same time or without a long interval which could explain the lapse of the earlier tradition and the gradual emergence of the later, for the one is not a logical development from the other. The two are distinct and neither leads into the other. In the case of people working with enormous monolithic blocks and with a minimum of tools and mechanical aids the importance of traditional techniques, and therefore of the related styles both of construction and of artistic representation, is far greater than when perfected mechanical methods afford greater versatility. In this matter the craftsman psychology of the stoneworker is more necessary to understand than the theoretical speculations of the modern archaeologist.

Both Tihuanacu styles differ profoundly from the Inca styles and indeed from stonework elsewhere in Peru. Except at Chavin and in certain sites closely related to Tihuanacu, such as Pucara, sculptural carving is not used for architectural purposes. There are a few stones still to be seen in Cuzco itself on which snakes are somewhat crudely carved in relief (I have seen rather similar snake carvings on natural boulders beside the upper Beni amid tropical jungle); but this is all. It is true that in their crusade for the extirpation of idolatry the Spaniards destroyed such images as they found. But destruction could not have been so complete without far greater constructional damage if sculpture had been integral to the buildings of the Incas. And in Machu Picchu, which the Spanish crusading ferocity never reached, there is a complete absence of carving, representational or geometrical. In Tihuanacu too the polygonal style and the style of construction with squared and faced blocks, which were the basis of all Inca building, is absent. The corbelled arch, used by the Incas, is also unknown at Tihuanacu. It was a generally accepted belief of the natives, repeated by Cieza de León, Garcilaso, Cobo and most of the chroniclers, that the Incas built Cuzco after the model of Tihuanacu. But these fundamental differences prove beyond doubt that Inca building depended upon a different and independent tradition of stone-working and was neither a copy of Tihuanacu (a copy of style and technique would in any case have been impossible to the times of which we are speaking) nor a development from the style and tradition of Tihuanacu.

Megalithic stonework presupposes social organization, a strong central government which can direct large-scale man-power into non-productive labour and sufficient productivity to support such non-productive man-power. In a region such as the Andean highlands this means a fairly extensive empire with a strong despotic centralized government, a fairly dense population and agriculture considerably above maintenance level. It is possible that some of the man-power was sporadic and seasonal, Indians working on construction only at the agricultural close seasons, as now many work in the mines part of the year and on their lands for the rest. But this can apply only to heavy unskilled manual labour. Stone working is a highly skilled technical craft, even in its engineering aspects. It cannot be performed as a spare time craft by unskilled agriculturalists. There must have been a large body of skilled workers with a long technical tradition behind them, helped by periodic influxes of unskilled man-power and supported by the State. For these reasons I hold with Julio C. Tello (*Antiguo Peru*, 1929) that there was certainly at a very early period in Peruvian history an extensive political unification of population in the form of a strong centralized empire with its nucleus not far from Lake Titicaca, of which we have little or no record in written chronicles or in surviving tradition. The marked differences in style and technique between the early and the classical period would indicate a very long history of development or more probably, since the two styles and techniques do not appear to have developed logically from each other, successive political organizations. They must have been highly centralized, with considerable man-power, and agricultural production must have reached the level at which it was capable of supporting a large body of non-productive labour. For an organization which is capable of planning and producing works of the size of Chavin or Tihuanacu, probably for religious or non-utility purposes, would inevitably have demanded a relatively high proportion of administrative and other non-productive man-power in addition to the labour actually engaged on construction. In a region so little conducive to agricultural surplus as the Central and Southern Andes this achievement implies far greater efficiency and pertinacity than in regions more naturally fertile. This political organization I call the Megalithic Empire—or Empires—and I am inclined to date it rather earlier than the time now generally ascribed to Chavin. A fuller presentation of the facts upon which this view is based will be found in Clements R. Markham, *The Incas of Peru* (1910), ch. 2, José de la Riva Agüero, *La Historia en*

MYTH AND ARCHAEOLOGY

el Peru, and Julio C. Tello, *Antiguo Peru* (1929). Although archaeological discoveries in the last thirty years have necessitated some modification for their view, I am convinced that the assumption of a great centralized Megalithic political organization is inescapable. It is possible that local variations occurred within this organization and that these attained prominence at various periods; and it is possible that Chavin may have to be included within this framework.[1]

It has sometimes been maintained that the climate of the Altiplano must in an earlier age have been more benign to support the population necessary to supply the stupendous man-power required for such constructional works. And indeed although the margins of Lake Titicaca are still said to be the most densely populated agricultural region in South America, such an achievement would be ludicrously beyond the capacity of the present meagre population. As will be seen, the first necessity of the political organization created by the Incas was to increase the area of arable lands by irrigation and terracing. Both terracing and irrigation were known to the builders of Tihuanacu, but it seems impossible that even with these aids the present unfriendly soil and climate could have supported the necessary surplus labour within the restricted region of the lake. Posnansky and others have supposed that at the time Tihuanacu was built the Altiplano was much lower, with a warm and fertile climate, and that it has since been elevated several thousand metres. Quite apart from the geological unlikelihood of such a supposition, it is certain that if Tihuanacu and the lake had risen several thousand metres above their former level, the constructions which now puzzle archaeologists could not have remained *in situ*. That they are there to constitute a problem is in itself proof that this explanation of the problem is not true. But if the climate and the land were then much as they are now, the political organizations of populations under the Megalithic Empire must have been very extensive.

There is evidence that the characteristic ceramic style of Tihuanacu extended as far north as modern Colombia, throughout the coastal region of Peru, south into northern Argentine and central Chile and to the eastern Cordillera of Bolivia, an area

[1] In the appendix to this chapter a reconstruction is suggested from Montisenos, the only literary record which preserves a tradition of a pre-Inca Megalithic Empire of the Andes.

hardly inferior to that later covered by the Inca Empire. But it must always be remembered that the distribution of ceramics and artifacts may be due to barter and commerce. It has also been argued from the etymology of place names, by E. W. Mindendorff and subsequent writers, that the influence of an Aymara-speaking people once extended widely over northern Peru and south of the Bolivian Altiplano. For what they are worth these arguments offer subsidiary support to the belief in an early Megalithic Empire of the Aymaras or a people speaking the same language.

Both the first and the second period at Tihuanacu appear to have been terminated abruptly by some catastrophe which stopped the work before completion. The interruption is proved by the large number of stones from both periods which have been left incompletely carved or shaped. About the nature of the interruptions it is possible only to guess. Most people, like Posnansky, have supposed either a great natural catastrophe such as the overflow of the lake or invasion and the disruption of the political organization which was responsible for the structure.

It is usually supposed that the Aymaras were responsible for one or both of the constructional periods at Tihuanacu, and therefore for the political empire which made them possible—but rather for lack of any other plausible alternative than because there are any strong positive reasons for attributing this achievement to the Aymaras. Aymara mythology and legend retain no memory of the origin of Tihuanacu but supply supernatural explanations for what seemed to them beyond human powers. The Aymara cosmological mythology refers the building of Tihuanacu to the time of *Chamac Pacha*, before or contemporary with the creation of the present races of mankind. One version of the myth explains the huge stone figures as a race of giants who lived before the creation of the Sun and were turned to stone by the creator God. It was often said by the Indians that the whole of Tihuanacu was built miraculously in one night. A story is recorded by several writers that the stones came down of their own accord, or at the sound of a trumpet, from the mountain quarries and took up their proper positions at the site. A curious belief survived Inca days that the ancient race had known the secret, later forgotten, of softening the stone with certain herbs so that it became easily workable. All these legends seem to indicate that the Aymaras were not themselves workers in stone and had no racial memory that they themselves had built Tihuanacu. It seems curious indeed that, if they were the builders, the tradition should have perished so completely, even to the memory they had once possessed the technique of stone-masonry, although under the Incas stone construction was active all around them. Cieza de León says that in response to a question whether Tihuanacu had been built in the time of the Incas the Aymaras who were living there laughed and replied: 'It had been built long before the Incas ruled but that they were unable to say who had built it.' Aymara tradition therefore makes no claim to have constructed Tihuanacu but regards it as miraculous. Added to this is the fact that the Aymara does not display the undeniable aesthetic sense and the feeling for orderliness which is reflected in the remains from Tihuanacu. Their pottery shows no inherent gift for form or design, their homesteads and settlements are without the most elementary sense for neatness or planning, and in their handicrafts they display less latent aesthetic talent than the Quechua. Although centuries of economic depression would inhibit aesthetic development, some latent sense of form would be expected inevitably to manifest itself if it ever existed in the race, as indeed the modern Quechua, although his life has been for centuries indistinguishable from that of the Aymara, often displays some feeling for orderliness and layout and some instinctive sense of aesthetic form. The Aymara children at Tihuanacu now carve small stone figures in the manner of the large monolithic figures of the classical Tihuanacu period for tourists and are not without mechanical skill. But their own carvings of their homesteads have none of the neatness and design of this derivative work. As Enrique Finot says: 'If the Aymaras had been the most remote inhabitants of Tihuanacu, it would mean that this people had retrogressed, contrary to the laws of progress.' Finally the features and dress of the sculptured figures from the first period of Tihuanacu do not seem to have anything in common with the Aymara. This has been noticed by Cieza de León and a number of early writers. Cieza de León says, 'One sees that they have long garments different from those which we see among the natives of these provinces; on their heads they appear to have their own type of adornment.' Posnansky has noticed that the hair style of some of these early statues, consisting of a very large number of thin tightly braided tresses, is still used among the Urus.

The difficulty is to find any trace of an earlier people capable of the necessary organization and technique, and if the Aymaras have forgotten that they were builders of Tihuanacu, they have also forgotten that they entered the highlands as invaders and all their mythology and legend represents them as autochthonous. The difficulty would not be helped by supposing that the Aymaras were invaders who overthrew the civilization which built the first period Tihuanacu before it was completed and themselves later built up there a new metropolis of the classical period. For the stone construction of the classical Tihuanacu period is superior to anything else in Peru. G. E. Squire, who visited Tihuanacu in 1877, gave it as his considered opinion that: 'In no other part of the world have I seen stones cut with such mathematical precision and such admirable skill as in Peru; nor in all Peru have I encountered any comparable with those which are scattered about the plains of Tihuanacu.' Wendell C. Bennett says of the classic Tihuanacu period in the *Handbook of the South American Indians*: 'The Classic Tihuanacu period places great emphasis on masonry. No other Peruvian period matches the exactness and precision of the stonework in its careful cutting, dressing, squaring, and notching. The nearest rivals are Chavin and Inca, but even in those cultures the masonry is inferior.'

It might seem most reasonable that the Aymaras were invaders who overthrew the civilization which built the Classical period of Tihuanacu, that these builders retired after defeat at the Apurimac Valley and later gave rise to the Inca Empire. But against this is first the fact that the Aymara agricultural knowledge and social institutions seemed to demand a far longer period than this would allow, as also does their rooted disinclination to move from the harsh and difficult soil of the highlands, which has persisted against every inducement up to the present day. They seem essentially a highland people and by no means relatively new arrivals in the Altiplano. The second difficulty is that there are no traces of any predecessors of the Aymaras on the Altiplano who could have been capable of constructing the civilization which produced Tihuanacu. The Urus seem to have been hunters rather than agriculturalists and even less capable than the Aymaras of what was required.

The racial problem therefore remains unsettled. It will be solved, if at all, only after much more work has been done on the civilization of which Tihuanacu was the central achievement. In particular much archaeological investigation remains to be done at Escoma and many other sites along the east and northern shores of Lake Titicaca.

Prescott wrote in his *Conquest of Peru*: 'We may reasonably conclude that there existed in the country a race advanced in civilization before the time of the Incas; and, in conformity with nearly every tradition, we may derive this race from the neighbourhood of Lake Titicaca; a conclusion more strongly confirmed by the imposing architectural remains which still endure, after the lapse of so many years, on its borders. Who this race were, and whence they came, may afford a tempting theme for enquiry to the speculative antiquarian. But it is a land of darkness that lies far beyond the domain of history.' In the century which has lapsed since these words were written, many new discoveries have been made; but nothing can be added with any security about the origin of the Aymara people.

After the fall of the empire which produced the classical period at Tihuanacu it is thought that there ensued a long peiod of disorganization with no outstanding achievement. To this period are usually assigned the Chullpas or large circular burial towers which are found on the west coast of the lake and in southern Peru. There is, however, no great certainty that these towers are in fact later than Tihuanacu or that they are characteristically Aymara. The Aymaras, a people who have a very retentive racial memory—they still commonly refer to La Paz as Chuquiapu after four centuries—and whose culture is largely based on respect for the dead, seem never to have regarded the Chullpas as sacred places or as burial places within the period of written history. Nor is it known that in fact they ever used this form of burial. There is, however, a striking similarity between the shape and structure of the Chullpas and the houses built by the Chipayas in Bolivia.

Appendix

THE MEGALITHIC EMPIRE OF THE PIRUAS

Who then were these great builders of old? This people who made their homes in the mighty Andes, this petricolous people who reared in very truth a culture of the stone?

Of one thing we may be sure. The vast man-power required for works such as have been described necessitated strong political centralization over a wide area, a dense population—the present population of the Altiplano would be insufficient for works of such magnitude even though it were to be mobilized in its entirety—and an economic organization able to support the very large surplus of non-productive labour that was needed. Even though there were no records of it, we are bound to assume that there existed centuries before the Incas a Megalithic Empire, or Empires, uniting and controlling the tribes of the Andes.

Were then the people whom we call Aymaras the founders of the early Megalithic Empire of the Andes which built Tihuanacu? Their present qualities certainly would not lead us to suspect that they were ever capable of such achievement. They have little sense of unity and integration, have no inherited mechanical skill and their aesthetic powers are rudimentary. Nor, long as their racial memories are, do their traditions ever claim that they were the builders. Rather, as the early chroniclers have recorded for us, the Aymara traditions handed down from father to son in their folk ballads and romances repudiated any knowledge of the builders of Tihuanacu and invented supernatural origins for the remains which caused them such wonder and astonishment. Yet Aymara traditions all claim that they were autochthonous in the land, created by the god Virajocha from the lake, and retain no memory that they migrated from elsewhere to the Altiplano or of a previous race whom they conquered there. We know that they did migrate to their present home because it is established that all the South American native peoples arrived by the migration of a Mongoloid stock across the Behring Straits at the end of the Neolithic age; but we do not know from where they reached the Altiplano or when. Nor have we any record or trace of an earlier

MYTH AND ARCHAEOLOGY 69

people capable of greater achievement. The almost extinct Urus and Chipayas, who seem to have been more primitive than the Aymaras, were at an even lower level of civilization than them; just emerging from the nomadic stage, they were hunters and fishers and even their agriculture was elementary.

The problem is made more complicated by the fact that at Tihuanacu there are two distinct building techniques and styles, so different that it must be assumed they were the work of different peoples or dynasties. The style of the second period, usually called the Middle or Classical period, was not a gradual and logical development from the first but a new start in a new building tradition. And still a further complication. Both periods were brought to an abrupt end before their work was finished. That this was so we know beyond question from the large number of individual stones which were left unfinished and abandoned before their shaping was completed. Even the Sun Door itself was never finished. While most of the carving of the frieze was cut with beautiful precision and exact care, a few of the panels at the ends were only drawn in with incised outline and work was stopped before the carving could be completed. In the second case destruction was not complete, for although work upon Tihuanacu itself ceased, the style of the second period continued in a derivative and debased form almost until the time of the Incas and spread over the Andean region northwards as far as Quito, up and down the advanced cultural centres of the Peruvian coast, southwards into northern Argentine and eastwards to Cochabamba and the Cordillera Real and even into the great tropical plains of eastern Bolivia. Various causes have been conjectured for the disasters which brought to an abrupt close the two periods of Tihuanacu. It has been thought that the first period came to an end from some gigantic natural calamity such as an inundation of the Altiplano from the overflowing of the lake. Others have attributed the disaster to an invasion of uncivilized barbarians from the Chaco in the south or from the forests of the Amazons or the migration of a new racial stock into the Altiplano. I have always felt that a strong element of romantic melodrama is involved in such conjectures. For, as we have seen, a strongly centralized empire must have been necessary to liberate the manpower required for such building, and without dramatic disasters of floods and invasions such an empire might well fail through a combination of external pressure and internal dissension or even through some economic affliction such as a pestilence or a series of drought years. Any weakening of the central power or worsening of the economic position would have been sufficient to interrupt a work which required such organization and such availability of labour.

Nor must we entirely neglect the possibility that the Megalithic Empire of Tihuanacu was set up by a small race of foreign and superior stock and advanced culture, who immigrated from without and imposed themselves as masters and rulers over the more primitive natives of the land, bringing with them their traditions and techniques of building. There is nothing inherently impossible or even improbable in such a supposition, and indeed there are those who have thought that the Inca rulers themselves were of foreign stock and immigrated from outside in small numbers but owing to their superior culture were able to dominate the native races of the Andes. There is, as I say, nothing inherently impossible in this supposition; but it becomes improbable to the point of absurdity when you find yourself supposing, as you must, that exactly the same thing happened three or four times over. For the two periods of Tihuanacu represent two separate and independent florescences; the one did not develop in unbroken line from the other. And the megalithic building of Peru, which was developed to such perfection by the Incas but which certainly had its origin and roots long before their time, represents a different tradition again. Despite the Indian legend that the Incas built Cuzco on the model of Tihuanacu, the Inca style of building was not developed from the Tihuanacu tradition but from an independent local tradition of Peru. We know this from the fundamental differences between them. Most typical of Peruvian megalithic building is the 'polygonal' style, which uses large building blocks of irregular shape and many angles meticulously and accurately fitted together. This style of building was never used at Tihuanacu and the Tihuanacu method of constructing a wall from squared blocks between huge monolithic upright columns was not used in Peru. Again representational carving, realistic in the first period and symbolic in the second, is the most characteristic feature of the Tihuanacu style; but from Peruvian building carving is almost completely absent. And finally Inca doors, windows and nitches were trapezoidal, wider at the bottom than the top, while those at Tihuanacu are rectangular. We have then to account for at least three different traditions of stone building, besides the emergence

MYTH AND ARCHAEOLOGY

of the Inca dynasty itself, and it would be absurd to the point of the ridiculous to seek an external origin for them all. Besides, what country in the world is more inherently likely to have produced great indigenous cultures of stone than the stern petrous wastes of the Andes?

We have already said that the chroniclers who wrote during the early years of the Conquest and were best situated to collect the historical traditions preserved by the native peoples are silent about an Andean Empire before the Incas. And the reason is not far to seek. For when the Incas began to systematize their historical records, they tried to suppress whatever had gone before the emergence of the Inca dynasty in favour of the myth that it was they who had first brought the blessings of civilization to peoples who until their time had lived in brutish barbarity. We know, however, from abundant archaeological evidence that there was a long history of cultural progress in the Andes before the Inca dynasty was founded at about A.D. 1200, some three centuries and a half before the arrival of the Spanish. There is, however, one historian who has preserved, almost accidentally, the tradition of the dynasty which ruled in the Andes before the Incas and which goes back to earliest antiquity, the dynasty which must have been that of the Megalithic Empire of Tihuanacu. The story of how this tradition was preserved is one of the strangest accidents in history.

Fernando Montesinos, a Jesuit and a licentiate of canon law, came to Peru in 1628, probably in the train of the Viceroy the Count of Chinchón, and remained there about fifteen years, returning to Spain between 1642 and 1644. During this time he was occupied in clerical work, in mining studies and in travelling. He was twice made 'Visitador' and explored the whole of Peru and Bolivia, travelling more than 1,500 leagues in the course of his duties. It is not known exactly at what time he wrote his *Memorias antiguas historiales del Perú*, which remained for many years in manuscript. The second part of the *Memorias* was published by Marcos Jimenes de la Espada at Madrid in 1882 and an English translation by Philip Ainsworth Means was issued by the Hakluyt Society in 1920.[1] This is the book which is composed about the tradition of the pre-Inca dynasty which every other chronicler neglects or dismisses with a passing reference.

Montesinos has been called the 'Münchausen of Peru'. He is

[1] The quotations from Montesinos that follow are taken from this translation.

credulous, unscientific and lacking in historical sense; as an authority he is less than light weight. But the skeleton upon which his work was moulded, the armature which supports the dull clay of Montesinos, is a list of ancient Andean rulers compiled by a certain Blas Valera, an authority of a very different calibre. Blas Valera was born near Cajamarca in 1540, the natural son of Luis de Valera, one of the soldiers who accompanied Pizarro in his conquest of Peru and was present at the historic meeting between Pizarro and Atahuallpa, and a Peruvian lady attached to the Inca court. Blas Valera was brought up in Cajamarca and Trujillo and in 1568 went to Lima and was received into the Society of Jesus, which had established the first Jesuit mission there. For the next twenty-three years he lived in Peru, preaching the Gospel of Christ, teaching and converting the Indians. In 1571 he was sent to Cuzco as a catechist with the founders of the new Jesuit college in that city and remained there until 1572, when he went to the Jesuit mission at Juli on the western shores of the lake. From Juli he made a number of trips across the Altiplano, visiting both Copacabana and La Paz. He left Peru for Spain in 1591 and was in Cadiz when that town was sacked by the Earl of Essex in 1596. His knowledge of Aymara and Quechua and his Indian blood were not only valuable to Blas Valera in his work of teaching the Gospel but placed him in an ideal position to collect the ancient traditions and history of his people from the first generation of *amautas*, or wise men, after the Conquest. He is known to have written three books on early Andean history: a *Historia del Perú* in Latin; a *Vocabulario Historico del Perú*, and a work *De los Indios del Perú sus costumbres y pacificación*. The *Historia del Perú* was partly destroyed in the sack of Cadiz but fragments of this work came into the hands of Garcilaso de la Vega and were later used by him in compiling his great *Comentarios Reales de los Yncas*, the richest and most readable story of pre-Columban Peru that was ever written. Garcilaso was also a mestizo, born in 1540, in Cuzco, son of a Spanish soldier Garcilaso de la Vega y Sotomayor Suarez and an Inca princess, a niece of Huayna Capac and granddaughter of the great Inca monarch Tupac Yupanqui. But Garcilaso left Peru for Spain at the age of twenty and wrote his Commentaries there forty years later. Blas Valera on the contrary remained in his own country and because his work brought him into constant close contact with the Indians, because he was half Indian himself and because he belonged to the first generation of

MYTH AND ARCHAEOLOGY 73

mestizos, he had advantages which no other historian has been able to claim. His authority is second to none.

Now the second work of Blas Valera, the *Vocabulario Historico del Perú*, was taken from Cadiz to the first Jesuit College in La Paz in 1604, and there it was studied by Montesinos and used by him without acknowledgment as the framework about which his own history is hung. And Blas Valera preserved in this work a tradition of the megalithic kings going back to very remote antiquity, a tradition from some local school of *amautas* outside the orthodox Inca tradition of truncated history. As a work of history the *Memorias* of Montesinos is trivial; but because it embodies this rare tradition preserved by Blas Valera, it is invaluable. Thus from lack of literary conscience much good has come.

Not that he was content to take the list as he found it. Montesinos was obsessed by the belief that Peru was colonized by Ophir, grandson of Noah, three hundred and forty years after the Deluge, which he placed at 2200 B.C., and in order to bring the Peruvian records into accordance with this curious Biblical chronology, all worked out from the supposed date of the Creation at 4004 B.C., he amplified the list of kings, padding it with many duplicates who are names only and introducing many figures who did not occur in the direct line of succession. His list contains 102 kings with an average reign of 27 years, so that if we took it as a literal transcription we should be carried back to a date about 1220 B.C.

From a careful analysis of the kings of Montesinos made by Philip Ainsworth Means, one of the leading authorities on early Andean history, emerges a dynasty dating from about A.D. 250 to the rise of the Incas between A.D. 1100 and A.D. 1200, and this is probably as near to the truth as it is possible to attain. In this reduced list fourteen names stand out as genuine historical rulers about whose reigns the tradition had something concrete to relate and dispersed between them a rather indefinite number of more shadowy figures of whom little except the names is known. Before the first of the figures who are definitely historical, Ayar Tacco Capac, to whom Means assigns the date A.D. 275, Montesinos gives the names of twelve kings from the founder of the dynasty, Pirua Pacari Manco. It is evident that the tradition he copied had no information about these early kings except their names, for Montesinos characteristically fills the gap by attributing to their reigns garbled versions of events which really happened during the thirteenth century in the reigns of the early Inca kings. But there is no reason to doubt that a genuine tradition had been preserved of a line of kings—though not necessarily twelve before Ayar Tacco Capac—going back to an eponymous founder Pirua, after whom the dynasty is named. Of him Montesinos naively remarks, 'and he was not an idolator, for he adored the God of the Patriarch Noah and of his descendants, nor was there any other God than the Creator of the world, whom he called Illatici Huira Cocha.' Montesinos writes as though the seat of this whole megalithic dynasty was at Cuzco, later the capital of the Inca Empire. But we know from the lack of archaeological background that Cuzco cannot have been an important centre of culture much before the twelfth century and that the seat of the pre-Inca dynasties must have been either at Tihuanacu or somewhere near Tihuanacu by the borders of the Lake.

In the reign of Ayar Tacco Capac—somewhere about the middle of the third century A.D.—Montesinos tells of the influx of peoples from the north, who settled in the coastal valleys of Peru and founded those flourishing nuclei of culture whose brave and versatile civilization through more than a thousand years has come to life for us again in the archaeological discoveries of the last thirty years. 'While Ayar Tacco Capac was reigning in Cuzco[1] in profound peace, the seers and wizards told him how, wishing to placate the wrath of Illatici, they found a very evil prognostication in the entrails of the ewes and sheep[2] which they had sacrificed. This greatly disturbed the king, and, at the end of several days, news was brought that a great throng of strange people had disembarked upon the coasts from balsas and canoes which formed a great fleet, and that they were settling in the land, especially along the water-courses, and that some men of great stature had gone in advance of the rest. And the *amautas* affirm that the tribes and nations which came at this time were without number. As soon as the king learned of their coming, he sent scouts to find out who these people were, what offensive and defensive arms they carried, and what was their manner of living. The spies returned, and said that wherever the giants arrived, if there were people there, the people of the land were despoiled and subjected; and that the giants were settling on the whole of the coast, and that some of them had gone up into the mountains, and that their government was all in confusion.' The highland

---

[1] Rather, it is believed, Tihuanacu.   [2] *i.e.* llamas.

MYTH AND ARCHAEOLOGY 75

peoples were alarmed by the news of this irruption, built fortresses to restrain the new immigrants within the coastal belt and for the next two hundred years clashes between them seem to have been frequent. But the coastal peoples do not appear to have made any serious attempt at a hostile penetration inland to the mountain region or to overthrow the mountain kingdoms.

It is within this period, roughly between A.D. 100 and A.D. 500, that we must place the first era of Tihuanacu.

The cause for the sudden break which brought to an abrupt end the building of Tihuanacu of the first period before its completion is not apparent in the narrative of Montesinos. Some writers have thought that the dynasty changed between the sixteenth king, Paullu Ticac Pirua, and the seventeenth, Lloque Ticac Amauta, because Paullu Ticac was the last of the kings to be named 'Pirua' and Lloque Ticac was the first to be named 'Amauta' and because Montesinos writes that Paullu Ticac left Lloque Ticac 'as his heir' without expressly stating that he was his son. If this *does* indicate a break between a 'Pirua' dynasty and an 'Amauta' dynasty it must have occurred, according to our dating, about A.D. 350. I am more inclined to attribute the weakening of the first dynasty to an invasion of barbarous races from the south—Chiriguani or Guarani from Paraguay and other tribes from northern Argentine and Chile—on to the Altiplano in the reign of Cayo Manco Amauta and his successor Marasco Pachacuti (A.D. 425 to A.D. 450). 'In the time of this king (Cayo Manco Amauta),' says Montesinos, 'there were great disturbances in the kingdom on account of the news that very ferocious and warlike people had marched through Tucuman, the Chiriguaynas and barbarians from Chile. Cayo Manco made himself ready, and in the act of preparing he died. . . . He chose as his successor in the kingdom Marasco Pachacuti. . . . In the time of this king it is said that the tribes which came again caused by force the establishment of great idolatries throughout the land. The king wished to make war upon them with a copious army, but his plan was spoiled by the people of the coasts, with whom he had many encounters, and he never could gain from the Chimos one palm of land, although he did curb them somewhat. The most important thing he did was to re-enforce the garrisons which he had between the two cordilleras, which lie along the borders of the coastlands as far as the Rimac river where the city of Lima now is, and back into the mountains as far as Huanuco. His troops had a very bloody battle in the Collao with the barbarians, of whom many were killed and captured. . . . So great was the corruption which the barbarians who entered the land practised in their idolatries that the ancient rites were almost forgotten by the Peruvians.' We do not have to suppose that the empire of Tihuanacu was broken or its dynasty overthrown. But the impression we are given, especially by the undermining of the Virajocha religion, is that the central power was weakened by this double trial of simultaneous invasion from the south and trouble with the Coast, so that amid such dangers and difficulties it may no longer have been possible to free and support the heavy drain of surplus man-power required for so ambitious a building project. Such weakening of cohesion, without outright overthrow of the empire, must have been quite sufficient to interrupt work upon the first Tihuanacu.

The second period, between about A.D. 500 and A.D. 900, represents a brilliant florescence both for the highland culture of Tihuanacu and for the coastal civilizations. The cult of Virajocha was firmly established with greater prestige than ever before in the highlands and an analogous cult of a creator-deity Pachacamac on the coast. During this period the buildings of Tihuanacu of the second or Classical epoch were begun to be erected with greater magnificence upon the old unfinished site. Hostilities between the coastal and the highland peoples seem to have ceased after A.D. 500. Astronomical science, the perfecting of the calendar and the determining of the solstices, was a predominant interest. To king after king in this period Montesinos attributes reforms of the calendar and of solar observations. Of Capac Raymi Amauta (A.D. 575), who succeeded Tupac Amaru Amauta remembered only because 'he lived in continual melancholy, without anyone having seen him laugh in all the twenty-five years of his reign,' Montesinos says, 'this king called a great assembly of his wise men and astrologers, and, with the king himself (who was deeply learned), they all studied the solstices with care. There was a sort of shadow-clock by which they knew which days were long and which were short, and when the sun went to and returned from the tropics.' These stone 'shadow-clocks', whose principle is not now understood, were built also by the Incas and many of them are still to be seen throughout Peru. They are now known as Intihuatana, 'hitching-post of the sun.'

The downfall of this second Tihuanacu Empire can be traced with greater precision. In the reign of Huillcanota Amauta

(A.D. 725) new invasions from Tucuman and the inflow of uncivilized peoples from the tropical forests of the east caused renewed disturbances. 'In the time of this king there came many hordes of people from Tucuman, and his governors retired toward Cuzco.[1] He assembled his forces and prepared a great army. He sent spies to find out what manner of men the enemy were. He learned that they were coming in two armies. He halted with his warriors on a high pass full of snow . . . which is called Huillcanota.[2] There, fortified, he awaited the enemy. He gave battle to the first army, which he conquered easily on account of it being in disorder. The second army, hearing the news, came very confusedly to aid their fellows, and it also was conquered. . . . Also at this time there came through the Andes[3] a large number of tribes who surrendered forthwith on condition that they be given lands for sowing, and they said that they did not come to bring war, but that they were fleeing from some men very large of body who had taken their lands from them, because of which they had come seeking some place where they might live. They gave information to the effect that, having left the plains where they lived, a very fine and rich land, they had passed, on their way thence, through many great swamps and thick jungles, full of wild animals, and that, without knowing where they were going, they had arrived in these parts.' This time the Tihuanacu kings survived and beat back the double invasion, though in the defence at Vilcanota the invading hordes from the south must have swept over Tihuanacu itself and passed the lake. The final fall of the empire occurred a century later in the reign of Tito Yupanqui Pachacuti (A.D. 825) and was also due to invasion from without.

'So great was the disturbance suffered at this time by the people of Cuzco[4] and of all the provinces of the kingdom as much on account of the marvels and portents which appeared in the sky every day with a great variety of comets and a continuous trembling of the earth and destruction of buildings, as on account of the multitude of tribes which came from all directions, publishing the tidings of destruction and expulsion of the inhabitants of the kingdom, that the king, Titu Yupanqui Pachacuti, was full of dismay and melancholy, and he did nothing besides offer sacrifices to the gods. The affliction increased because the seers, tarpuntaes, alcahuizas and other wizards and priests told him that

---

[1] Tihuanacu.   [2] Vilcanota.
[3] *i.e. Antis*, the eastern Cordillera.   [4] Tihuanacu.

the entrails of animals gave evil prognostications and foretold ill fortune in everything and that *chiqui*, as they call ill fortune, was predominant in all matters relating to the king. Therefore this king, Titu, ordered that warning be given to all his governors and captains, and he made preparations and defences, fortifying the camps and fortresses, and commanding that everyone should be on the watch and that the number of the spies should be increased everywhere. While these preparations were being made, news was received that many hordes of warriors were marching through the Collao, and that the ferocious men who were going through the Andes were approaching, and that they had some black men among them; and the same was said of the coasts. And they had all prepared great armies and were laying waste the fields as they came, taking possession of the villages and cities. The governors of the lands through which they passed had not been able to resist them. And so the king determined to assemble all his forces in order to oppose these people.' The decisive battle took place at the fortress of Pucara to the east of the lake, where Titu was heavily defeated and killed. The survivors fled to Tamputtocco in the valley of the Apurimac, south of Cuzco, and there established a small court with a boy king. The invaders do not appear to have established themselves in the land and certainly founded no new empire. But the defeat marked the final break-up of the old Tihuanacu Megalithic Empire. Pestilence broke out from the many unburied corpses, centralized control was lost and the empire split up into a number of decentralized regional powers under independent local chieftains. 'The provinces of the kingdom, learning of the death of the king, all rose up in rebellion, and the people of Tamputtocco had many dissensions among themselves as to the choosing of a king. Thus was the government of the Peruvian monarchy lost and destroyed.'

So the period of decline, the Dark Ages of the Andes, began. The old dynasty of Tihuanacu, its glory gone, continued for some three centuries more as a small local kingdom at Tamputtocco in the valley of the Apurimac, until from it rose the Inca dynasty which moved to Cuzco and later built up an Andean Empire greater than anything which had been before.

Thus in outline we may reconstruct the history of the great Megalithic Empire of Tihuanacu in its greatness and its decline. At one time it must have controlled the whole Andean region of what is now Bolivia and Peru, with the exception of the coastal belt, where it maintained amicable relations with advanced centres of coastal culture. Fuller knowledge of the early stages of this empire and of its period of decline can now only come from further archaeological research not only at Tihuanacu itself but even more importantly at the very many places round the whole lacustrine basin which still await exploration.

Chapter Four

THE INCA IN LEGEND AND HISTORY

1. LEGEND

Inca history has its origin in myth and continues in legend. History was memorized and handed down by trained professionals with the aid of the *quipu* and was embodied in epic poems and romances which are lost. It has been suggested that the Inca preoccupation with history may have been derived in the first place from the coastal peoples—in the kingdom of Chimu, particularly, great importance was attached to genealogy and genealogy among primitive peoples involves both history and legends of the deeds of ancestors. As has been said in an earlier chapter, at some time during the Inca dynasty, perhaps in the reign of Pachacuti, the Incas began to centralize and formalize historical records and in doing so adapted history to their own ends. In particular they abstracted all history which was not Inca history and so telescoped the 'official' memories, leaving a gap between the semi-mythical period before the emergence of settled communities with political organization and the beginning of the Inca dynasty, thus representing the Incas as contemporary with the emergence of civilized life.

Two legends of the origin of the Inca dynasty were allowed to survive. One lies mainly in the region of myth, although it may embody a vague legendary memory. The other appears to be true legend, that is to represent actual historical events in the form of story. In addition Montesinos has preserved what appears to be genuine remembered history of the period between the fall of the Tihuanacu civilization and the origin of the Incas, probably some local historical tradition which was not suppressed by the centralization of official Inca history by Pachacuti.

There are then two legends of the origin of the Inca dynasty.[1]

One tells how when the races of men were sunk in ignorance and barbarism the Sun God, taking compassion upon them, brought

---

[1] Legends of the Inca origins are reproduced more fully in the appendix to this chapter.

THE INCA IN LEGEND AND HISTORY

forth from the Island of Titicaca (now called the Isla del Sol) his son and daughter, Manco Capac and Mama Ojllo, husband and wife, to bind the scattered peoples together and to teach them the arts of civilization. Manco Capac carried a golden staff and had orders to journey until he reached a place where it would sink of its own accord into the ground and disappear; there he was to found the capital of his empire. Travelling northwards along the heights which border the lake, the divine pair came first to Paccarictampu and thence to Cuzco, where the miracle occurred and the golden staff sank into the ground. (The story of the sinking of the golden staff into the ground is surely a legendary embroidery upon the very rational search for fertile soil by testing its depth with a stick.) At Cuzco they founded the seat of the future empire and set about their beneficent mission to mankind, Manco Capac teaching the men the art of agriculture and Mama Ojllo initiating the women into the arts of spinning and weaving.

The second legend is more specific and seems to contain some measure of genuine historical reminiscence. I summarize here the version of Sarmiento. It is given also by Cieza de León, Betanzos Cobo, Poma, Morúa and others.

Six leagues (thirty kilometres; others say eight leagues) to the south-west of Cuzco is a place called Paccarictampu, which means 'Place of Origin', where there is a peak called Tamputtocco, which means 'Place of Windows', in which peak are three windows (*i.e.*, entrances to caves or tunnels), called Marasttocco, Sutticttocco and the middle one Ccapacttocco, which means 'Rich Window'. From Marasttocco came out the Indian people called Maras, from Sutticttocco came out Indians called Tambos and from the greatest window Ccapacttocco came out four men and four women, brothers and sisters, and they had appeared by order of Ticci Viracocha and had no parents. The men's names were Manco Ccapac, Ayar Aucca, Ayar Cachi and Ayar Uchu. The names of the women were Mama Occllo, Mama Guaco, Mama Ipacura and Mama Raua. These eight brethren decided to leave Paccarictampu in search of fertile lands to conquer and make themselves rulers of a new and better kingdom. By promising them lands and wealth from the people they would conquer they persuaded ten *ayllus*, or tribal groups, of the people of Paccarictampu to follow them and set forth towards Cuzco. They advanced slowly, stopping at several intermediate places and overcoming opposition on the way. Their journey and adventures are given in considerable detail. At Tamboquiru (Tampo-kiro) Mama Ojllo bore a son Sinchi Rocca to Manco Capac. Ayar Cachi made himself unpopular by his feats of strength and his ferocity and the brethren, fearing that he would cause their followers to desert, persuaded him to return to Tamputtocco to fetch some gold vessels (*tapacusi*), some seed and the sacred llama of the Incas, called Napa, which they had left behind there. They sent a companion back with him, who according to secret orders shut him up inside the mountain cave, where he still remains. At Huanacauri Ayar Uchu was turned into stone and remained as a *huaca* or cult object of Inca religion. On the outskirts of Cuzco Ayar Aucca turned himself into boundary stone (*Cozco Guanca*) indicating possession of the land. Manco Capac then advanced with the women into Cuzco itself and after a war of extermination and terrorization against the local inhabitants, established himself there and built a city. The site was chosen by the use of a golden rod which at Cuzco sank into the earth.

Sarmiento represents this as a war of conquest and in accordance with his general practice to represent the Incas as tyrants and oppressors, emphasizes its cruelty and horrific character. Others represent it rather as a semi-peaceful penetration, beneficial to the existing inhabitants of the Cuzco valley. There seems no real reason to believe that this story does not contain genuine reminiscence of an expedition from Paccarictampu, in which part of the population of the latter under leaders of their own made for themselves a new settlement, from which originated the Inca dynasty, at Cuzco. José de la Riva Agüero seems justified when he says, in his prologue to Urteaga's *El Imperio Incaico*, 'it is not a myth but a legend, with solid and abundant basis in fact.' The identity of the site of Paccarictampu and Tamputtocco has long been sought, and Hiram Bingham rather wildly suggested in *The Lost City of the Incas* that it was to be found in Machu Picchu. Two years earlier an article had appeared by Luis A. Pardo in the *Revista de la Sección Archeológica de la Universidad Nacional del Cuzco* for 1946, describing the remains at the modern Maukallacta and Pumaorcco, forty kilometres to the south-west of Cuzco, which I think he is almost certainly right in believing to be the site of the Paccarictampu and Tamputtocco of the Inca legend.

Although the majority of chroniclers are consistently silent about any development of civilization in Peru before the Incas, recent archaeological discoveries have shown beyond doubt or question that a relatively high level of civilization and cultural achievement had been reached before the Inca Empire. We have seen, moreover, that the magnitude of the ruins of Tihuanacu and the work which they represent necessitate the assumption of a not inextensive political organization. We shall give reasons later for believing also that it is quite necessary to attribute much of the megalithic building of central Peru to pre-Inca times. This also makes it necessary to assume fairly wide-scale political organizations before the Incas, because in a country which is habitable only in small, scattered and not very fertile valleys, works of the volume and extent of these megalithic structures could not be achieved without an organization of man-power which would demand the political integration of small groups over an extensive area.

Montesinos is the only early historian who appears to know of any extensive political organization on the central Andean highlands before the Incas. But as we should be compelled by the evidence of surviving facts to suppose a pre-Inca dynasty even were there no recorded evidence for it at all, we may in this case give very serious attention to the tradition which he perpetuates. Montesinos tells of a Pirua dynasty which ruled on the Altiplano for many centuries at least, which was ultimately overthrown by an invasion of barbarians from Brazil and the Chaco and which then established itself as a small local state in the valley of the Apurimac. After the defeat at Pucara the old Pirua Empire on the Altiplano broke up and after a period of anarchy there emerged a number of rival and warring territorial units under local chieftains. Meanwhile the remnant of the Pirua dynasty continued in relative obscurity beside the Apurimac for some four hundred years, until from it emerged the new Inca dynasty. The chronicle of Montesinos thus serves too to bridge the gap between the fall of Tihuanacu and the emergence of the Inca—the Dark Ages of Andean history. What he has to say is not much and not very reliable; but it gives a general picture which in its main outlines accords with the known facts and may well be true. While it would be rash and presumptuous in the present state of our knowledge to guarantee dogmatically the truth of Montesinos, his story does at least enable us to build a coherent skeleton of pre-Inca history which does no obvious violence to known facts.

Certain Peruvian historians who accept this version of events, such as Horacio H. Urteaga, Luis A. Pardo, etc., speak of the Pirua dynasty as 'palaeo-Quechuan'. In the sense that the Pirua dynasty in decline gave rise to the Inca dynasty, this term is not wholly without meaning. But there is absolutely no evidence that the founders of Tihuanacu were racially Quechuan. There is in fact some evidence that they were linguistically Aymara. The name of the first Inca monarch 'Manco' may be the Aymara word *Mallcu*, which means 'authority' or the bearer of authority, and is applied to the chief of a *marca*. The *amautas*, who under the Incas became a special class in the governing hierarchy, were of Aymara origin. Montesinos speaks of them as a priestly caste in association with the Piruas and the equivalent of the *amauta* on a small scale survives today in the typical Aymara *ayllu*. *Amauta* is an essentially Aymaran word. From the root '*am*' derives a large number of cognate terms (*amuta*: memory; *amasa*: secret; *amuya*: meditation; *amutu*: thoughtful person, etc.), and from the verbal form *amzutta* comes *amauttana*: meditate, teach, calculate, and a number of others. It does not follow that the modern Aymaras are identical with the people who formed the empire of the Piruas and built Tihuanacu. Those may have been superseded by the invaders who destroyed the Pirua empire. But it seems most probable that after sweeping over and destroying the political unification achieved by the Piruas, the invaders either receded or were partly overcome by the conditions of the country to which they were not used and partly absorbed into the existing population. It seems unlikely that they brought with them any linguistic change.

2. HISTORY

The foundation of the Inca dynasty in Cuzco is dated about A.D. 1200 and the most generally accepted list of Inca kings is as follows:

1. Manco Capac
2. Sinchi Roca
3. Lloque Yupanqui
4. Mayta Capac
5. Capac Yupanqui
6. Inca Roca
7. Yahuar Huacac
8. Viracocha Inca
9. Pachacuti Inca Yupanqui
10. Topa Inca Yupanqui
11. Huayna Capac
12. Huascar
13. Atahuallpa

Pachacuti is thought to have come to the throne about 1440. Huayna Capac died in 1527 and after four years of civil war Huascar was killed by Atahuallpa in 1532 and was himself killed by Pizarro in the same year.

There are two contradictory schools of Inca history among the early chroniclers. Garcilaso and those who follow him date the expansion of the Inca Empire from near the beginning of the dynasty and make it more or less continuous from the years following the foundation of Cuzco until the Spanish invasion. According to the other school the Inca state remained small and localized around Cuzco until the reign of Pachacuti. Modern historians tend to prefer the latter version, and there is no doubt that their case is a good one. But, as will be maintained later, if the Inca expansion did not get under way until well into the fifteenth century, most of the megalithic building of Peru must have been pre-Inca. It is unrealistic to crowd into the short century between the accession of Pachacuti and the Spanish invasion the vast territorial expansion, the astonishingly meticulous and enduring social organization and the enormous volume of constructional work as well. We adopt here—though without complete conviction—the view that expansion began with Pachacuti, but reject the view that the megalithic building achievements of Peru can have been entirely due to the Incas.

Up to the time of the Inca Pachacuti, then, the Incas ruled over a small localized state at Cuzco.

J. H. Rowe says: 'Down to the reign of Pachacuti, towns very near to Cuzco preserved complete freedom of action and raided one another's territory whenever there seemed to be a good opportunity for plunder.' But 'neither the Inca nor any of their neighbours thought of organizing their conquests as a permanent domain.' During the reign of the two predecessors of Pachacuti the Inca state gained somewhat in importance, without extended territorial acquisitions. In the time of Viracocha two Aymara groups rose to prominence on the margins of Titicaca, the Colla with their capital at Hatuncolla and the Lupaca with their capital at Chucuito. In rivalry with each other both sought an alliance with Cuzco and Viracocha, who had began to make conquests southward, entered into an alliance with Cari, the chief of the Lupaca. Before the Inca's armies arrived, however, Cari had defeated the Colla and sacked Hatuncolla. Why when the Aymaras were brought into the Inca Empire by Pachacuti this southern section was called Collasuyu after the defeated Collas, is not known.

Cuzco was bulwarked to the north-west by the strong and friendly state of the Quechua. But early in Viracocha's reign the Quechua were defeated by the northern tribe of the Chanca, who attacked Cuzco in Viracocha's old age. Viracocha together with his heir Urcon abandoned Cuzco, but the two old generals, Apo Mayta and Vicaquirao, who had been responsible for the growth of Inca power, remained to defend Cuzco together with two other sons of Viracocha, Roca and Yupanqui. Under the leadership of the young Yupanqui, the Chanca were eventually beaten off and Yupanqui had himself crowned in the stead of his brother Urcon and took the name Pachacuti (Reformer).

Pachacuti did not rest upon his laurels but consolidated his power around Cuzco by a campaign in the Urubamba valley and in Vilcapampa, proceeding then through the territory of the Quechuas and the Chanca to the north. His general Capac Yupanqui pushed his way northwards probably as far as Lake Junin, while he himself conquered the Lupaca and campaigned along the eastern and southern shores of Lake Titicaca. From about 1463, Topa Inca, son of Pachacuti, took command of the armies and carried the northern conquests as far as Quito, then turned to the west near Manta and swept down the coast, subduing the kingdom of the Chimu and the coastal valleys as far south as Lurin, near the modern Lima. In a second campaign from Cuzco he made himself master of the coast from Nazca as far north as Lima. Pachacuti now abdicated and in about 1470 Topa Inca assumed the throne of an empire which extended as far north as Quito, which covered the whole of the coast south to Nazca and which in the southern highlands included much of the Titicaca basin. His first expedition after his accession was into the eastern tropical jungles of the Madre de Dios, but he was compelled to interrupt it and return to cope with a rebellion in the Titicaca basin led by the Colla and the Lupaca. The Incas, as the Spanish after them, were never very successful in their military attempts upon the jungle tribes. The rebels fortified themselves at Pucara but were defeated by Topa Inca, who occupied the territory of the Colla and turned south to defeat the remaining Lupaca and Pacasa again at the river Desaguadero, which flows out from the south of Lake Titicaca, not far from the modern port of Guaqui. Not stopping there, he swept over the whole of the

Altiplano of modern Bolivia, down into Chile, and southwards as far as the river Maule, where is the modern town of Constitución. He covered also Tucuman and most of the highland country of north-west Argentine. Topa Inca now held a nominal empire reaching from Quito in the north to Constitución in the south and devoted the rest of his reign to organization.

About 1492 he was succeeded by his son Huayna Capac, who pushed his conquests north of Quito to the boundary between the modern Ecuador and Columbia and conquered the coastal region of the Gulf of Guayaquil and the island of Puna. Huayna Capac spent the last years of his life in Quito and died there in 1527 from a sudden outbreak of pestilence. Before his death he received reports of Pizarro's preliminary expedition which penetrated as far as Tumbez and is said to have predicted the fall of the Inca Empire to the white invaders. It is extremely probable that the Inca had even earlier intelligence of the establishment of the Spanish in the New World and it would be interesting if reliable records had survived of the reactions of this Inca king to the earliest reports of the white conquerors. Unfortunately accounts are contradictory and veiled in marvel, mystery and the supernatural.

Huayna Capac's legitimate heir was Huascar, who succeeded him in Cuzco. But he had another son, Atahuallpa, according to one story by a princess of the royal family of Quito, of whom he was very fond. On his death-bed he left the dominion of Quito to Atahuallpa, according to some historians as deputy to Huascar, and the rest of the empire to Huascar. Apparently for some while the two brothers remained in amity; but later jealousy and rivalry broke out owing to the aggressive ambition of Atahuallpa, who eventually revolted against Huascar. Atahuallpa had the advantage of the large and well organized Inca army, which had been stationed at Quito at the time of Huayna Capac's death, and the support of the two most experienced generals, Quisquis and his maternal uncle, Challchuchima. After a series of battles in the north, including a heavy victory near Chimborazo, his enemies finally defeated Huascar in the valley of the Apurimac outside Cuzco. Huascar was taken prisoner and many Inca nobles who supported him were put to death by the two generals. These events occurred very shortly before the arrival of Pizarro and Atahuallpa had not yet had time to consolidate his victories when he met the Spanish adventurers. Huascar was put to death on the orders of Atahuallpa while the latter was Pizarro's prisoner in Cajamarca and Atahuallpa was executed shortly afterwards by Pizarro.

Thus the Inca state grew from a small local principality to an empire extending some two thousand miles along the Andes in the space of three reigns lasting ninety years. At the accession of Huascar the Tawantinsuyu or Four Corners of the World, as the empire was called, extended from southern Colombia in the north to the site of the modern Constitución of Chile in the south and from the Pacific coast to the Amazonian jungle, including the eastern Cordillera of Bolivia and northern Argentine to the region of Mendoza. These conquests were achieved so far as is known without any military innovation of tactics or armaments, by organization and discipline. While many of the conquests were in the form of peaceful penetration or ceremonial victories only, in some places they had to overcome embittered resistance. The policy of the Incas was always, however, to introduce peaceful and stable conditions as rapidly as was practicable, to avoid plunder, looting and oppression, and to reign by acceptance rather than by overt force. The speed and thoroughness with which their empire was organized and the successful unification within the short period of its survival were even more remarkable than its sudden expansion.

3. SOCIAL ORGANIZATION

The Inca polity has frequently been represented as communism or as state socialism. It is true that there was some communal ownership of land, and it is true that the state diverted to its own purposes all surpluses, including all labour surplus above the basic needs of maintenance. But like all loose classifications, it is more misleading than helpful to rank the Inca state as either socialist or communist in terms of modern political ideology. For the state was not the people but the Inca. And the socialism of the Incas was not egalitarian. Equality was not its ideal. Rather the Inca state was organized as a strong hierarchy with an exceptionally wide differentiation between the privileged and the unprivileged classes. Democracy or equality of opportunity were contrary to its principles. It was an aristocracy of birth set above the subject masses. What seems remarkable in these days of reluctant democracy is that the system was good, the aristocracy was responsible and beneficent, the masses flourished and there was no oppression.

At the head of the hierarchy stood the Inca, who was accorded divine honours as the descendant of the Sun God, and who was the sole fount of authority and law. The law was the will and command of the Inca and right consisted in obedience to the law. The absolutism of the Inca was unlimited in theory and was in practice limited only by a strong sense of continuity and by the expectation that he would govern with the welfare of his subjects at heart. Respect for existing institutions was a dominant feature of Inca policy even in conquered territories and the stability of the state grew out of the contentment of the populace; but both these were obligatory only because successive Incas chose to make them so. The Incas had a small advisory council of leading nobles which they consulted before undertaking important campaigns and on similar occasions—but only because they wished to do so. The Inca had but to lift a finger to ordain the death of the most prominent noble or the most successful general. His word literally was the law. The semi-divine position of the Incas was real. They were not puppets dignified with mysteries and divine attributes for the purposes of some clique by whom they were controlled. For the most part, at any rate, the Incas seem to have been men of strong and dominant personality with genuine gifts of leadership and to have been adequate to the position in which they were placed. They were the real and not merely the symbolic heads of the state.

The Inca married his eldest sister, who became the reigning queen or *coya*, and he was expected to have a large number of subsidiary wives. Limited polygamy was customary among the small local chieftains before Inca times and polygamy on a larger scale had been practised in the coastal kingdoms which had developed great pomp and regal ceremony. Thus polygamy was no strange custom, although monogamy was normal among the rank and file. Succession was ordinarily through the eldest son of the reigning Inca by the *coya*, although if he were judged to be unsuitable to the very high standard which was set, he could be put aside in favour of another. The members of the royal family formed an aristocracy and the higher administrative class. Polygamy in the royal family had an obvious function in so rapidly growing an empire with need for a constantly increasing administrative and governing personnel.

A very elaborate court ceremonial grew up around the Inca's person, emphasizing his divine character and uniqueness. The separateness of the ruling nobility, who were in theory blood relations of the Inca, was emphasized by magnificence and luxury in contrast with the simple austerity of the people. Precious metals, jewels and all luxury articles throughout the realm were reserved for the court. The Inca wore clothing of specially fine vicuña wool and sandals of white wool woven for him by women of the court. His personal appointments were of gold. He ate from gold dishes, sat upon a low throne of solid gold and was carried in a litter covered with gold plaques, while attendants swept the road clear before him. He never drank twice from the same dish, or wore the same clothes twice.

The following account by Pedro Pizarro of the state kept up by Atahuallpa in captivity has the interest of an eye-witness description. 'This Atabalipa was a well set up Indian, of good presence, medium figure, not over stout, comely of countenance and serious withall, his eyes florid, much feared by his people. (I remember that the Lord of Guaylas once asked leave to visit his estates and he granted it, giving him a limited time in which to go and return. He took rather longer, and when he came back —I was present—brought a gift of fruit and arrived in his presence began to tremble in such a manner that he was unable to remain on his feet. And Atabalipa raised his head a trifle and smiling signed to him to go.) When they took him out to execution all the people in the Plaza, which was crowded with natives, fell to the ground as though they were drunk. This Indian was waited upon by his women, a different sister taking duty by rota every eight days with a large number of the daughters of the nobility in attendance on them. These women were always present to wait on him and no male entered into his presence. He had many caciques (*i.e. curacas*) with him; they remained outside in the patio and when any of them was summoned to his presence, he entered barefoot; if he came from afar, he had to enter barefoot and carrying a burden. And when his general Challicuchima came in to see him with Hernando Pizarro, he entered as I say with a burden and his feet bare and threw himself at the Inca's feet and kissed them. And Atabalipa with serene countenance said "Welcome, Challicuchima!" This Indian wore on his head *llautos*, which are braids made of coloured wools, half a finger thick and a finger in breadth, made in the form of a crown rounded and without

THE INCA IN LEGEND AND HISTORY

points, a hand's width, which fitted his head, and on the forehead a tassel (*borla*) sewn onto this *llauto*, a little more than a hand's width, of very fine wool, cut very regular and adorned to the middle very subtlely with bugles of gold: this wool was spun and below the bugled fringes was unravelled and it was this which fell on the forehead, for the gold bugles covered the whole of the *llauto* aforesaid. This *borla* hung to just above the eyebrows, one finger in thickness, and covered the whole forehead. And all the nobility went with their hair cropped short. They wore very fine and soft raiment, they and their sisters, whom they made their wives, and their kinsmen, the chief nobility; and all the rest wore coarse clothing. This lord put on his cloak over his head and fastened it beneath his chin, covering his ears. He wore this to cover one ear which was torn, as Huascar's men split it when they captured him. This lord wore very fine raiment. One day he was eating a meal which the above mentioned ladies used to bring and place before him on very thin and small green rushes; this lord was sitting on a wooden stool a little more than a palm in height; this stool was of very lovely red wood and they always covered them with a very fine rug even although he was sitting upon it: these above mentioned rushes they always set before him when he wished to eat and on them they placed all the victuals on gold, silver and pottery and he would make a sign that they should hand to him whatever took his fancy and taking it one of the above mentioned ladies would hold it in her hands while he ate. One day, as he was eating in this manner, and I present, while raising a piece of food to his mouth a drop fell onto the robe he was wearing and handing it to the Indian woman he rose and retired to the inner chamber to change his robe and he returned wearing an under-robe and a mantle (dark brown). Going up to him I felt the mantle which was softer than silk and said to him: "Inca, what is this mantle made of that it is so soft?" He said to me: "It is from certain night birds of Puerto Viejo and Tumbez which bite the Indians." As I got it clear he meant it was made from the skin of bats. When I asked him how it was possible to collect so many bats, he said: "What had those dogs of Tumbez and Puerto Viejo to do but collect bats to make robes for my father?" It is so that those bats of those regions bite the Indians and Spaniards and horses and extract so much blood that it is a wonderful thing and thus was it confirmed that that robe was of bats' skins and its colour was the same as theirs of which there are many in Puerto

Viejo and Tumbez and their environs. And it happened one day that an Indian came to complain that a Spaniard had taken some garments of Atabalipa, so the Marquis bade me go and find who it was and summon that Spaniard for punishment. The Indian took me to a hut where there was a vast quantity of chests, for the Spaniard had already gone, telling me that he had taken a garment from there; and when I asked him what was in those chests, he showed me some in which was stored everything that Atabalipa had touched with his hands and clothes which he had used; in some the little rushes which they set before his feet when he ate; in others the bones of the fowl or flesh he ate, which he had touched with his hands; in others the cobs of the maize he had taken in his hands; in others the clothing he had discarded; in fine, everything he had touched. I asked him why they kept it there. They replied in order to burn it because every year they burnt all this, because everything touched by the Lords who were children of the Sun had to be burnt and made to ashes and scattered to the winds, for no one else could touch it. And in charge of this was a Chief and Indians who guarded it and received it from the women in attendance on the Inca. These lords slept on the floor on large cotton mattresses. They had large woollen blankets with which they covered themselves. Nor have I seen in all this Peru an Indian like unto this Atabalipa either for his fierceness or for his air of authority.'

The nobles had the lobes of their ears pierced and from them hung precious stones (whence the Spanish term *orejones*, or 'big ears'), and the Inca the largest of all. His hair was cut short and his head covered by a multicoloured turban, above which were two feathers from the sacred curinquingue bird. The insignia of royalty was the *lauta*, called *borla* by the Spanish, a narrow red tasselled band around the forehead. The Inca was served only by women of the royal family. No one could look him in the face, but all approached him barefoot, with downcast face and with a burden on their back. This ceremonial was kept up even for Atahuallpa in his captivity.

The magnificence, the ceremonial and the formalities of the Inca court were saved from Arabian Nights unreality by the high characters of the Incas. Most of them seem to have been men of dignified presence, of natural authority and with outstanding gifts of leadership. The duties of the ruling nobility were taken seriously and the education and training both of the Incas and the children

THE INCA IN LEGEND AND HISTORY

of the nobility were formidable. There can be no reasonable doubt that the Incas did seem to be superior beings to the majority of their people. It has even been conjectured that they were of a different race from the common people, perhaps immigrant families from outside South America. But a similar magnificence and separateness between royalty and subjects was characteristic of the coastal kingdom of Gran Chimu, whence it may have been copied by the Incas.

At the other extreme were the commons, the *hatunruna*, who had few rights and no luxuries.

The unit of social organization, which seems to have been aboriginal in the highlands and upon which the structure of the Inca state was later built, was the *ayllu*. The *ayllu* was a group of extended families, united by supposed kinship, probably by common ancestor worship and common worship of natural objects or *huaca*, and by communal ownership of an area of land. The *ayllu* was directed by a chief, elective or hereditary, called *mallcu* or *jilakata*, and by a council of wise men and elders, called *amautas*. The individual families owned their houses, tools, domestic furniture, agricultural implements, clothes, a few animals and the fruits of their own labour on the land. The land itself and all natural resources, as also the flocks of llamas and alpacas, were the communal property of the *ayllu*. In the autumn of every year the communal land was divided up among the families (*lihua*), each family receiving plots (*catu*)[1] in accordance with the number of mouths to be fed. After the partition each family was responsible for working its own plot and retained the fruits as its own. There was, however, a voluntary system of mutual help (*ayni*) so that a number of friends would help in turn with the cultivation of their respective *catus*.

There was no actual shortage of land, although the soil was poor and the climate unreliable. Every *ayllu* had more land than was necessary to cultivate at one time and in the annual repartition only a part was divided up (*aynokas*) and the remainder left to lie fallow (*pharalaya*). There was no real system of crop rotation as has sometimes been said, since the only crops of the sierra were potatoes, *oca* and the two cereals, *quinoa* and *cañahua*, and land which would grow the one usually would not grow the other. But land was regularly allowed to fallow. If more land became necessary, it could be obtained by clearing a larger area of stones,

[1] Called *tupu* in Quechua.

additional terracing (*sucres*) and increased irrigation. The soil of the highlands demands heart-breaking toil for small returns. The work of clearance, irrigation and terracing is necessarily communal and must be constantly renewed. One may now see in Bolivia, particularly on the southern and east shores of Lake Titicaca, whole hillsides which have been cleared with certainly generations of work and which are now for lack of manpower reverting to their primitive state. This communal work which was necessary to every *ayllu* was undertaken by assigning to each member a certain labour-duty or *mit'a*. The *catus* assigned to the chiefs and to widows and the infirm were also tilled on their behalf by communal labour, which fell within the *mit'a*. Thus the very nature of the country impelled communal labour as a necessity. The communal system of land tenure may therefore be interpreted as a concession to the inevitable by people naturally inclined to private ownership just as well as a natural inclination to communism. From my own knowledge of the Indians today, who still retain a sense of communal land tenure combined with a very strong feeling for personal property, I should regard the former as the more likely.

Among the Aymaras a rather larger territorial group, formed by the coalescence of a number of *ayllu* for war, defence or other purposes, was called *marca*, seems to have been primarily a territorial unit and the *ayllu* a kin-group owning territory collectively. The chief of a *marca* was called by the general name of *curaca* under the Inca Empire and later by the Spanish *cacique*. The latter was a native name from San Domingo and was improperly applied in Peru.

This system of collective land tenure arose spontaneously from the conditions of the country long before the Incas and was not invented or imposed by them. In fact it was never very thoroughly established in the northern territories, where it was not aboriginal. The Licentiate Francisco Falcón, who in 1582 wrote a *Representación hecha en concilio provincial sobre los daños y molestias que se hacen a los Indios*, specifically says that the annual repartition of the communal lands was a custom dating from before the Incas, which they allowed to remain. Ondegardo describes it as an invariable rule in Chucuito and elsewhere, where he saw it in operation. That it was a more firmly engrained racial custom than it could have become had it been imposed from above during the last three Inca reigns, is proved from the fact that amidst the unfavourable environment of the Spanish organization it has persisted in purely Indian communities to this day, and that Bolivian law has recently recognized collective land tenure by Indian communities after it had been legally abolished in 1824. Some chroniclers, among whom are Acosta and Cobo, have said that under the Incas the Indians had no titular possession of anything at all but received everything by favour of the Incas, in whom was vested the sole ownership of all land. This is a tendencious mistake which was used to defend the argument that the Spanish Crown, as the successor to the Incas, was legal owner of all lands in the Colony. It is specifically contradicted by Ondegardo, who states that 'the lands were the property of the Indians and their forbears and their communities themselves', and goes on to say that to deprive the Indians of their title to their lands and tax them in addition was in fact to impose a double tribute upon them.

There is no reasonable doubt that communal land tenure was current before the Incas and was undisturbed by them in their territorial organization, which separated the lands of each community into three parts, one belonging to the Sun (*i.e.* religious lands), one belonging to the Inca (*i.e.* State lands), and one belonging to the community. There has been much futile discussion whether these three divisions were equal or whether they varied from district to district according to the fertility of the soil and the density of the population. In fact the Indian before and since Inca rule has never except under compulsion cultivated more land than was necessary for his own maintenance, having in view the need to build up stocks against bad years. It was and is foreign to the Indian mentality to amass wealth by surplus production. Hence the first concern of the Incas was to increase the amount of cultivated land in each community, for it is agreed by all writers that the communal lands of every village under the Incas were sufficient for its support. Cobo says clearly: 'It cannot be said whether this share (*i.e.* that of the commune) was equal to the others or greater, but it is certain that sufficient lands were given to each province and town to support its population, and these lands were distributed each year among the subjects by the chief, not in equal parts, but proportionate to the number of children and relatives that each man had; and as the family grew or decreased, its share was enlarged or restricted.' Since the cultivated lands before the Inca re-organization were only enough for the maintenance of the people, and since the heavy tribute exacted by the Incas to support the social edifice were exacted in the form of labour upon lands earmarked for specific purposes, it is obvious that the Incas must have increased the amount of land under cultivation. There was no lack of land for this purpose; it only needed to harness the available labour. And that this is what was in fact done, Garcilaso makes clear. In the first chapter of his fifth book he says: 'Having conquered any kingdom or province, the Inca . . . commanded that the worked lands should be increased and for this purpose commanded irrigation engineers to be sent. . . . Having cut the irrigation canals, they levelled and squared the ground so that it should benefit from the irrigation. In the mountain slopes and peaks where the soil was good they made terraces. . . . Thus little by little they covered the whole hill, clearing the land by their terraces in the form of steps and obtaining the use of all the soil which was good for sowing and could be watered. Where the land was covered with rocks, they removed the stones and brought soil from elsewhere to make terraces and make use of the site, so that it should not be lost. . . . Having increased the land, they measured all that there was in the whole province, each village separately, and divided them out in three parts: one for the Sun, the other for the King, and the other for the natives.' The increase of cultivable land came before reorganization and partition.

The tribute exacted by the Incas from their subjects took the form of personal labour upon the new lands brought into cultivation. It thus appeared as an extension of the *mit'a* and did not threaten the land or the sustenance of the community. As Garcilaso says: 'The principal tribute was working, cultivating and harvesting the lands of the Sun and the Inca.' And: 'From the produce of their private lands the subjects paid the Inca nothing.' To a people already accustomed to the *mit'a* upon the more modest public works of the commune and on the lands assigned to the chief, the elders and the widows and helpless, the tribute demanded by the Inca state would seem but the extension of an obligation already familiar and accepted. Tribute was also exacted in the form of labour service on national works, military service, personal service to the nobility and a number of minor duties. Those engaged on a *mit'a* which took them away from the *ayllu* were assured of their keep while on duty and that their own land parcels would be cultivated on their behalf by communal

THE INCA IN LEGEND AND HISTORY 97

labour during their absence. To a people who, although constitutionally inclined to laziness, were capable of hard work and did not dislike work, who were entirely without ambition to accumulate wealth by surplus production, this tribute, though heavy to our ideas, was probably not felt as burdensome. At the same time they saw the arable land increased visibly before their eyes and were given assurance of protection against famine and drought by the stocks accumulated on a national basis—an assurance which to them was every bit as important as would be a guarantee against unemployment to the modern urban worker.

From the lands of the Inca and the Sun were supported all the tax-exempt classes, the nobles and the court, administrative and religious personnel, and all commoners while engaged upon national service. Stocks were built up against the needs of war and were drawn upon if any community or district were threatened with famine from failure of the harvest. Public granaries and storehouses were built throughout the empire, which aroused the admiration of the first Spaniards to see them. Francisco de Xéres describes the storehouses at Cajamarca as 'piled to the roof, as the merchants of Flanders and Medina make them.... The Christians took for themselves all that they wanted, and they still remained so full that it seemed as if nothing had been taken from them.' Cobo says that they were stocked with maize, quinoa, *chuño* (dried potatoes), *charqui* (dried meat), dried vegetables, fish, cords, hemp, wool, cotton, sandals, arms and even shells. Garcilaso says that the goods were stored in containers called *pirua*, made of adobe with plenty of straw, which were shaped in moulds to fixed sizes and each size stored in an appropriate warehouse so that the amount in stock could be estimated at a glance (Book V, chap. 5). This nationalization of surpluses was particularly important in a country such as Peru which has many different climates within a relatively small area. The maize and *aji* (pepper) which grew in the temperate valleys, the cotton and fish of the coast, were regular articles of consumption in the highland regions, which in turn supplied potatoes and the wool of llamas and alpacas. The interchange of products on a national basis was a welcome increase of the small trading which had preceded Inca organization. Every three years the *tucricuc* or official inspector arranged on behalf of the Inca distributions of the surpluses from the state stores. It is said that the state had stocks for ten years ahead, in proportion to the normal and predictable calls upon them.

Between the *hatunruna*, or commons, and the Inca king-god stood the privileged nobility, also called 'Incas', or *orejones* by the Spanish because the piercing of the ears and insertion of jewelled pendants was the badge of entry into the privileged class. Theoretically the Incas were all of royal blood and formed an aristocracy of birth. From them were recruited the higher governing and administrative personnel and they were in fact rigorously trained in childhood for the part they were to play in later life in the state. So far as is known, there never grew up a privileged nobility without functions and duties.

Polygamy in various degrees was usual among the Inca class. Each monarch started a new royal clan or *ayllu* at his accession and on his death his personal property passed not to his successor but to his *ayllu*. Thus each monarch on accession built himself a new palace in Cuzco, and probably other palaces elsewhere. Sarmiento says that there were ten of these *ayllus* deriving from the companions of the first Inca and eleven royal *ayllus* originating subsequently from various monarchs. Owing probably to the practice of polygamy the Inca class seems to have increased considerably in numbers. But even so the very abrupt expansion of the empire caused the demand for administrative personnel to outstrip the supply, and it became necessary to supplement the true Inca class by a regional nobility. The chiefs or *curacas* of communities incorporated into the empire, when confirmed in office by the Inca, were often brought into the Inca class. The monarch would give them a woman of royal blood as wife and their sons were brought to Cuzco to be educated along with the sons of the Inca aristocracy. It seems too that others could be granted Inca privileges for outstanding services or as the result of exceptional ability, particularly in the military sphere. Several of the most famous generals of the Inca armies are said to have risen from the *hatunruna*.

The duties of the governing class were taken seriously and their education was rigorous. Special training schools under the *amautas* were instituted for them in Cuzco. Morúa says that the first year was devoted to literature, the second to religion and ceremonial, the third to the *quipus* and the fourth to history. Physical and practical training also bulked largely and a high standard of intelligence, physical endurance, skill, courage and stoicism in face of pain was demanded. At the same time an ideal

THE INCA IN LEGEND AND HISTORY 99

of chivalry, duty and *noblesse*, which was characteristic of the Inca attitude, was developed and inculcated. It was only after having passed a stern examination, or *huaracu*, at the completion of their training that the youths were accepted into the Inca nobility. No formal education was provided for the *hatunruna*.

An analogous hierarchy of the women was also carefully selected and subjected to strict training for special duties in special establishments set apart for them. Along with the girls of royal blood, children of the nobility, were educated girls of the common people, chosen for outstanding beauty or physical perfection at the age of ten. After the initial period of training some, called *mamacunas*, became wives of the Inca nobility or royal concubines and others, called *ñustas*, embarked on a sort of conventual existence vowed to perpetual virginity in the service of the Sun.

4. UNIFICATION OF THE EMPIRE

The unification and solidification of the enormous territories incorporated into the empire proceeded according to settled plan from the time of Pachacuti onwards. The Incas were not merely military conquerors but were outstanding even more as organizers. This process of unification was still incomplete when the empire was disrupted by the Spanish.

(*a*) It was Pachacuti who first began to extend Quechua throughout the empire as a general language. It is not certain whether Quechua was the language of the Incas themselves or whether they also spoke an esoteric tongue. But as a universal language of the empire it took great steps forward in the three generations from Pachacuti to Atahuallpa. It was the language of administration and no state official was admitted without a knowledge of Quechua. Teachers of Quechua were sent to the outlying provinces. And by settling colonies of Quechuas among other peoples nuclei of the Quechua language were created throughout the empire.

It is not certain whether it was ever the intention that Quechua should supersede the many other languages spoken within the Inca Empire or whether it was only intended to create a universal second language. It is certain that no attempt was ever made to forbid or suppress any other language. And when the Spanish took over they found a vast number of regional languages still in use. The missionaries indeed found their work of evangelization seriously hampered by the large number of different languages spoken in the coastal belt and they themselves did much to generalize Quechua for their own convenience. The early chroniclers speak of three 'general' languages in Peru, Quechua, Aymara and Uru. Aymara has still survived as the normal language of the Aymara people and Quechua is general among the other amalgamated peoples of Peru. Both languages have resisted the influence of Spanish.

(b) A uniform system of administration was evolved from existing customs of land tenure, social and political institutions and morality and was applied with sufficient elasticity not to do violence to regional variation and custom. Deference to existing institutions was basic to Inca administration and no attempt was made to impose a rigorous uniformity which would alienate the subject peoples. The ideal was rule by consent rather than by compulsion.

The empire, which was called Tawantinsuyu or the Four Quarters of the World, was divided into four departments. The north-western division, called Chinchasuyu, covered central and northern Peru and Ecuador; the southern department, called Collasuyu, and later Collao by the Spanish, was the largest and included the Titicaca basin, modern Bolivia except the portion which lies east of the Cordillera Real, northern Argentine and the northern half of Chile; the south-west department, called Contisuyu, included the coastal region; and the eastern division, called Antisuyu, covered the Amazonian forest. But except for some of the deep and fertile valleys in the eastern slopes of the Cordillera, the Incas, like the Spanish after them, did not succeed in putting their military conquests of the jungle tribes on a permanent basis. Within this general classification administration was conducted by a very elaborate hierarchy of territorial officials, from the viceroy of each of the four departments through the governor, or *tucricuc* ('he who sees all'), nominally ruler of four *hunu* or divisions of ten thousand families, to the *chunca-camayu*, the head of ten families. It seems, however, that this decimal system of categorization was not allowed in practice to override existing local hierarchies. Alongside the local officials were a number of visiting inspectors and interpreters of the law, who represented the central government directly and whose business was to examine the efficient working of the system in practice. In *L'Empire Socialiste des Inka*, Louis Baudin estimates that without counting the viceroys, governors, inspectors and special functionaries, there were 1,331 officials for every 10,000 families.

The whole system was able to work by means of meticulous statistics which in detail and exactness seems to have been better than anything that has existed since. It is a perpetual miracle that so large a self-contained military empire, with such perfection of public works and so high a standard of luxury and culture among the privileged classes, could have been constructed upon so poor a soil. For tribute was always exacted in the form of labour and conquered peoples were not placed under any obligations to contribute except their services. Baudin says, 'Never had any great civilization of antiquity such reduced means at its disposition.... The pressure of the population upon the means of subsistence was one of the determining elements of the Peruvian policy.' The whole system of statistical planning was raised to an unrivalled level of perfection from the necessity of eliminating wastage and making the utmost use of the poor resources of the country, while ensuring that the population everywhere was adequately provided for.

(c) It is difficult to judge to what extent the imposed worship of the Sun, with the Inca as the divine representative of the Sun on earth, acted as a unifying principle of empire. There was no attempt to suppress local and regional religious cults. Instead they were incorporated into the official religion and the local deities were given a place in the Sun-cult at Cuzco as subordinate deities. It is probable that there was a large degree of religious uniformity over the central part of the empire owing to the pan-Peruvian cultures which had preceded the Incas, though with regional variations which also persisted under Inca rule. The Incas themselves claimed to come as the bearers of a new and higher religion to the subject peoples and there is every evidence that their claims were received without hostility. Their methods were undoubtedly superior to those of the Christian missionaries who came with similar claims later. The three generations of Inca dominion were too short a time to produce any great measure of religious unification, although had the empire persisted longer the generalization of the Sun-cult might have done more than anything else to mould into one the heterogeneous peoples which composed the empire. As it is, the pre-Inca religious ideologies have survived in amalgamation with Christianity and the Inca religion of the Sun has left little permanent mark.

(d) The finest achievement of the Incas was the great system of arterial roads by which the material unification of the empire was fostered. Road building is the most intractable of modern problems in this country. In the mountainous Andean regions a road is normally five times as long as the distance as the crow flies and presents engineering problems of astonishing complexity. Owing to the instability of the soil subsidences and landslides are an annual occurrence every rainy season. Bolivia is still without a useful modern network of roads which are serviceable all the year round and in Peru the good modern roads are a recent achievement and limited to the coastal region.[1] The Inca roads were superior to the Roman roads for their purpose. They ran straight, surmounting obstacles rather than avoiding them. Where the slope was too steep the road zigzagged to lessen the gradient. In the mountainous districts it was supported by strong sustaining walls and defended against landslides from above by bulwarks. Where necessary the road ran through a tunnel cut in the hillside and bridges were maintained over the rivers. Occasionally steps were cut up a hillside and enormous monolithic seats were disposed along the mountain roads for rest or enjoying the view. The Incas had, of course, no wheeled vehicles and no motorized traffic; their roads were kept smooth but were not metalled. As foot passengers were expected to spin as they went (as is still done by all Indian women), and the roads were used by the fleet couriers, they were required to be kept permanently clear of obstacles.

The key of the network consisted in two great arterial roads running north and south. The mountain road ran south from the present frontier between Colombia and Ecuador through Quito, Huancapampa, Cajamarca, Huanuco, Jauja to Cuzco. South from Cuzco it forked at Ayavire and ran round both the east and the west shores of Lake Titicaca, thence to Sucre, the capital of modern Bolivia, and on through Tupiza to Tucuman in the Argentine. The coast road ran from Tumbez in the north through Chimu and Pachacamac to Nazca, whence a branch ran up through Vilcas to Cuzco. From Cuzco it was continued to

---

[1] It takes an hour today to fly from La Paz to Cochabamba in Bolivia, twenty hours to make the journey by train and anything from two days to two weeks by road, according to the season. The flying time from Lima to La Paz is five hours; the adventurous motorist may cover the distance under favourable conditions in a week.

Arequipa and perhaps on to Arica, Tarapaca and Atacama and down into Chile. The coast road was six to eight metres wide, bordered by mud walls where it ran through agricultural land, with a channel of water and trees beside. In rough country the roads were narrowed sometimes to one metre. In regions subject to inundation they were raised on a foundation and were carried on culverts over irrigation canals. In parts they were paved with stone slabs.

Along the roads, at distances of some fifteen or twenty miles, were built large *tampus*, a combination of lodging- or rest-house and storehouse. Here travellers might rest for the night with their herds of llamas and officials could obtain food and stores. Along the roads too was organized an official system of couriers or *chasquis*, by which messages or light produce could be carried with surprising speed. Courier posts were established at intervals of two or three miles along the roads, where runners were always in readiness to take on in relays. The couriers were specially trained and fed for speed and endurance from childhood. It is estimated that they covered an average distance of about 150 miles a day. We know that the Inca received in Cuzco fish from the coast in two days and it is said that messages between Cuzco and Lima took three days and between Cuzco and Quito ten days, which compares favourably with any modern system of transport except the aeroplane.

(*e*) The famous Inca policy of transplanting populations within the frontiers of the empire also had its analogy in pre-Inca times. Many of the Aymara *marca* on the frigid Bolivian Altiplano had colonial offshoots in the warmer coastal regions, which supplied the parent community with the much desired products of these territories—maize and *ají* (pepper) in especial. The Chibchas and Chimnes of the coast possessed lands in the highlands, where they pastured llamas and alpacas for their wool. But the Incas organized and systematized this population movement in accordance with a centralized plan.

Their colonies, called by the Spanish *mitimacs* from the Quechua word *mitmac*, were of three kinds, military, political and economic. The military colonies were in the nature of outposts, placed to guard the frontiers or important bridgeheads from attack, particularly from the Amazonian tribes or the warlike peoples of the Chaco. The political colonies were settlements of the quieter and more civilized tribes among the more restless and newly conquered peoples. The purpose of the economic colonies was to people thinly populated districts with the object of increasing the total productivity of the empire. Many colonies of course combined a political and an economic purpose and it is probable that the large Quechua population in the southern and eastern districts of the Bolivian Altiplano originated from such colonization by the Incas. The colonies carried the Quechua language and customs among the outlying peoples or brought the latter under Quechua influence and so contributed to the unification of the empire.

In this way the Inca Empire began to become a vast melting-pot of populations. Ondegardo says that there was hardly a valley or a *pueblo* in all Peru which had not an *ayllu* of *mitimacs*. Cuzco itself was a true cosmopolitan city with inhabitants drawn from all parts of the empire and there were others, like the holy city of Copacabana, which is said to have been founded with *mitimacs* from forty different tribes.

The unification of populations cannot be said to have more than begun by the time the empire was broken by the Spaniards. The northern peoples of Quito remained distinct and even within the modern Bolivia Aymaras and Quechuas have refused to coalesce. But within the central portion, which is the modern Peru, the many different tribal and racial groups were so merged that within a short time after the Spanish rule only the Aymaras in the south remained distinct and the rest were merged together homogeneously as Quechuas.

The Andean peoples have little natural or spontaneous sense of unity and even the four centuries of oppression to which they have been subjected by the white invader has created no more than a passive sentiment of common destiny. The Indian will still readily side with his master and oppressor against his fellow Indians. But there is a sense of the unity of Indian culture which has nothing to do with race-consciousness or common political ideals; one Indian who meets another in friendship or in enmity meets a man of his own kind. And this consciousness of fellowship is due to the Incas. Rowe exaggerates somewhat but is basically correct in the following summary. 'Inca policy thus not only brought efficient administration and material well-being to the provinces, but unified the whole Empire. The unification was so carefully done that local nationalistic feelings were not aroused, and when a revolt did take place, the tribes were so scattered that it could hardly acquire the force of a national movement. One short century of Inca rule completely altered the course of Andean cultural history. To this day, Inca provincial boundaries and names are widely used, and the Inca language flourishes, while even the memory of the older states and languages has vanished. . . . The feeling of solidarity is certainly present among the modern Indians, and can be traced back at least into the nineteenth century. It is a direct result of the unifying policies of Pachacuti and Topa Inca, and its existence in the modern world is their justification, their glory, and their fitting monument.'

To four things we attribute mainly the success of the Inca state: (1) the complete system of road communication throughout the country; (2) emphasis on the general welfare of the people as a basis on which to build an aristocracy of privilege and luxury; (3) the planned development of the resources of the country, in order that the surplus only should be used for the needs of the state and the aristocracy after the needs of the producers had been satisfied; (4) the constant adaptation of central organization to regional variants to avoid unnecessary conflicts with local custom. It should be added that while the needs of a hard-working people were few, the privileged classes were functional and not drones. It is one of the greatest tragedies of human history that so fine a beginning was smashed so soon to make way for careless and unproductive exploitation. The Incas had something to contribute to humanity which was wantonly broken by ignorance, greed and complacency.

Appendix

LEGENDS OF INCA ORIGINS

The legend of Manco Capac and Mama Ojllo, who were created by the Sun from Lake Titicaca to found the Inca dynasty and bring the blessings of civilization to mankind, is told as follows by Garcilaso, who claims to have heard it from his royal Inca relations.

'After having made many plans and tried many ways to tell of the origin and beginning of the Inca kings of Cuzco, it seemed to me that the best plan and the simplest and smoothest way was to relate what I heard many times in my childhood from my mother and her brothers and uncles and other relations about this origin and beginning, for everything which is told elsewhere reduces itself to the same that we shall say and it will be better that it be known in the very words which the Incas tell than from foreign writers. So it is that, my mother residing in Cuzco, her native city, there came to visit her nearly every week the few relations who had escaped the cruelties and tyrannies of Atahuallpa (as we shall relate in his life), during which visits their most usual topic of conversation was to discuss the origin of their kings, their majesty and the greatness of their empire, their conquests and mighty deeds, their government in peace and in war, the laws which they appointed for the advantage and welfare of their subjects. In sum, there was nothing which they omitted to recount of the days of their prosperity.

'From their past greatness and prosperity they came to the present, wept for their dead kings, mourning the fall of their empire and commonwealth, etc. This and other talk the like the Incas indulged in their visits and with the memory of the good that was lost they always ended their conversation in tears and weeping, saying, "Our royal estate has been changed to servitude". Etc. During these talks I, as a boy, went in and out often and I took much delight to hear them, as children delight in fables. Then as the days passed, and the months and years, when I was not sixteen or seventeen years of age, it happened once that, my relations being one day upon this their conversation of the

THE INCA IN LEGEND AND HISTORY

kings and their ancient history, to the oldest of them, who was repeating the story to the others, I said:

' "Inca, my uncle, since there is no writing with you, which is what preserves the memory of things past, what intelligence have you of the origins and beginning of our Kings? For over there the Spaniards and the other nations, their neighbours, as they have written histories, divine and human, know by them when their own kings and those of other peoples began to reign and the changing of one empire for another, and even how many thousand years ago God created the sky and the earth. For all this and much more they know through their books. But you, who have no books, what memory have you of our ancient history? Who was the first of our Incas? What was he called? What was the origin of his line? In what manner did he begin to reign? With what people and arms did he conquer this great Empire? What was the origin of our mighty achievements?"

'The Inca, as though pleasured to hear my questions for the much delight he took in relating them, turned to me (who had already heard him many times but never with the same attention as then) and said to me:

' "Cousin, gladly will I tell you; and you it behoves to hear and store my words in your heart (which is their word for memory). You shall know that in the centuries of old all this region of the earth which you see was covered with great mountains and scrub and the peoples in those times lived like wild animals and beasts without religion or polity, without village or house, without cultivating or sowing the earth, without clothing or covering their bodies, for they knew not how to work cotton or wool to make clothing. They lived in twos or threes as they happened to join together in the caves and crevices of the crags and caverns of the land. Like beasts they ate herbs of the field and roots of trees and the wild fruits which grew of themselves and human flesh. They covered their bodies with leaves and bark and skins of animals; others went naked. In a word, they lived as the wild animals and the animals that are hunted and even with their women they were as the beasts, for they knew not to have and to recognize wives of their own."

'That it offend not that these words "Our Father the Sun" be so often repeated, note that it was the language of the Incas and their manner of veneration and respect to use them whenever they mentioned the Sun, because they prided themselves on being descended from him and that he who was not an Inca was not permitted to utter these words, for that were blasphemy and such a one they stoned.

'Said the Inca: "Our Father the Sun, seeing men as I have described them, commiserated with them and took pity upon them and sent to the earth from the sky a son and a daughter to instruct them in the knowledge of Our Father the Sun, that they should adore him and have him for their God; and to give them laws and precepts in which they should live like men in reason and civility, that they should live in houses and cities, that they might learn to till the lands, cultivate plants and crops, breed cattle and enjoy them and the fruits of the earth like rational men and not beasts. With this order and injunction Our Father the Sun brought forth these two children of his in Lake Titicaca, which is eighty leagues from here, and bade them go where they would and wherever they halted to eat or to sleep, they should attempt to sink into the soil a golden rod half a yard long and two fingers thick which he gave them for a signal and a sign that in the place where the rod should bury itself in the soil with but a tap, there Our Father the Sun wished them to stay and make their home and their court. In conclusion he said to them: 'When you have reduced these races to your service, you shall maintain them in reason and justice, with benevolence, clemency and kindness, acting in everything as a fond father to tender and beloved sons, in my likeness and semblance; for to the whole world I do good, giving them my light and brightness that they may see and do what they have to do, and warming them when they are cold and nourishing their pastures and seedlands; I make their trees to fructify and multiply their cattle, bringing rain and fair weather each in its season, and I am careful to circle the world every day to see the necessities that are in the lands, to succour and sustain them as the friend and supporter of mankind. I wish you to imitate this example as my children sent to earth solely to teach and aid those men who live like beasts. And I therefore appoint and name you Kings and lords of all races whom you thus instruct in your good reason, works and government.' Our Father the Sun having declared his will to his children, dismissed them. They went forth from Titicaca and journeyed towards the north and throughout all the way, wherever they stopped, they tried to sink the bar of gold and never did it bury itself in the ground. Thus they entered a small natural inn, seven or eight leagues to the south of

THE INCA IN LEGEND AND HISTORY

this city, which today is called Pacacc Tampu, which means 'Inn of the Dawn'. From there they arrived, he and his wife, our Queen, to this valley of Cuzco, which was then entirely wild scrub.

'"The first stop which they made in this valley," said the Inca, "was on the hill called Huanacauri, to the south of this city. There the bar of gold sank into the earth with great ease at the first blow they gave it, so that they saw it no more. . . .

'"Together they founded the city. Our Inca taught the male Indians the offices pertaining to the male, as to break and cultivate the soil, to sow the crops, seeds and vegetables, which he showed them were good to eat, for the which he taught them to make ploughs and the other necessary tools and instructed them the manner of making irrigation canals from the streams which flow through this valley of Cuzco, even showing them how to make the footwear we use. For her part the Queen set the women to work on feminine tasks, spinning and weaving cotton and wool, making garments for themselves, their husbands and children; and she taught them how to manage the other domestic duties. In short, nothing which belongs to the life of man did our chiefs fail to teach their first subjects, the Inca King instructing the men and the Coya Queen instructing the women. . . .

'"These were they who held this our great, rich and famous Empire of which your father and his comrades deprived us. These were our first Incas and Kings, who came in the first centuries of the world, from whom are descended the other Kings who have ruled over us and from them we ourselves are descended. How many years ago the Sun Our Father sent these his first children I could not tell you exactly, for they are so many that the memory has been unable to keep the count. We believe that it was more than four hundred. Our Inca was called Manco Capac and our Coya Mama Ocllo Huaco.'"

This is the legend of the origin of the Inca Empire which was preserved by the Incas themselves. Another version is given by Garcilaso which he attributes to the Aymaras.

'Another legend is told by the common people of Peru about their Inca Kings, the Indians who lie to the south of Cuzco, which is called Collasuyu, and those of the west, which is called Cuntisuyu. They say that after the flood, about which they are unable to say more than that it took place, nor is it agreed whether it was the universal flood of the time of Noah or some other regional flood, wherefore we shall omit what they relate about it and other similar matters which from the way in which they tell them appear rather as dreams and clumsy fables than historical events; they say, then, that after the waters ceased, there appeared a man in Tihuanacu, which is to the south of Cuzco, who was so powerful that he divided the world in four parts and gave them to four men whom he called Kings; the first was called Manco Capac and the second Colla and the third Tocay and the fourth Pinahua. They say that to Manco Capac he gave the northern part and to Colla the southern part (from whose name that great province was later called Colla); to the third, called Tocay, he gave the part of the east and to the fourth, whom they call Pinahua, that of the west; and that he ordered them to proceed each one to his district, and to conquer and govern the races they found there. And they advise not to say whether the flood had drowned them or whether the Indians had come to life again to be conquered and instructed, and this is all that they say of those times. They say that from this repartition of the world arose later the division which the Incas made of their kingdom, called Tahuantinsuyu. They say that Manco Capac went to the north and reached the valley of Cuzco and founded that city and subjected those that dwelt around and instructed them. And with this beginning they say of Manco Capac almost the same as we have said of him, and that the Inca Kings are descended from him and of the other three Kings they do not say what became of them.'

Here you have the legend which traces to the sacred Lake the supernatural origin of the Incas, whose supreme talents for organization constructed one of the most complex and most successful examples of a non-democratic socialistic regime that the world has known, under whom the nations of the Andes reached the peak of their cultural and political development.

There exists too another cycle of legend—perhaps closer to the historical truth of what happened—about the origin of the Inca state, deriving it from Tamputtocco where, as Montesinos tells us, the old Pirua dynasty of Tihuanacu had established itself in its decline three centuries before as a small local kingdom. Starting out from Tamputtocco, this form of the legend tells us, under the leadership of four brothers and four sisters, who claimed to be the children of the Sun, ten tribes, or *ayllus*, of the Tamputtocco people made their way to Cuzco and there established the nucleus of their new kingdom, which was to grow into the greatest empire of them all.

THE INCA IN LEGEND AND HISTORY

I will give the version of this legend as it is told in the Second Part of his *Crónica del Perú* by Cieza de León, who says that he had it from Cayu Tupac, a descendant of the great Inca monarch Huayna Capac, and other Inca nobles in Cuzco in the year 1550.

'With the best interpreters that could be found, I asked these lords Incas of what race they were, and of what nation. It would seem that the former Incas, to magnify their origin and great deeds, exaggerated the story they had received, in their songs. It is this. When all the races who lived in these regions were in a state of disorder, slaughtering each other and sunk in vice, there appeared three men and three women in a place not far from the city of Cuzco, which is called Pacarec Tampu. And according to the interpretation Pacarec Tampu is as much to say the House of Production. (The Quechua means "House of Origin".)

'The men who came forth from there were, as they relate, the one, Ayar Ucho, and the other, Ayar Cachi Asauca, and the other, they say, was named Ayar Manco. Of the women, one had the name of Mama Huaco, the other Mama Cora, the other Mama Rahua.

'Some Indians give these names after another fashion, and in greater number, but I have put them down from the informations of the Orejones,[1] who knew better than anyone else. They say that these people came forth, dressed in long mantles, and some vestments like a shirt without collar or sleeves, made of very fine wool, with patterns of different kinds, which they call *tacapu*, and in our language the meaning is "vestures of kings". And each of these lords held in the hand a sling of gold with a stone in it. The women came out dressed very richly like the men, and they had much gold. Going forward with this, they further say, they obtained great store of gold, and one of the brothers named Ayar Ucho spoke to his brethren that they should make a beginning of the great things they had to do; for their presumption was such that they thought they had to make themselves sole lords of the land. They were determined to form in that place a new settlement, to which they gave the name of Pacarec Tampu; and this was soon done, for they had the help of the inhabitants of the surrounding country. As time went on, they put great quantities of pure gold and jewels, with other precious things, into that place of which the fame goes that Hernando Pizarro and Don Diego de Almagro the lad, obtained a large share.

[1] Large Ears or nobles.

'Returning to the history, they say that one of the three, named Ayar Cachi, was so valiant and had such great power, that, with stones hurled from his sling, he split the hills and threw them up to the clouds. When the other brothers saw this they were sorry, thinking that it was an affront to them who could not do such things, and they were enraged by reason of their envy. Then they asked him sweetly, and with gentle words, though full of deceit, to return and enter the mouth of a cave where they had their treasure, to bring out a certain vase of gold that they had forgotten, and to pray to their father the Sun that he would prosper their efforts so that they might be lords of that land. Ayar Cachi, believing that there was no deceit in what his brothers said, joyfully went to do what they required of him, but he had scarcely got into the cave when the other two so filled up the mouth with stones that it could not be seen. This done, they relate that for a certainty the earth trembled in such a manner that many hills fell into the valleys. ...

'As soon as Ayar Cachi was secured in the cave, the other two brothers, with some people who had joined them, agreed to form another settlement, to which they gave the name of Tampu Quiru, which is as much as to say, "Teeth of a residence or a palace", and it may be supposed that these settlements were not large nor more than sufficient for a small force. They remained at this place for some days, being now sorry at having so made away with their brother Ayar Cachi, who was also called Huanacaure.

'Proceeding with the narrative that I took down in Cuzco, the Orejones say that, after the two Incas had settled in Tampu Quiru, careless now about seeing Ayar Cachi again, they beheld him coming in the air with great wings of coloured feathers, and they, by reason of the great fear that this visit caused them, wanted to flee away; but he quickly removed their terror by saying to them, "Do not fear, neither be afflicted; for I only come that the Empire of the Incas may begin to be known. Wherefore leave this settlement that you have made, and advance further down until you see a valley, and there found the Cuzco, which will be of great note. For here are only hamlets, and of little importance; but that will be a great city, where the sumptuous temple must be built which will be so honoured and frequented, and where the sun will be so worshipped. ..."' Cieza then goes on to tell how Ayar Cachi from the sacred Hill of Huanacaure gave instructions for the Inca ceremonies of state. He then goes on: 'Returning to

THE INCA IN LEGEND AND HISTORY

those who were on the hill of Huanacaure, after Ayar Cachi had spoken of the order that was to be taken for the arming of the knights, the Indians relate that turning to his brother Ayar Manco, he told him to go on with the two women to the valley he had pointed out, and to found there the Cuzco, without forgetttng to come and perform sacrifices in that place, as he had commanded. And as soon as he had done speaking, both he and the other brother were turned into two figures of stone in the shape of men. This was seen by Ayar Manco, who, taking the women with him, went to the place where Cuzco now stands and founded a city, naming himself from that time forward Manco Capac, which means the rich King and Lord.'

When we compare this story with the versions given by Garcilaso, Sarmiento, Morúa and other chroniclers, the central fact that the Inca dynasty in this legendary cycle traced its origin from the relics of the Tihuanacu dynasty at Tamputtocco stands out clearly. As Cieza himself says 'That which, for my part, I hold to be the truth in this matter is that as Zapana rose up in Hatuncollao, and other valiant captains did the same thing in other parts, these Incas must have been three valiant and powerful brothers with grand thoughts who were natives of some place in those regions, or who had come from some other part of the mountains of the Andes; and that they, finding the opportunity, conquered and acquired the lordship which they possessed'.

Montesinos distorts and transfers this legend to the beginning of the ancient Pirua dynasty and in its stead tells an amusing story of the origin of the Incas which was obviously invented to 'debunk' their claim to be the divine descendants of the Sun-god. When king Toco Cozque reigned in Tamputtocco (about A.D. 1000), says Montesinos, there entered Peru 'by way of Panama' hordes of cannibals who 'lived like beasts, without decency or government, and they ate human flesh'. The king was not powerful enough to oppose them, but 'received them in a friendly manner, and they mingled with them, avoiding almost all their vices and idolatry'. But as time went on bad example corrupted good manners, and in particular the vice of homosexuality festered and rotted the roots of society. 'Every day the affairs of Peru went from bad to worse, and the kings were kings in name only, because the vices had taken all obedience from them, so that decency was brought to an end and confusion prevailed. The chief interest of everyone was bestiality, the origin of all the misfortunes which afflicted the kingdom.' During this period of social degeneration, some time in the twelfth century, a reformation in manners was instigated by a lady of royal family, Mama Ciuaco, and her sister, 'who was a great sorceress who had had dealings with the Demon'. Mama Ciuaco had a son, Roca, a well-built and handsome youth of lofty ideals, 'which gave value to his twenty years', and he was a leader of a group of men who also 'greatly deplored the vices that prevailed'. Mama Ciuaco plotted with her sister to make Roca king and through him impose the reforms they desired. The two women therefore secretly had made for Roca a 'curious shirt' covered with delicate sheets of very fine gold, with many brilliant gems and precious stones, so that it should shine refulgent in the rays of the sun. They then hid Roca in a cave Chingana and put about the story that the Sun had come down to earth wrapped in brilliant light and had transported the youth into the sky, saying that within a short time he would be restored to rule over them, for he was the child of the Sun. The two women then stage-managed the reappearance of Roca in the mouth of the cave with his gold tunic flashing in the bright sun before the assembled people. The people were struck with awe, believed the story and hailed Roca as their king. Roca married his sister Mama Cura in order to ensure her silence because she had learnt of the fraud, and thus originated the custom for the Inca monarchs to marry their sisters of the royal blood.

We have already seen in the story of the Pirua dynasty that Montesinos, through Blas Valera, had access to an ancient tradition from the lake which had survived the Inca attempt to suppress all historical traditions anterior to their own dynasty. It is not too rash to speculate that this tradition of the old Tihuanacu kings must have been preserved by some local school of *amautas* on the borders of the lake, who were too wise and independent to submit to the orthodox Inca rewriting of their history, and that it was picked up and transcribed by Blas Valera while he was teaching in the Jesuit Mission at Juli. From this sceptical, iconoclastic story of the Inca Roca we see that their sturdy independence was not content with a passive refusal to accept the Inca suppression of their history of past greatness but with typical Indian humour they retaliate by inventing a legend of Inca origins which mocked the elaborate Inca assumptions of divinity as a gross and gigantic fraud.

Chapter Five

UNDER INCA RULE

THE LIFE OF THE PEOPLE

THE life of the highland Indian is hard and unlovely. Although the Inca nobility achieved a measure of refinement and even opulence, the existence of the common man knew few graces and his wants were few. It would savour of complacency to assert that any human society does not aspire to an amelioration of its lot, yet the ambitions of the Indian are modest. The betterments for which he has longed are minor improvements within the way of life he knows and not a radical change of that way of life for the refined and showy luxuries of the Incas or the mechanical comforts of modern urban civilization. The Indian mentality is of the so-called oriental type which finds happiness in limiting its desires within the bounds of possibility to the provision that is available instead of proliferating ever new desires which awake a restlessness for new fulfilments. He is not ambitious for new comforts and new relaxations, desires only enough of what he knows, resents rather than welcomes innovations. Outwardly agrarian life has changed rather little on the Andean uplands from Inca times until today. But under the Incas the common man was contented and even gay; life seemed good. Since the fall of the Incas his existence has become burdensome, his life sombre and his character resentful and sad.

The houses of the workers were the same in Inca times as they are today. They lived in one-roomed hovels, built of adobe bricks or field stones, roofed with thatch and without windows. The door was so low that it was often necessary to enter on all fours. The floor was of bare beaten earth without covering. There was no furniture but a few niches built into the walls to serve as cupboards and protuberant bosses on which to hang gala clothes, implements or musical instruments. Household possessions consisted of a few cooking pots. Cooking was done in general out of doors and the Indians ate from the pot, squatting on the floor. Several of these houses were usually built together in a compound with a corral for domestic animals and were occupied by the parents and married sons of one family. Some of the better urban houses were faced with coloured stucco but little attempt was made to decorate or beautify the houses in the country or to make them comfortable or livable. For the life of the Indian was passed out of doors and the house was used only for shelter and sleeping. The main function of the house was to give protection against the biting cold and winds at night after the hot daytime sun. Very large settlements of adobe houses have survived from Inca and pre-Inca times in the coastal regions of Peru, but few in the highlands. For in the highlands the life of adobe is short; under the influence of the wind and the rain it soon returns to the soil from which it was formed. I have seen mining towns on the Altiplano of Bolivia which after being abandoned for no more than fifty or a hundred years now retain no more than a foot or two of decaying and crumbling walls. Adobe ruins are without dignity or grandeur, a perpetual reminder of the fleetingness of human endeavour. So the paucity of adobe remains from Inca times is no indication that it was not then as now the main form of common building on the uplands.

The Indian dress was practical and unpretentious. The men wore a breach-clout, which was assumed on reaching maturity, and a *chusma*, a kind of sleeveless waistcoat which was made by folding a square of cloth down the middle, sewing up the edges with a gap before the fold through which the arms were inserted and cutting a slit for the head in the fold. The now ubiquitous poncho, which was introduced only after the Conquest, is like a *chusma* without the edges sewn. Above the *chusma* was worn a loose woollen cape, called *yacolla*, the ends of which were thrown over one shoulder while working. The women wore a loose unshaped tunic (*anaco*) flowing to the feet and above it a shawl (*lliclla*) of woven material and sometimes a stomach band (*chumpi*). Both men and women normally went barefoot. The Indian had no reserve wardrobe but kept a few finer clothes for gala occasions. His working clothes were worn until they would no longer hold together and were then discarded, but as they were very durable a person would rarely have to renew them after reaching adult age. They were made mainly from llama wool or from cotton where there was trade with the coast; the finest clothes of the nobility were from the beautiful wool of the vicuña. They were gaily and tastefully coloured and beautifully patterned. The art of weaving achieved a perfection both in technique and in design which has been rarely equalled and the textile fragments recovered from tombs are genuine museum prizes. Gold, silver and copper pins and brooches, often set with coloured stones, and gaudy feathers were used for adornment. The aesthetic gifts of the Quechuas were directed to personal adornment, the love of flowers, which were assiduously cultivated, and to music and dance.

Ondegardo remarks with surprise on the little food with which the Indian can maintain his strength and the conquerors in general took for granted that the native race required less sustenance than themselves, although their physical output was greater. Modern medical opinion which has concerned itself with native diet concludes that the Indians have been undernourished since the Conquest, though it is known that Indians who acquire extra money through work in the mines will spend it on drink or on fiestas rather than to improve their basic diet. There are, however, no statistics which would tell us what quantities of nourishment would be consumed spontaneously in an agrarian Indian community not stinted by penury or how much was normally eaten in Inca times. Certainly the variety of food was very limited and the Indians are still reluctant to accommodate themselves to unfamiliar dishes.

The climate of the Andes varies greatly within short distances according to differences of altitude and the regional diet varies correspondingly. In the valleys maize has always been the staple cereal and was eaten also on the high tableland when it could be obtained by barter. But in the highlands its place as a staple was taken by quinoa and cañahua. The second great stand-by was the potato, which originated in the Andean country and of which several hundred varieties were cultivated, divided into two main types, 'white' and 'bitter' (called in Aymara *saya chokke* and *lukki chokke*), together with two tubers rather similar to the potato, the *oca* and the *ulluca*. Potatoes were generally eaten in the dried and dehydrated form called *chuño*, white or black, a custom which is still universal. In order to make white *chuño* the potatoes are soaked in water for a week or two and then exposed for several days and nights in the open, where they are alternately dried by the hot daytime sun and chilled by the nightly frost. After this process the remaining moisture is squeezed out by trampling them with the feet and they are then left on the fields for three weeks to dry out. The black *chuño* is made in the same way but without the preliminary soaking. The Indians believe that potatoes so prepared will last for centuries, though it is doubtful whether the process would succeed elsewhere than in this intense solar radiation by day and extreme contrast between the day and night temperatures. Garcilaso gives this interesting account of the potato for a European audience to whom it was still fairly unfamiliar: 'In all the province called Colla, more than a hundred and fifty leagues in length, maize is not produced because the land is too cold; much quinoa is harvested, which is like rice, and other grain and vegetables which fructify beneath the soil and among them is one which they call *papa*; it is round and very moist and because of its great humidity apt to spoil quickly. To preserve it they spread it on the ground on straw, which is very good in those parts. They allow it to freeze for many nights, for in that province it freezes hard all the year, and after the freezing has softened it as though it had been cooked, they cover it with straw and tread it carefully and gently to remove the moisture which the potato has in itself and which the freezing has caused; and after they have extracted all the moisture they place it in the sun and keep it in the open until it is completely dried. Prepared in this way the potato lasts a long time and its name changes to *chuñu*.'

The food was mainly boiled and eaten either as a soup (*chupi*) or dried after the water was poured off. The green leaves of the quinoa were also boiled as a vegetable. Meat was seldom eaten, though the guinea-pig, which was kept as a domestic animal, was regarded as a delicacy for special occasions. Then as now the Indians liked their food highly condimented with a kind of chilli-pepper called *aji*, which was one of the main articles of barter from the warm valleys to the highlands. From the evidence of food offerings placed in tombs, representations on ceramics and the records of the first Spanish to arrive in Peru, we know what fruits and vegetables were cultivated in pre-Columban times; but we do not know to what extent these were reserved for the nobility or whether they were generally available in Inca times. We are told that the Incas passed elaborate sumptuary laws covering diet among other things and that State inspectors were appointed to see that these laws were respected; but with so poor a variety and with the limitations imposed upon barter by the monopolization of trade by the State, it is not easy to imagine great scope for dietetic luxury.

Then as now the national drink was *chicha* (called *k'usa* in Quechua and *akjga* in Aymara), a fermented beverage made from maize or quinoa. The habit of masticating *coca*, a shrub whose leaves contain a narcotic and stimulant alkaloid which is the basis of cocaine, pre-dated the Inca regime. We are told that the Incas restricted its use as a privilege of the nobility, as a reward for special services or as a provision for those who, like the *chasquis*, were required to make feats of exceptional physical endurance; but the habit was so universal and so deeply engrained at so early a period in the Colony that it is difficult to believe any restriction was seriously maintained. Coca was also generally used in local religious practices for purposes of propitiatory sacrifice, purification and divination.

Like agricultural peoples the world over the Indian did not resent hard and grinding toil and could relax from toil with equal intensity. His toil and his relaxation were ritualistic both. The Christian division of work and worship into separate compartments has never been understood by the Indian; for him work that is not a ceremonial lacks sense and meaning. This attitude fitted into the Inca organization of society designed to eliminate all wastage and to make the utmost use of all available resources, with human labour as the supreme and greatest of the country's resources. Unlike modern society in which work is regarded as a necessary evil undertaken in order to secure a leisure which society is untrained to utilize, in Inca society work was regarded as an end in itself and leisure was ritualistically regimented in a unified life of service. If the tradition is true that the Inca would on occasion create work artificially to keep occupied the *mit'a*, this was not, as Baudin has said, a device of good government adopted in pursuance of the precept that a fully occupied people has not time for discontent; it was much more fundamental to the attitude of people and rulers alike. The nobility themselves took their duties seriously and never degenerated into an idle and parasitic class. The people were happy in work so long as their work was ritualistically controlled in a society within which they were harmoniously incorporated and tradition was respected. But the habitual laziness of which they are accused in colonial and modern times is a form of passive resistance against demands which were felt to be alien and unjustified in a society which had disrupted their traditions and offered nothing in exchange.

The great bulk of the work was inevitably labour on the land.

And despite the great development in agricultural engineering, the superlative skill in clearing and terracing the soil and in irrigation, both agricultural implements and methods of working remained elementary. The main tool was the digging-stick (*huysu* in Aymara and *tajlla* in Quechua), a three-foot pole about the thickness of the wrist, with a hardened point of bronze, stone or hardwood (*chonta*), a stirrup (*ttijlla*) for the foot near the base and a curved handle at the top. With this the men would break the soil as with a spade, a team of men working rhythmically together to a chant. The women followed behind the men with clod-breakers, formed from a rough stone head bound to a two-foot pole, and broke up the clods as they were turned up by the digging-stick. The only other tools in common use were a broad-bladed hoe (*lampa*) and a threshing stick for harvesting the grain. The plough was not known. The Andean Indians have always been deeply attached to the soil and agriculturalists in heart as well as of necessity. Agricultural labour was turned into a festival and every act had its ritual consecrated by tradition. One of the main causes of the success of Inca government was undoubtedly the care which it took to incorporate traditional agricultural rituals into the national religion of the Sun, giving greater glamour to the former and enriching the latter.

Cobo describes as follows the order of cultivation of the three-fold division of the land within each commune. 'If the Inca himself, or his governor, or some high official happened to be present, he started the work with a golden digging-stick, which they brought to the Inca, and following his example all the other officials and nobles who accompanied him did the same. But the Inca soon stopped working and after him the other officials and nobles stopped also, and sat down with the king to their banquets and festivals, which were especially notable on such days. The common people remained at work and with them only the curacas-pachacas, who worked a little longer than the nobles; thereafter they supervised the work, giving such orders as were necessary. The hilacatas and decurions in charge of ten subjects worked all day, as did the ordinary Indians who had no official position. These divided the work they had to do by lines, each section being called a *suyu*, and after the division each man put into his section his children and wives and all the people of his house to help him. In this way the man who had the most workers finished his *suyu* first, and he was considered a rich man; the poor man was he who had no one to help him in his work, and had to work that much longer. Each official or curaca followed the same system in his district, the most important man starting the work and soon leaving it and the nobles following him according to their rank. When the *chacras* (fields) of religion were finished, the fields of the Inca were immediately sown and in their cultivation and harvest the same order was followed. All members of the community who were present assembled and with them the officials up to the most important chiefs and governors dressed in their best, singing appropriate songs. When they cultivated the fields of religion their songs were in praise of the gods, and when they cultivated the King's fields in his praise. . . . When it was time to sow or cultivate the fields all other tasks stopped, so that all the taxpayers might assemble to take part, and if it were necessary for someone to do something else in an emergency, like war or some other urgent matter, the other Indians of the community worked the fields of the absent man without receiving any compensation beyond their food, and this done, each cultivated his own fields. This assistance which the community rendered to its absent members caused each man to return home willingly when he had finished his job, for he might find on his return home after long absence that a harvest which he had neither sown nor reaped was gathered into his house.'

Garcilaso also emphasizes the communal work upon lands of the aged and infirm and the absent and gives the same picture of delight in work which was made a ceremony. He differs from Cobo in stating that the lands of the Inca were worked last. 'In working and cultivating the land they also had order and method. They worked first those of the Sun, then those of the widows and orphans and those incapacitated by age or sickness. . . . Each one had to bring his own food in order that the infirm should not be troubled. They said that the widows and orphans and the aged and infirm had enough with their own misfortune without having to trouble about others. If they had not seed, it was provided from the public stores. The lands of the soldiers who were away at the wars were also worked by the community, like the lands of the widows, orphans and infirm, since while the husbands were away on active service their wives were regarded as widows. They took great pains with the educations of the sons of those who were killed in war until they married. When the lands of the infirm had been worked, each worked his own, helping each other turn and turn about. Then they worked those of the curaca, which had to be the last in each community. In the time of Huaina Capac in a community of Chachapuyas, because an Indian director put the lands of the curaca, who was his relation, before those of a widow, they hanged him as a disturber of the order which the Inca had enjoined for working the land and set up the gallows on the lands of the curaca himself. The Inca ordered that the lands of his subjects should have precedence over his own, because they said that the welfare of the subjects was a condition of good service to the King; if they were poor and needy, they could serve but ill in war or in peace. The last lands to be worked were those of the King. They worked them in common; all the Indians went to them, and to those of the Sun, in a body with the utmost joy and content, clothed in the garments which they kept for their greatest festivals, covered with silver and gilt ornaments and with great plumes on their heads. When they ploughed (which was the work which pleased them most) they sang many songs composed in praise of the Incas; they changed labour into festival and rejoicing, for it was in the service of their god and their Kings. . . . The songs which they sang in praise of the Sun and the Kings were all composed upon the idea of the word *hailli*, which in the general language of Peru means "triumph", because they triumphed over the soil, ploughing it and disembowelling it, in order that it should bear fruit. In these songs they interposed witty sayings about shy lovers or valiant soldiers, all anent the triumph over the land which they were working.'

The system of communal work, each man's portion being worked by a team in common, and the ritualistic and festival character of agricultural work survive to the present day in the typical Indian agrarian community. Though something of the joy in work has been eradicated by crushing indigence, they still work to the music of flutes and the public festivals with song and dance and drink are still associated with the important agricultural occasions. There is no reason to believe that in Inca times agricultural labour was not a delight as Garcilaso pictures it or that the common tradition so frequently reported by the chroniclers was over-idealized. Unfortunately in the absence of a written literature almost all the native poetry and song is lost; but one Hailli which is probably pre-Columban is quoted in Appendix I to this chapter.

The penal regulations of the Incas were simple and strictly

UNDER INCA RULE

enforced. And they were successful because they sprang from the moral consciousness of the people. The Incas systematized the administration of justice but did not impose an alien moral code. While almost all writers have admitted the high moral standard which prevailed under Inca rule, most have supposed that it was maintained by the stern rod of fear. Morúa says, 'Fear made everyone walk in the path of right and there was neither thief nor vagabond in the land'. Baudin takes the same view, going so far as to say that the chief merit of the Incas was to have given the people a moral code which was based on prohibition, enforced by sanctions and had no seat in the individual conscience. This view is incorrect. The penal code of the Incas was an expression of the collective conscience of the *ayllu* and in this lay its strength. Had it been otherwise, the moral code could not have endured through four centuries of oppression and bad example after the fear by which it had been bulwarked was removed. Three generations of external rule cannot implant in a people so strong and enduring a moral sense. For the morality of the Indian community today, a morality which depends upon tradition and a social sense, is very much what we are told was the morality guaranteed by the Inca penal code and is superior to the practical morality of the post-Conquest state. It must have existed in the collective consciousness of the people long before it was systematized by the Incas.

The Inca code consisted in a few simple rules condemning murder and violence, theft, lying and adultery, and in Inca times these were practically unknown. One of the earliest soldier Conquerors, Mancio Sierra de Leguizamo, having grown old in the land and observed the damage done by the Spanish, wrote to relieve his conscience in the preamble to his will: 'The Incas governed in such a way that there was not a thief, not a criminal, not an idle man, not a single adulteress or woman of evil life in the kingdom.' He says too: 'The Indians left the doors of their houses open or put a broom or a small stick crosswise in front of the door as a sign that the owner was not in and on this according to their custom nobody could enter, and when they saw that we put gates and locks to our houses they thought that it was through fear of them, so that they should not kill us, not because they thought that anyone would rob or burgle another man's house.' I have seen this Indian practice still prevalent, even in the town of La Paz. The merit of the Incas was to organize the country in such a way that there was virtually no want and therefore no temptation to steal among a people who held the main necessities of life in common and had no incentive to accumulate material possessions. The weak, the sick and the infirm, and those absent on national service, were maintained by communal labour. Theft became an aberration which held no sense. Murder and injury were wrought mainly through black sorcery and the employment of black magicians ranked as one of the most heinous offences. Whether sorcery was in fact effective owing to the belief in its effectiveness or whether death, illness or accident from natural causes only were attributed to sorcery, there is no means of knowing; for the belief in black magic and its condemnation were shared by the chroniclers who are our sources of information. The Incas are said to have added to the list of crimes idleness and drunkenness. But in a highly communistic system of shared labour individual idleness is obviously a social crime affecting the community of which the culprit is a member; and the same is true of drunkenness in so far as it interferes with the capacity of the individual to contribute his share towards communal production. Many chroniclers, knowing the seasonal addiction of the Indians to drink, were puzzled by this regulation and some have said that it was applied only in so far as drunkenness rendered a person incapable of work. This is a misconception. There was a time for work and a time for relaxation with intoxication; during the relaxation of the fiesta the Indian was expected to become intoxicated, just as he was expected to refrain from drink and idleness during periods of work. Intoxication at its proper time has always had a ritual necessity. This principle has maintained itself right through to the present time and it is clear that the Inca condemnation of drunkenness *at the wrong time* and idleness *at the wrong time* had its roots in the social consciousness and merely formalized what was generally condemned. Perhaps the only crime which the Incas added to the common sentiment of *ayllu* tradition was the crime of evil-speaking or disloyalty against the Emperor.

The administration of justice was rapid and ruthless but impartial. Antonio de Herrera says: 'After the Incas conquered the land they retained the curacas in their office; but their authority was restricted and they were unable to exert tyranny, for they had visitors and superintendents over the curacas to see that they did no outrage against the subjects.' And again, the Inca administrators of justice were 'so honest that they received a handful of maize as a present from nobody, nor was justice nor pardon sold in any way, nor was there bribery nor any thought of it, and there was no traffic in anything'. A stern system of justice strictly and impartially administered, a code based upon the collective moral consciousness and allowing for regional variants and the removal so far as possible of the ordinary incentives to crime, produced an ordered society which gave the impression to the more thinking at any rate of the Spanish of a state in which crime had been abolished. But underlying the Inca achievement was a strong communal moral sense which has survived without outside sanctions wherever Indian society survives intact.

URBAN BUILDING

Francis Violich says[1] that: 'The Incas were undoubtedly the best planners South America ever knew.' And he adds that: 'Today, in spite of four hundred years of European domination and almost complete rebuilding under the Laws of the Indies, the urban spirit of the Incas still pervades Cuzco and many smaller towns in the region.' In their town planning the Incas used the gridiron scheme of streets converging round a central plaza with secondary plazas arranged according to the geography of the site. The main avenues were wide and spacious, the secondary streets narrower. The main public buildings were located in the central plaza or on the main avenues; they included a temple, a governmental residence and a large public building used as a storehouse, an inn for travellers and guests and a hall for pubilc meetings. In many towns the Incas built their palaces. Water was brought down the middle of the main streets and great care was always taken to distribute it through the town. The towns were generally undefended but a strongly walled fortress was built on a neighbouring hill and as this was intended to serve as a temporary refuge for the population in case of emergency, it had often streets and plazas, houses, temples, and so on—a town in miniature. Such may still be seen at Ollantaytambo in the valley of the Urubamba, where the fortress has survived more completely than the ancient town.

The Inca urban sense, which was little short of genius and far in advance of European town planning at the same date, is the more

[1] *The Cities of Latin America* (1944).

remarkable in that no hint of any similar gift can be discerned in the Indian settlements of the highlands. From the earliest pre-Inca vestiges right through to the present day Indian settlements have displayed a striking uniformity and nowhere is there much evidence of planned design. They proliferate at random, grow up higgledy-piggledy as house is added to house in a purely haphazard way, guided only by the need for expansion, the availability of space, the topography of the hilly, irregular terrain and the position of agricultural terraces and the *pucara* or fortress. Except in the many towns built under instruction from the Incas, the Indian agglomerations are of rather exceptional untidiness and irregularity of design. Nor indeed—again with the exception of the Incas and the people of the coastal belt—do the Indians appear to have developed an urban sense. The *marca* consisted of a large conglomeration of isolated *ayllu* settlements; but these were not naturally or normally assembled into larger constructional units of village or town. In my view this sense of order and plan which pervades everything the Incas did from the smallest fortress to Cuzco, their capital, should be one of the strongest arguments for those who still maintain that the Inca rulers came from outside the Andean region.

The sheer quantity of Inca urban building which survives today is astonishing and no attempt can be made here to give a complete account of it. Cuzco itself, the cosmopolitan capital of the Inca Empire, is still hardly less an Inca than a Spanish colonial city, with modernism but beginning to creep in on the outskirts. The Inca plan essentially remains; the main squares and streets in Inca Cuzco are the main squares and streets in the Cuzco of today. The colonial churches and buildings are constructed on Inca foundations and along the streets may be seen the walls of the Inca buildings. A short distance to the north of the present city still stand the remains of the stupendous fort Sacsahuaman, built by Pachacuti, which aroused the admiration of the first Spanish to see it. Cieza de León says that in his time, although the greater part of it had been destroyed, the enormous foundations and the principal towers remained; and Garcilaso says that the three great towers were standing in 1560, the year he left for Spain. Today visitors may see the cyclopean Megalithic walls and gateways and the groundwork of the towers, with stone watercourses and a few piles of polished stonework. Like so much of Inca building this marvel of construction has perished by wanton destructiveness, the greed of treasure hunters and from the pillage of those who sought an easy quarry for building stone. At Kenko may be seen the impressive tomb of the Inca Pachacuti, with its great amphitheatre enclosed by a convex niched wall and a huge natural rock about twenty feet high set on a platform of carved stone. At Tampumachay exists a beautiful example of an Inca bath and close by is a small fort or *pucara* in scenery of singular beauty. The visitor who wishes to range further may explore the three cities of the Urubamba valley—Pisac, Ollantaytambo and Machu Picchu. There is much still to be discovered, cities of the mountain ranges which are known to the Indians but which have not been located or excavated. What exists within relatively easy reach is a veritable paradise for the amateur archaeologist. When the Inca Empire was at its height the intensity of urban building must have been quite exceptional for a people at this period of their history. It is certain that in sixteenth-century Europe no area could have been found of equal extent with so rich an efflorescence of urban construction.

It requires no expert eye to distinguish the various styles of construction used in pre-Columban Peruvian building. First there is the crude method of putting together rustic dwellings or barns by fitting together irregularly shaped field stones, much as country walls and barns are made in the north of England, although the Indians gave greater attention to interlocking and permanence. This method is often used in combination with others for constructing less important parts of fortresses and examples can be found at Ollantaytambo and Machu Picchu. As larger and heavier stones are used with greater care in fitting them together, this crude style merges into the 'polygonal' style proper, in which large irregularly shaped stones are faced in accordance with their natural contours and fitted together with minute exactness. The skill and precision with which these irregular stones were adjusted without the use of mortar or cement with such accuracy that it is impossible to push a razor blade between them has become a byword. This style is often combined with the use of blocks of enormous size and has therefore been known also as the 'Megalithic' style. The builders in this style, whether using Megalithic blocks or large polygonal blocks only, possessed a practical knowledge of thrust and of strength by interlocking which has not been surpassed to this day. It is a knowledge which could only have been acquired by generations of practical and loving craftsmanship. Very different in style is the method of building with roughly squared stone blocks, which too were set together with minute precision and without cement, sometimes skilfully keyed. The squared blocks were sometimes chamfered at the edges where they join, while the outer faces were left rough and bulging, the effect being to emphasize the lines of the joints and break up the surface of the walls into patterns of light and shade. Different again is the style of building with highly burnished blocks roughly cubical in shape. For Megalithic building limestone or diorite porphyry seems to have been preferred and basalt or black andesite for polished work, but there is no invariable rule. There was always, however, the craftsman's sure knowledge of the quality of the stone; you never find used blocks with blemishes or cracks and the quality selected is always such that centuries of weathering do not cause serious deterioration. The strength of this early building was practically demonstrated in the great earthquake which hit Cuzco in 1950. The Inca structures stood foursquare while the Spanish colonial and modern edifices toppled to the ground.

Archaeologists used to distinguish these different styles chronologically and it seems reasonable to suppose that the crude rustic style, of which we have examples in the primitive Neolithic settlements in the valleys round Potosi and elsewhere on the Altiplano, was the earliest in time and that the polygonal technique was a development from it, when something stronger and more permanent, such as a fortress or defence wall, was needed. And the Megalithic style, which is regularly found in conjunction with the polygonal except at Tihuanacu, may logically be supposed to have developed from the same technique when greater resources of man-power were made available by the growth of more extended political centralizations. Building with squared blocks, again, would appear to be a later technique. In Inca building, however, all these styles are used together, each being adapted to the use for which it is most suited. At Machu Picchu and Ollantaytambo two or three of these styles are often used in one and the same wall or in adjacent buildings. It is therefore very difficult to distinguish a typically 'Inca' style from 'pre-Inca' styles, for even the style of building with polished blocks, which seems logically to be the latest, was carried out at Tihuanacu long before the Incas to a greater perfection than was ever achieved by the Incas themselves. Nor is it easy to say when the Incas added to a construction already in existence and when they were responsible for a whole structure built in a variety of styles.

The tendency of contemporary Peruvian archaeology is, indeed, to deny that the Megalithic style was pre-Inca and to attribute almost all the building to the late Inca period, that is, to the ninety years or so which elapsed from the time when Pachacuti began to extend the Inca Empire beyond Cuzco until the Spanish Conquest. In the *Handbook of South American Indians*, J. H. Rowe writes: 'The best-known Inca buildings were constructed wholly or partly of stone and all stone buildings between Pucara in Puno and Ayacucho, of which any illustrations have so far been published (with the exception of constructions at Chanapata and possibly also at Pikillacta and Huata) are of late Inca style. These include Machu Picchu, Sacsahuaman, Ollantaytambo, and all remains in the city of Cuzco proper. It is necessary to stress this point because there is a widespread belief that some or all of these ruins are pre-Inca.' While strong technical arguments have been found for this view, common sense tells us that it is impossible that all the stone building we know could conceivably have been erected in the three generations which elapsed since the time of Pachacuti. In the first place such mastery of technique and sureness of style, such practical knowledge of the engineering possibilities of stone, such ingenuity in its utilization for a variety of purposes for which we should expect the use of timber or metal, such instinctive feeling for the aesthetic possibilities of the *quality* of stone, could only be acquired through long generations of experience and craftsmanship; it is not a thing which could be worked out in a moment even today. And the technique of craftsmanship was not inherited from the Tihuanacu builders, for they did not know the polygonal technique while the builders who worked for the Incas had inherited no tradition of architectural sculpture. They could cut a stone block and assemble it so that the join was unnoticeable, bore the inside into complicated channels and shapes, but always for a practical purpose. Decorative carving was not used. Without a long practical development in stone-masonry, which was not a continuous development from Tihuanacu, the experience and ability could not have been suddenly achieved in the time of Pachacuti, before whom the Incas ruled only a small territory around Cuzco. It is impossible to escape the assumption that Pachacuti and subsequent Incas must have been able to draw upon the services of a large body of skilled and experienced stone workers who had generations of tradition behind them. The other consideration which renders the contemporary view ludicrously impossible is the consideration of time and man-power. In the ninety years after the accession of Pachacuti the Incas were almost continuously at war; they reduced enormous territories by means of large armies, not by any new discovery in offensive armaments. In a country like Peru, which does not give lavishly to support unlimited man-power, the strain of such large forces as the Incas are known to have kept almost continuously under arms must alone have been made possible only by the scientific developments of agriculture introduced on a larger scale than ever before by the Inca rule. The Inca administrative system, though well justified in its results, imposed a heavy additional burden on the agricultural productivity of the country. In addition to this the Incas achieved a hitherto unknown perfection of public works and services—roads which are a marvel today, courier services, stores and inns—an unprecedented luxury for the ruling class, an opulent and wealthy State religion, and reserves to last the whole empire some ten years. The *mit'a* call is agreed to have been one-tenth. Administrative staff must have been one in ten. And the call of military needs must have been equivalent to as much again. All this was achieved in a land which depended upon agriculture under difficult and unfavourable conditions, which was not and could not be densely populated and which was entirely self-sufficient. Consider then the demands of the building programme. The fortress of Sacsahuaman is said to have required 50,000 workmen; the rebuilding of Cuzco by Pachacuti is said to have taken twenty years with 40,000 workers —and these estimates of tradition are most reasonable when one bears in mind the magnitude of the tasks and the slowness of the work with primitive stone-working tools. There simply could not have been the man-power available for all the multifarious building which is attributed to this busy ninety years—the present Peru with all modern engineering devices certainly could not face such a task with equanimity. The Incas must certainly have followed up a tradition of stone building which was widely spread long before they extended their empire—but who were the peoples responsible for this tradition we do not know.

RELIGION

The religion of the Andes was already complex when it came into contact with the proselytizing Christianity of the Spanish missionaries. It had grown up gradually from constant additions and accretions through the centuries, like some old and venerable mansion which moulds in plastic union the diverse contributions of different styles and ages. For the Indian character is syncretic, receptive; integrating the new without ever discarding the old; prepared to conjoin the incongruous and marry the incompatible into a polycladous tradition multiradicate in the distant past. Pliant to new doctrines and cults, the Indian moulds them into new shapes of his own and no force can compel him to desquamate what he has once made his own. His most distant traditions may be driven underground but survive to emerge in moments of stress. Ecdysis is never complete. Hence his religious history combines the most primitive stages of development alongside the more advanced and each new step does not exclude what has been before.

In antiquity Andean religion consisted of a large number of decentralized cults, as many cults as there were tribes or communities, all very similar in their main features but not organized into any formal unity or conforming with any larger orthodoxy. The most pervasive, primitive, fundamental and enduring religious idea of the Andean peoples, hardly less prevalent today than in the past, is the *huaca*, which combines our ideas of 'holy', 'magic', and 'charm' in a primordial synthesis in which the conceptual differences of content have never been made analytically distinct. *Huacas* were so numerous and so varied that they are almost impossible to classify, and their influence reached into every sphere of life. Prominent natural features very easily became *huaca*—mountains, crags, rivers, lakes, springs, caves, or indeed any natural object which tended to arouse the feelings of reverence, mystery or awe (what modern students of comparative religions call the sense of the 'numinous'), or any place associated in popular memory with an historical event handed down in remembered legend. One class of such local *huaca*, called *pacarina*, were associated with the legendary origin of the community or tribe and perhaps regarded as the home of the ancestral spirits of the tribe. The belief in *pacarina* is embodied in the Aymara cosmogonical myth, which tells how the creator god Virajocha sent out his lieutenants from Lake Titicaca north, south, east and west, with orders to call into being the races of men from the rocks and caverns, the lakes, rivers and springs, with the names which Virajocha had ordained for them. The analogy with the belief of the Amazonian Indians that each tribe has as its ancestor some particular jungle animal is too obvious to escape notice, but among the highland Indians the *pacarina* from which each community derived its legendary origin was a fixed natural object. Even in colonial times the belief in the *pacarina* exerted a strong influence in the choice of abode and made the communities reluctant to be uprooted for the convenience of the Spanish. Many other natural *huacas* were simply holy places. Snow-capped mountain peaks were, and still are, objects of worship. Natural features associated with history or legend—bridges, rivers, stones such as the stones near Cuzco believed to have turned into men to help Pachacuti in the defeat of the Chanca—became holy. Perhaps the most famous of all was a curiously shaped stone on the hill Huanacauri, which was associated with one of the legendary brothers of Manco Capac and became a prominent feature in the maturity rites of the Inca youth. Temples and shrines, cities and forts; Cuzco itself was *huaca* and in colonial times the new mining city of Potosi became *huaca*—proof that the religion of *huaca* was not merely a survival but remained active and creative long after the Conquest. A curious development of the *huaca* idea was the custom, which again survives into the present and has been remarked on by many travellers, to build piles of stones at the top of a pass or at critical stages in a road, where the traveller, having reached this stage in safety, would make a small sacrifice to the *huaca*—called *apacita*—perhaps only a gob of coca or the addition of a stone. There is no doubt that the instinct of topolatry was strongly developed among the Andean peoples.

Another class of *huaca* were those associated with agricultural ceremonial. For as the life of the highland peoples revolves around agriculture, so agricultural beliefs, superstitions and ritual have always occupied a central place in religion. In a sense everything connected with agriculture was holy in some degree, for there was no separation between religion and life. There was not one religious tradition and one secular tradition interacting and interpenetrating at certain points; tradition was one and all tradition was religious. Religion was practical and life was religion. Thus agriculture as such was holy and everything connected with agriculture or agricultural ritual became *huaca*. With this background, the most prominent particular agricultural *huaca* were the boundary stone, or *sayhua*, and the stone guardian of the field, the *guanka*. The earth itself was worshipped as Pachamama, the Earth Mother, and a number of celestial bodies were the objects of ritual in connection with the agricultural seasons and their supposed influence on the weather.

Perhaps the only aspect of Andean religion which was not severely practical in intention was the reverence paid to the ancestors of the family or *ayllu*; outside the practical affairs of life *cuyaspa*, or respect for the dead, was the Indian's most important preoccupation. Not that this was entirely without its practical implications, but it seems not to have been purely practical in origin and purport. The spirits of the dead, or some of them, were believed to be able to cause sickness or death by stealing away the souls of the living or to bring calamity and misfortune. But there is no sufficient evidence at all that the Andean cult of the dead was—as is the case with some primitive peoples—entirely or largely propitiatory or motived by fear of the dead. The preserved bodies of forefathers, past members of the *ayllu*, called *mallqui*, were *huaca* in a very high degree and objects associated with them acquired *huaca* by reflection. In Inca religion the ancestor cult was to blossom into one of the main pillars of the national religion, bringing into visible relation the worship of the Sun and the divinity of the dynasty. The mummies of past Incas acquired great sanctity, were preserved with great opulence and pomp, and were brought forth in processions to participate in great public ceremonies. In the month of Ayamarka, corresponding with November, the *mallqui* or bodies of the dead (literally 'fruit-bearing trees') were brought out and taken in procession for the blessing of the fields throughout the land, a ceremony which has now merged into the pious adoration of the dead with gifts on All Souls' Day. During early colonial times the Indians would secretly remove the bodies of their dead from the Christian cemeteries to deposit them in the mountain caves where their tribal *huaca* were preserved, explaining this action when apprehended as a manifestation of *cuyaspa*.

Finally there were innumerable portable *huaca*, called by the general name *conopa*, which appear to have been something akin to our good-luck charms and amulets. They had personal *conopa*, family *conopa*, portable house-guardians, *conopa* connected with the rituals of birth and maturity, and many more. These were small carved figures in the shape of men or animals, curiously shaped stones, representations of food objects to ensure fertility, amulets against disease and accident and innumerable others.

In a word everything which was strange or grand, everything which inspired awe, everything which was significant from historical or legendary associations, everything which aroused a sense of attachment through familiarity, everything which was connected with ritual or superstition, might acquire *huaca* and become important in the religious life of the people. The Spanish believed that the *huaca* were inhabited by devils and attacked the *huaca* religion as a form of devil-worship; but there is not good reason for thinking that the Indians before Spanish influence imagined all *huaca* to be inhabited by disembodied or 'free' spirits. They certainly believed in malicious and dangerous spirits, called *supay*, which could be controlled by black magicians for evil; and the Aymaras today believe that some local *huaca* are the homes of 'earth spirits', while in some regions it is believed that they are occupied by the spirits of the primitive race of men who lived before the creation of the Sun. But while some place-*huacas* were believed to be spirit-homes, it is unlikely that all *huaca* were thought of as enshrining a spirit. It is probable that belief was much more vague and at a more primitive level, more nearly akin to the belief which many people retain in 'lucky charms'.

This then was the popular foundation of belief upon which the Incas erected their grandiose superstructure of Sun-worship and divine Kingship. But it is almost certain that before the Incas some form of universalized cult and central priesthood had been imposed upon the popular religion, probably by the political organization which we have called the Megalithic Empire, because many of the enormous surviving stone structures, such as Chavin and Tihuanacu, seem to have been primarily religious in their purpose. And it is certain that this pre-Inca universal cult was associated with the worship of a feline deity—whether deriving from the tropical interior and, if so, whether introduced and spread by a migration of conquering peoples from the interior to the highlands is still a matter of speculation. But at least it is curious that the worship of the jaguar was not only at one time widespread throughout the highlands but even today all the tribes of the Amazonian jungle, whatever their particular totem-animal, agree in according special worship to the jaguar.

The worship of the feline god, the jaguar or American tiger, the puma or American lion, or the mountain cat, was far more ancient than the Inca religion of the Sun and sank more deeply into popular belief and custom, leaving its mark after the worship of the Sun had been forgotten. The feline symbol is ubiquitous in the archaeological remains of the Andes, both in the coastal civilizations and on the highlands, in regions where neither the jaguar nor the puma is known to have been indigenous, and although the Inca religion superimposed itself upon and to some extent ousted the old cult of the Jaguar, even in Inca religious symbolism itself the feline motif retained a position of prominence. According to legend the 'Island of the Sun' was a sacred centre of the Jaguar cult many centuries before the famous temple of the Sun was built there and the very name Titicaca—which originally belonged to the Island and was later transferred to the Lake—means 'Jaguar Rock'. In Aymara *titi* is a general term for feline. In the primitive period of Tihuanacu the sculptured Jaguar head is dominant and there has been discovered a special type of ceramic jar (called *zahumador*), in feline shape, in which the remains of charred ash seem to indicate that they had a ritualistic purpose. At Tihuanacu have been found zoomorphic stone figures, called locally *Chacha-puma*, or 'Lion-man', usually about three feet high, representing a man with feline head and an expression of exaggerated ferocity. Some carry a cudgel in the right hand and a human head in the left. Two of these Lion-men, badly weathered, may still be seen in the enclosure popularly known as Puma Punku—the Gate of the Puma—at Tihuanacu. Others have been set up in the open-air museum at Miraflores in La Paz. One, discovered by D'Orbigny in 1883, was displayed in the Musée de l'Homme at Paris. They are thought to have been connected with a blood-thirsty feline cult associated with Tihuanacu. And even the stylized figures carved in low relief on the famous Gate of the Sun, from the Classical period, are now explained as stylized Jaguars and not as figures of the Sun-god. (In my opinion, while the Jaguar motif is undoubtedly present, the stylizations may represent a fusion of the feline motif with the new symbolization of the Sun-god.) In the Chavin culture again the feline figure was omnipresent and as a decorative and religious design spread throughout the coastal belt and over large stretches of the highlands.

Garcilaso says that the Indians of northern Peru worshipped the tiger, the lion and the bear before the coming of the Incas, and that if a man met one of these animals, he would fall down and worship and allow himself to be killed by it instead of trying to escape (Book I, chap. 9). In another place he says that the Antis, the inhabitants of the Bolivian Altiplano, worshipped in antiquity the tiger and the boa, believing these to be indigenous and to have owned the land before their own arrival. Cieza de León and Bernal Diaz de Castillo mention sacrificial worship of the tiger after the fall of the Incas, the former as far north as Quito. In the *Religión y Gobierno de los Incas,* Polo de Ondegardo mentions forest-dwellers who worshipped a star called Chuqui-chinchay, which 'is a Tiger, in whose charge are the tigers, bears and lions'. In the *Extirpación de la Idolatria del Perú,* José de Arriaga says that the Devil appeared to the native priests in the form of a lion or a tiger. Guaman Poma asserts that in the earliest times the Yarohuillka had a complete hierarchy of the puma and Juan de Betanzos mentions a city which was called the 'Body of the Lion' and its inhabitants the members of the body. In his *Descripción biográfica, histórica y estadística de Bolivia,* Alcides D'Orbigny describes survivals of a tiger cult as late as 1815. And to this day in the traditional fiesta dances which are performed by the Indians in the towns and villages throughout the length and breadth of the Altiplano, often accompanying processions of the Virgin or saints, the mask of the Jaguar is the most prominent and active of all the costumes. I have myself known men in eastern Bolivia who have won respect by going out into the jungle and wrestling barehanded with tigers or killing them with only a wooden spear, such men who in the past became priests. Indeed D'Orbigny says that in his time men who had escaped the claws of a tiger were held in respect and considered deserving of priesthood, while the Bolivian archaeologist Leo Pucher mentions a belief that such men are able to turn themselves into tigers at night. The tribe of the Chiriguani still believe implicitly in a fabulous 'green tiger', Yaguarogui, which causes eclipses of the sun and the moon by attempting to eat them (Dorotéo Giannecchini, *Diccionario Chiriguano-Español* (1916)) and a ceramic representation of what is believed to be the Jaguarogui was found by Julio Tello at Chavin. Certain it is that at least from Inca times until today the custom of howling and screaming at eclipses in order to frighten away the Jaguar which threatens the sun or moon has prevailed throughout the Andes country. These are but a few evidences from many which show that some form of Jaguar worship had proliferated from times immemorial not only among the highland peoples who were the originators of agriculture, settled community life and civilization, but also among the untamed jungle peoples who were never brought within the orbit of a civilized and politically stable culture. About the time of Chavin and the first period of Tihuanacu, whether or not the Jaguar cult was then first introduced to the Andean region from outside, it was organized into a universal religion with a regular priesthood which knit together the scattered communities and tribes as well as the outposts of more advanced civilization into some sort of politico-religious unity. In its decline it was amalgamated with the Inca religion of the Sun and deeply influenced Inca ritual. And since the collapse of the Inca State it has continued to exercise a deeper influence on popular superstition and religious practice than the later religion of the Sun.

The agricultural and pastoral peoples who dwelt in the Andes country were as dependent in primitive times as those of today on the annual rains for their crops and the pastures for their flocks. In times of drought, and every year in the months before the beginning of the rains, the *puna* becomes a desert without a vestige of vegetation. Yet the rainy season in the Andes is notoriously irregular and variable. If the rains come too early or too late, or if they come in inadequate quantity, the result may be disastrous for the coming year. Many an *ayllu* has been compelled to migrate even in modern times by a couple of years of drought, which bring starvation, disease and despair. In Inca times and before, their irrigated lands, or *moyas*, were more extensive and they were in a better position than now to lay in a provision to tide over the bad years; but the fundamental dependence upon the rain was the same. If the rainfall is too plentiful or too sudden, torrents swirling down from the mountains may carry away the carefully prepared top soil, destroy the young crops, sweep down agricultural terraces, destroy roads, barns, houses. In La Paz itself, the modern capital of Bolivia, I have seen how a heavy rainstorm can cause floods and landslides, carrying away houses in the suburbs, blocking roads, strewing trees and boulders over the fields. Hence the constant preoccupation of native religion with weather conditions and with everything which influences, or is thought to influence, the annual rains. The lightning, the thunderbolt, the hailstorm and the wind were attributed to divine agencies and were objects of propitiatory worship long before the Incas. Julio C. Tello says that according to tradition the divinities of rain and storm were embodied in a monstrous Jaguar, which comes roaring and bellowing from the direction of the eastern jungles, climbs the peaks of the eastern Cordillera and wrapped in thick black cloud hurls lightning and thunder, storm and rain. If in fact the Jaguar cult came from the tropical jungles of the Amazon to the highlands, it is unlikely to have been a rain and storm symbol in origin, for in the jungle these weather conditions are different and less important to survival. Yet when the cult became established in the highlands it may well have taken on this symbolism, for so long as rain has so important a practical significance in the lives of the people—so long that is as they remain agricultural and pastoral—their religion must be largely preoccupied with the attempt to control and regulate the seasons.

Of the origins of Inca religion we know even less than we know of the origins of the Inca Empire. We know that as they created a single empire throughout the Andes country, so they created a single State religion, established a national priesthood and elaborated a cult rich in ceremonial, complicated in its ritual and magnificent in its impressiveness. We know that their religion was a highly typical and highly developed form of Sun worship combined with divine kingship, which ethnologists associate with the emergence of settled agricultural communities from the food-gathering stage. But in the Andes this religious development came many centuries, perhaps a millennium, after the change-over from the hunting and food-gathering stage to the stage of settled agricultural communities. Of its source and inspiration we know next to nothing. Possibly the Tihuanacu political centralization was controlled by priest-kings, but its religion was probably not Sun-worship. The institution of divine kingship had been highly developed in some of the coastal centres of pre-Inca civilization, notably at Chimu, but before the Incas the worship of the Sun had not apparently ever been dominant in Andean religion.

The Incas not only posed as political benefactors but were imbued with religious missionary zeal and taught that religion of the Sun was ethically superior and practically more powerful than the old cult of the Jaguar. They did not, however, as did the Christians later, attempt to suppress and stamp out the earlier religious habits or the religions of conquered peoples. The religion of the Sun was superimposed as a national cult but was rich to embrace within itself the regional rites as subordinate cults. It was not exclusive; in Cuzco was a place for every local deity and cult. Apparently Inca religion was much less highly developed doctrinally than in ceremony and ritual, making it the easier to incorporate harmoniously the many warring and jarring elements in one rich and fertile syncretic whole. But however politically effective this system was, it would be mistaken to regard it as pure political expediency; for the spirit of Andean religion has always been plastic and syncretistic, including all and rejecting nothing. What the Incas did with the worship of the Sun had been done before with the cult of the Jaguar.

The supreme deity of the Incas was Virajocha or Ticci-Virajocha, the creator-god. For the word *Virajocha* is not a proper name distinguishing one god in particular from another, but a term of respect like our word 'Lord', while the word *Ticci* or *Tice* means 'creator'. Diego Gonzales Holguin says in the *Diccionario Quechua* (1608) 'Ticci: principal origin; cause'. And the word still bears this sense in both Quechua and Aymara. Thus *Ticci-Virajocha* simply means 'Creator-Lord'.[1] It is unlikely that the worship of Virajocha was first introduced by the Incas. In pre-Inca aetiological myths we hear of a creator-god who is called Virajocha and there is some evidence that the Jaguar was also addressed as Virajocha. The innovation for which the Incas were responsible was to make the Sun the supreme object of worship, whether as identified with the creator-god Virajocha or as the chief agent of Virajocha is never made very clear. Thus the Sun-god Inti, Inti Virajocha or Cori-Inti (Golden Sun), became supreme, a national deity in a very real and lively sense. He was the ancestor of the Inca royal house, who derived their divinity through direct descent from him, and the reigning Inca was thought to be in some sense the embodiment of the Sun-god on earth. In his honour was built up a large and powerful priesthood, an order of Holy Women or *ñustas* vowed to perpetual virginity

[1] The derivation of Virajocha from 'vira', *tallow* or *grease*, and 'cocha', *sea* or *lake*, is common among the early chroniclers, although Garcilaso points out that Viracocha, if so derived, would mean 'lake of tallow'. ('Foam of the sea' would be *Cochap-vira*, as the genitive is placed first in Quechua.) Furthermore, while the 'cocha' of Viracocha is pronounced with an aspirated guttural like the Scottish 'ch'—represented in Spanish sometimes by 'c' and sometimes by the aspirated 'j'—the word 'cocha' meaning 'lake' is pronounced with a double guttural—'k' followed by the Scottish 'ch'. The derivation 'sea-foam' is certainly wrong, and though the derivation of 'vira' from 'pirua' by Montesinos is not certainly right, it is at least more reasonable.

in his service, temples and shrines throughout the land and an elaborate and imposing ceremonial. The cult was supported from lands set aside in every commune as the property of the Sun.

There is every reason to believe that the national religion of the Sun was readily accepted throughout the greater part of the empire as a superior ceremonial to which the peoples did obeisance without abandoning or being asked to abandon their traditional regional cults. It was established far and wide not only by the temples with their attached priesthood but by the movements of population, the *mitimaes* organized by Pachacuti and his successors. Although Inti was supreme, other gods were worshipped. There was a cult of the Moon, who was a male deity, and worship was accorded to the Storm-god Illapu (in Aymara *Thunupa*), later identified with Santiago of Spain, and to the Pleiades and certain other stars. A coastal deity Pachacamac, described as a spiritual invisible god who gave life to the universe, was accepted into the Inca religion. Every local *huaca* of importance had its shrine and cult in Cuzco under imperial patronage. Indeed ceremonial was so manifold that it is difficult now to say where ritual merged into worship of an independent deity.

Laying its main emphasis upon ritual and organization, Inca religion went far towards systematizing the ceremonial year as a counterpoint to the main agricultural events in the cultivation of maize. The Inca year had twelve months, each named after its appropriate ceremony, each containing three ten-day weeks, with a short intercalated week of five days. The Inca months as they correspond with our own are given in the following table by Luis E. Valcarcel:

Gregorian months	*Peruvian months*	*Translation*
December	Kapaj Raymi	The principal festival
January	Juchuy Pokoy	The small ripening
February	Jatun Pokoy	The great ripening
March	Paukar Waray	The garment of flowers
April	Ayriway	The dance of young maize
May	Aymuray	Song of the harvest
June	Inti Raymi	Festival of the sun
July	Anta Situwa	Earthly purification
August	Kapaj Situwa	General purification
September	Koya Raymi	Festival of the Queen
October	Uma Raymi	Festival of the water
November	Ayamark'a	Procession of the dead

The most important ceremony was Kapaj Raymi, the Great Festival, in December at the beginning of the year, when the work of preparation had been done, the earth was loaded with seed, pregnant and in gestation and all magic rituals had been accomplished at their appropriate times; then came the great all-inclusive ceremony in the period of waiting, a ceremony to propitiate all the supernatural powers jointly and to ensure that the season of rains already begun would continue normally and profitably for the harvest. For the greatest danger to Andean cultivation is that the rains having begun in October will cease prematurely in December or else that continuing too heavily they will lead to violent floods from the mountains in January and February which will wash away the young harvest. Hence this festival was specially devoted to the Storm-god Thunupa, and at one time perhaps to the Jaguar. The Incas combined it with the maturity rite of the royal youths, when they were given breechclouts and ear-plugs as a symbol of admission to the Inca nobility with full adult status. Thus the festival acquired political and national significance and very elaborate ceremonial was evolved.

From January to May the festivals followed the gradual development of the maize plant from its first sprouting to the harvest. Following the harvest came the great festival to the Sun, the Inti Raymi, in June, which was the cardinal festival of the national religion and in later Spanish times was amalgamated with Corpus Christi. Sometimes it coincided with the ploughing and sometimes it included ceremonial to protect the remaining crops against frost and drought, but its agricultural importance was not of the greatest.[1] July was the time of clearing and purifying the land in preparation for the next year's harvest. August was the month of the main ploughing and the early maize crop was then sown. In August, the earth, Pachamama, came alive, libations were poured to her and ritualistic purification of people, houses and animals was necessary. In September, the Raymi of the Queen, the main crop was sown and it was necessary to study the moon with divination in order to select favourable days for work. October was the time when the early rains were expected and the first ceremonial for the coming rainy season fell due. In November came the blessing of the now fertilized fields and the processionals of the *mallquis* of the dead to vitalize the now buried seed. A rite to ensure fertility of the livestock later became amalgamated

[1] A description from Garcilaso is given in Appendix 2 of this chapter.

with the ritual of the night of San Juan. Thus agricultural significance controlled the rituals the year round and it was the main innovation of the Incas to have given to them a national and political significance without interfering with the agricultural motive.

All these festivals and many others both fixed and occasional were celebrated with great pomp and meticulous ritual, with holidays, processions, singing, dancing and drinking. Lasting from a single day to a full week of ten days, they provided for the worker relaxation and approved licence from the daily routine and a relief from monotony. In their total Inca holidays were very much less than Catholic holidays in Colonial times, which with Sundays diminished the working days of the year by one-third. And while the Christian festivals were regarded as times of worship divorced from work, the Indian regarded his festivals and ritual as no less essential to agricultual success than the physical labour upon the land itself.

Inca religion was not without its moral aspect. Confession, penance, purification from sin and fasting were all practised. The priests in charge of local shrines acted as confessors and were bound to secrecy. Penance usually consisted of prayer and fasting. The person making confession would often hold in his hands a wisp of straw into which he would spit and then cast it into a stream as a symbol of release from his sins—whence comes the name *ichori*, or 'straw man', applied to the Aymara confessors, who were the most popular. In Colonial times religious teachers found it necessary to define the Catholic rite of confession with especial care in order to avoid confusion with the native rite practised under the Incas.

Divination safeguarded every important action at all levels of society from the Inca downwards and was practised by a variety of means. Professional diviners were employed by the nobility and divining sorcerers, or *yatiri*, served the generality. Divination by studying the phases of the moon, by dreams or by direct inspiration decided the appropriate day for all agricultural events. Local oracles or *huacas* were thought to tell the future and some acquired widespread reputation. Sorcerers were believed to have the power to invoke the supernatural powers and commune directly with them. Divination by enteroscopy, by fire and by coca were common and are practised today. Malicious spirits (*supaya*), ghosts and evil influences were dreaded and were believed to be the main causes of disease, accidents and ill luck. Sorcerers were ubiquitous and either employed white magic (*pako*) against the malicious spirits and the influences of black magicians (*laika*) or employed black magic for the hurt of their fellow men. Black magicians were hated and feared, though used, and were reprobated by the Inca code. It was one of the achievements of the Incas that they created a sacerdotal caste distinct from practising magicians and sorcerers. Yet despite strong measures by the Incas and veritable witch-hunts by the Spanish, the belief in magic and witchcraft survives in every Indian community. Our knowledge of the details of early Indian sorcery, white and black, is somewhat vague since the abundant references in the chroniclers tend to be distorted by their own belief in demonology; for at this date demonology, magic and witchcraft were firmly believed, though condemned by the Church. The interpretation of modern survivals even by the practitioners themselves tends also to be influenced by Christian demonological doctrine. Yet allowing for all distortion one cannot but be profoundly surprised by the many similarities between early Andean and medieval European belief and practice in all aspects of sorcery, divination, demonology, necromancy and other forms of intercourse with the marginal spiritual forces. It is astonishing indeed that beliefs and practices so similar grew up among branches of the human race out of contact for twenty millennia.

From this very summary survey of Indian religion we may draw the general conclusion that the Indian devotional habit was eminently practical. Despite the cult of the dead, it was a religion of a practical people concerned with the practical preoccupations of this life. Belief in a future life, if not entirely absent, had little influence upon the conduct of the present life. Work and worship were directed to the accomplishment of the same ends, worship was ritual and ritual predominated over doctrine. Metaphysical and mystical content seems to have been small. It is true that the almost complete loss of the unwritten literature of the Quechuas may have obscured metaphysical and mystical thought, but the few examples which have survived, while showing great poetical feeling, do not reveal doctrinal or mystical interest. And the reaction of the modern Indian to four centuries of Christian teaching agrees with the conclusion that his religious temperament is practical and ritualistic rather than mystical and speculative.

Appendix I

EXAMPLES OF QUECHUA POETRY

1

Pacha Kamaj	*Pachacamac*
Ayauya waqaylli	Pity my tears,
Ayauya puypuylli	Pity my anguish.
Lluttu puchaj	The most distressed
Wamrayki	Of thy children,
Lluttu puchaj	The most distressed
Wajchayki	Of thy servants,
Waqallamusunkin	Implores thee with tears.
Unujsaykita	Grant the miracle
Yakujsaykita	Of thy waters,
Kachallamuway	Grant the gift of rain,
Wajchayki	To this unfortunate
Runayki	Person,
Llajta runa	To this creature
Kamasqaykiman	Thou hast created.

(From *Guamán Poma de Ayala*.)

2

Runa Kamaj	*The Creator of Man*
Pacha paqarin	The earth dawns
Lliphipirintaj	Is covered with light
Upaykunanpaj	In order to honour
Runa kamajta	The Creator of man.
Janaj pachari	The high heaven
Phuyun chinkachin	Clears its clouds
Kkumuykunanpaj	Humiliating itself
Pacha rurajman	To the Creator of earth.
Qoyllurpaj Inkan	The lord of the stars
Inti yayanchis	Our father the Sun
Chujchan masttarin	Spreads out his hair
Paypaj chakinman	At his feet.

Wayrari tantan	The wind as well
Saccha purata	Shakes the treetops
Rijranta chhajrin	Tosses their branches
Janaj pachaman	Breaks them to earth.
Sacchaj sunqonpi	In the bosom of the trees
Takikun pichiu	The birds sing
Ancha upaykun	Doing their homage
Pacha kamjta	To the ruler of earth.
Tukuy ttikantin	All the flowers
Sumaj sumajlla	Proud and beautiful
Llanqa llimpilla	Display their colours
Qqapay samakun	And all their perfumes.
Qhocha ukhupi	The bosom of the lake
Rirppu unupi	A mirror of water
Challwakunapas	Is the happy home
Kusitan wayttan	Of the lucky fishes.
Nanaj mayupas	The brisk torrent
Rakhu takinwan	With its hoarse song
Añayñispanñan	Is singing the praises
Wiraqochata.	Of Virajocha.
Qaqa rumipas	The crag as well
Qqomer ppachallin	Is decked in green
Wayqqo sacchapas	And the forest in the ravine
Wataj ttikarin	Offers fresh flowers.
Orqopi kausaj	And the mountain dwellers
Katarikuna	The snake people
Paypaj chakinpi	At his feet
Qhatatakunku	Are gliding along.
Purun wikkuña	The vicuña on the desert heights
Qaqa wiskkacha	The viscacha of the rocks
Uywaman tukun	Make their homes
Paypaj qayllanpi	Around him.
Sunqoypas kikin	So too my heart
Sapa paqarin	At every dawn
Añayñisunki	Gives praise to thee
Yayay kamaqiy	My father, my Creator.

(Collection Vásquez. From Jesus Lara's *La Poesia Quechua*.)

3
Agricultural Jailli

Qharikuna	Men
Ayau jailli, ayau jailli!	Ho! jailli [Victory], ho! jailli!
Kayqa thajlla, kayqa suka!	Here is digging-stick, here the furrow!
Kayqa maki, kayqa jumppi!	Here the sweat and here the toil!
Warmikuna	Women
Ajailli, qhari, ajailli!	Huzzah, men, huzzah!
Qharikuna	Men
Ayau jailli, ayau jailli!	Ho! jailli, ho! jailli!
Maypin ñustta, maypin sijlla?	Where the Ñusta, where the fair one?
Maypin muju, maypin jailli?	Where the seed, where the triumph?
Warmikuna	Women
Ajailli, muju, ajailli!	Huzzah, the seed, huzzah!
Qharikuna	Men
Ayau jailli, ayau jailli!	Ho! jailli, ho! jailli!
Quapaj Inti, Apu Yaya,	Great Sun, Mighty Father,
Qhawaykuriy, samaykuriy!	Watch the sowing, that it prosper!
Warmikuna	Women
Ajailli, Inti, ajailli!	Huzzah, Sun, huzzah!
Qharikuna	Men
Ayau jailli, ayau jailli!	Ho! jailli, ho! jailli!
Pachamama wisallanman,	In the belly of Mother Earth
Yurinanman, rurunanman!	May it germinate and fructify!
Warmikuna	Women
Ajailli, Pachamama, ajailli!	Huzzah, Earth Mother, huzzah!
Qharikuna	Men
Ayau jailli! ayau jailli!	Ho! jailli, ho! jailli!
Kaymin ñustta, kaymin sijlla!	Here the Ñusta, here the fair one!

UNDER INCA RULE

Warmikuna	*Women*
Kaymin qhari, kaymin jumppi!	Here the man, here the toil!
Ajailli, qhari, ajailli!	Huzzah, man, huzzah!

(Collection Méndez. From Jesus Lara, *La Poesia Quechua*.)

4

(The following is from the Colonial epoch and was set to traditional music by Teófilo Vargas in *Aires Nacionales de Bolivia*.)

Manchay Phuito

Uj kata kusiyniy kajta	What cruel land has buried
Mayken jallppa mullppuy-kapun?	Her who was my only joy?
Sakerkani kallallajta.	Fresh I left her like a flower.
Sajra huayrachu apakapun?	Has some cruel wind carried her off?
Puriskan pallani	I will follow my lady
Llanttunta maskkani	Where her shadow stays.
Kikin pay llanttuy kuanchu	Is it she who gives me shade in the way
Huakayniypay ayppullanchu?	Or is it but the screen of my tears?
Moskochakus muchaykuni	I see her and kiss her in my dreams
Ttukuni chay, parlaykuni	In my trouble she speaks to me
Musppani ichas pa rikuni	In my hours of grief I see her
Kkanchaskaj ppahuaykamun	In a halo of light she descends to me.
Huañuchikujmanchu?	Am I to seek my own death?
Ppiñakujanmanchu?	Would my death vex her?
Huañuchikuspa kayllayman	By death could I approach her.
Astahuanchus karunchayman	But perhaps she would prefer me afar.
Ppampaskannejta jasppini	I scrabble the tomb where she sleeps
Huakaspa param paranta;	While my tears flow like rain endlessly;
Unuyanchus jallpa nini	Thus should the earth be softened

Maskarkonaypaj uranta	To seek my beloved in its depths.
Ñoka mayllapipis	Wherever you be, my beloved,
Jallppaj sonkonpipis	In the broad bosom of the earth,
Ñokalla munakuskayki	I only shall adore thee,
Sapallay huayllukuskayki.	None other but I may attend thee.
Aswan kkoñi samayniyuan	With the tender warmth of my breath
Ppukuykus kutirichisaj	I will succeed to bring her to life.
Ojllaykusaj mucchayniyhuan	I will embrace her and with my kisses
Alliyman rijccharichisaj	Falling softly will call her to life.
Manachayri jamuy	But if this is not to be,
Muyoj huayra uskamuy	Delay not to come, thou whirlwind,
Lakhayajniyki upiykuhuachun	Let thy black darkness absorb me
Ukhunpi chinkacjihuachun	And in darkness my life disappear.
Huakayniyhuan jokkochaska	Earth moistened with my tears
Khuyaj jallppa khataykuhuayku	Shelter us, thou generous earth!
Karkaykumin ujllachaska	United with thee in the universe
Ujllapuniña kaskayku	Thus to remain for ever.
Ñoka tuta kani	I am night unplumbed,
Cchintamin maskani	Solitude unbounded,
Llakiy kani yuyayniyta	I am the very flesh of anguish,
Munani chinkarichiyta.	I flee from my own thoughts.
Tullumtapis sikkisaj	But something from her I desire, I must draw out a bone;
Ojllayniypi kakunampaj	I will cherish it in my bosom, as though I held her herself.
Qenamanmin tukuchisaj	It will become a flute in my hands
Huakayniyhuan huakanampaj	And weep my own tears
Janaj pachamanta	From all eternity,
Llippipej chaymanta	From the origin of light,
Paymin sina huajyanaskan	Perhaps it is she that is calling.
Manan Kenallay huakaskan.	No, it is the lament of my flute.

Appendix II

THE FESTIVAL OF THE SUN

(Garcilaso, Book VI, Chapters xx–xxiii.)

The name *Raimi* has the same significance as Pasch or solemn festival. Of the four festivals which the Incas celebrated in the city of Cuzco, which was another Rome, the most solemn was that in honour of the Sun in the month of June, which they called Intip Raimi, which means solemn Pasch of the Sun, and they called it Raimi pure and simple, which has the same significance, and if they called other festivals by this name it was by analogy with this festival, to which the name Raimi belonged rightly. They celebrated it after the June solstice.

They held this festival to the Sun in recognition that he was adored as the supreme, sole and universal God, who by his light and strength created and sustained all things in the world.

And in recognition that he was the natural father of the first Inca Manco Capac and of the Coya Mama Occllo Huaco and of all the Kings and of their sons and descendants, sent to the earth for the universal benefit of mankind, for these reasons, as they say, this festival was the most solemn.

There assembled for it all the chief captains of war who had retired or who were not occupied in warfare and all the curacas, lords of vassals, of all the Empire; not by any order which obliged them to attend but because they took delight in being present at the celebration of so great a festival; which since it involved the adoration of their God, the Sun, and the veneration of the Inca, there was no one who did not take part. And when the curacas were unable to go owing to age or illness or because of important business in the service of the King or because of the great distance to travel, they sent to it their sons and brothers, accompanied by the noblest of their kin, to attend in their name. The Inca was present in person unless he was prevented by war or absent on tour in his kingdom.

The first ceremonies were performed by the King as chief priest because, although there was always a chief priest of royal blood who had to be a brother or uncle of the Inca fully legitimate on both father's and mother's side, in this festival, since it was the special festival of the Sun, the King himself performed the first ceremonies, as first-born of the Sun in whose honour the festival was principally solemnized.

The curacas came with all the finest attire and devices they could; some wore robes overlaid with gold and silver and coronets of the same on their heads over their head-gear.

Others came looking exactly like the paintings of Hercules, clothed in a lion's skin and with their head enclosed in the lion's head, because these pride themselves on being descended from a lion.

Others came garbed like the paintings of angels, with great wings of a bird which they call *cuntur*[1]—these birds are white and black and so large that many killed by the Spanish have measured fourteen or fifteen feet from wing-tip to wing-tip—for they boast that they are descended and derive their origin from this bird.

Others wore masks in the most horrid shapes they can make and these are the Yuncas. They entered the festival with gestures and grimaces of madmen, fools and halfwits. For the which they carried in their hands suitable instruments such as flutes, and tabours badly tuned, pieces of pelts, with which they cut their clownish capers.

Other curacas came with their several heraldic devices. Each tribe bore its characteristic weapons of war: some carried bows and arrows, others lances, throwing spears, long arrows, maces, slings and short-handled axes for use with one hand or long-handled two-handed axes.

They brought pictures of the deeds they had done in the service of the Sun and of the Incas; they brought large drums and trumpets and many servants to play them; in a word each tribe came as finely arrayed and with as fine a retinue as it could, each competing to excel over its neighbours, or over all if it should be able.

All alike prepared for the Raimi of the Sun with a strict fast, and for three days they took nothing but a little uncooked white maize and a few herbs which they call *chucam* and pure water. During all this time no fire was lighted in all the city and they refrained from sleeping with their wives.

After the fast, the night before the festival, the Inca priests deputed for the sacrifice were in charge of making ready the sheep and lambs which were to be sacrificed and the other offerings of

[1] *i.e.* Condor.

food and drink which were to be offered to the Sun. All the which was arranged in advance after it was known the numbers who had come to the festival, for the offerings had to suffice for all the tribes, not only the curacas and ambassadors but the relations, subjects and servants of them all.

The women of the Sun had the duty that night of making very large quantities of a maize paste which they call *cancu*; they made round rolls the size of a common apple and it should be remarked that these Indians never ate their corn made into dough and bread except in this festival and another which they called Citua and they did not eat this bread all through the meal but only two or three mouthfuls at the beginning; their usual food instead of bread is roasted or boiled maize in the grain.

The flour for this bread, principally that which the Inca and those of the royal blood were to eat, was ground and cooked by the chosen virgins, the women of the Sun, and they too cooked all the other food of that festival; for it seemed rather as though that banquet were given by the Sun to his children than by his children to him; and therefore it was cooked by the virgins, as they were the wives of the Sun.

For the rest of the people the bread was prepared and cooked by a large number of other women deputed for this purpose. But although the bread was for the common people, they paid great attention that it should be prepared by maidens, for they held this bread to be a holy thing, which was not permitted to be eaten during the year but only at this festival, which was their festival of festivals.

When the necessary preparations had been made, the following day, which was the day of the festival, at dawn the Inca came forth accompanied by all his family, which came in order conformable with the rank and age of each one, to the great Square of the city, which they call Haucaipata. There they waited for the Sun to appear, and all were barefoot and with great reverence, looking towards the east, when the Sun first began to appear all squatted on their heels (which with these Indians is the same as falling to their knees) to adore him and opening their arms with the hands raised one each side of the face, giving kisses in the air (which is the same as kissing one's own hand or the robe of the King in Spain), they adored the Sun with the utmost devotion and respect in sign that they held him as their God and natural father.

The curacas, since they were not of royal blood, went to another square adjoining the main square, which they call Cussipata; they made the same adoration of the Sun as the Incas. Then the King rose to his feet, the rest remaining crouched on their heels, and took two large golden goblets, which they call *aquilla*, full of the draught they brew. He performed this ceremony (as firstborn) in the name of his father the Sun and with the goblet in his right hand invited him to drink, which is what the sun should do, the Inca inviting all his relations, for this ceremony of offering an invitation to drink was the greatest and most usual symbol they had of the satisfaction of a superior with an inferior and of friendship one with another.

After the invitation to drink he poured the right-hand goblet, which was dedicated to the Sun, in a large golden jar and from the jar it came out through a pipe of very beautiful workmanship which ran from the great Square to the House of the Sun, as though he had drunk it. And from the other goblet, that in the left hand, the Inca took a draught, which was his share, and then shared the rest among the other Incas, giving each one a little in a small vessel of gold or silver which he had ready to receive it; so that little by little all received something from the principal goblet which the Inca had held, in order that the liquor, sanctified by the hand of the Sun or the Inca, or the two together, should communicate its virtue to those who participated. Of this draught drank all the Incas. To the other curacas who were in the other square they gave to drink of the same beverage which the women of the Sun had made but not of the sanctified liquor, which was only for the Incas.

This ceremony completed, which was a kind of promise of what was to be drunk thereafter, all went in order to the House of the Sun and two hundred steps before the door all took off their shoes except the King, who remained shod until the very gate of the temple. The Inca and those of the blood entered inside as natural sons and made their adoration to the image of the Sun. The curacas, as unworthy of so high a place, remained outside in a large square which exists today before the gate of the temple.

The Inca offered with his own hand the golden vessels which he had used in the ceremony; the other Incas gave their vessels to the Inca priests who were appointed and dedicated to the service of the Sun, for those not priests, even though of the same blood of the Sun, (as laity) were not permitted to perform the office of priests. The priests having offered the vessels of the Incas, came out to the door to receive the vessels of the curacas, who came forward according to their seniority, in the order in which they had been brought into the Empire, and gave their vessels and other objects of gold and silver which they had brought from their lands to present to the Sun, such as sheep, lambs, lizards, toads, snakes, foxes, tigers, lions and a great variety of birds; in a word all that most abounded in their country counterfeited in silver and gold with great naturalness though each thing in miniature.

When the offering was completed they returned to the squares in their order; then came the Inca priests with a great quantity of farrow sheep[1] and rams and lambs of all colours, because the indigenous livestock of that country is of all colours, like the horses in Spain. All this livestock belonged to the Sun. They took a black lamb since these Indians preferred that to all other colours for sacrifices, for they held it to be of greater divinity because they said that the black beast was completely black and that the white, though white in all its body, always had a swart muzzle, which was a defect, and was therefore regarded as inferior to the black. And for this reason the Kings dressed in black most of the time and their colour for mourning was undyed wool, which they called dun colour.

This first sacrifice of the black lamb was to examine the auguries and prognostications of their festival. For in everything of importance which they did, both in peace and in war, they almost always sacrificed a lamb in order to inspect and assure themselves by the heart and lungs if it was acceptable to the Sun, that is whether that day's warfare was to be fortunate or no, or if they were to have a good harvest that year. For some things they took their auguries from a lamb, for others from a ram and for others from a barren ewe; for when they said 'ewe' a barren ewe was always understood as they never killed the fertile ewes even for their food, but killed them only when they were useless for breeding.

They took the lamb or the ram and placed it with the head towards the east; they did not tie its feet but three or four Indians held it fast; they opened it up alive on the left side, put in a hand and took out the heart with the lungs and windpipe, pulling it out with the hand and not cutting it, and it had to come out entire right up to the palate.

[1] 'Sheep' here means llama. The sheep was introduced into South America by the Spanish.

They regarded it as the luckiest omen if the lungs came out palpitating, not quite dead, as they said, and having this good omen, even though they should have other contrary omens, they took no account of them. For they said that the goodness of this fortunate omen conquered the badness and ill-fortune of all the bad omens. When they had removed the organs they blew them up and kept the air inside by tying the pipe or gripping it with the hands, and then inspected the channels by which the air enters the lungs and the little blood-vessels in them to see whether they were very swollen or whether there was little air in them, for the more swollen they were the better was the omen. Other things also they inspected which I am unable to tell because I did not pay attention to them; of those mentioned above I remember that I saw them twice when as a child I managed to enter a corral where old Indians, still not baptized, were performing this sacrifice—not that of the Raimi because it was already finished before I was born; but in other private matters they used to inspect the auguries and to do so they sacrificed lambs and rams, as has been said of the sacrifice of the Raimi; for what they did in their private sacrifices was a replica of what they did in their principal festivals.

They regarded it as the most unfavourable omen if the beast rose to its feet while they were opening its side, overcoming the strength of those who held it fast. It was similarly a bad sign if when they pulled at the pipe it broke and did not come out entire. It was a bad augury too if the lungs came out broken or the heart damaged and other things which I did not notice or ask. I remember these because I heard the Indians whom I found making the sacrifices speaking of them and asking each other about the good or bad omens and they did not bother to conceal it from me because I was such a child.

Returning to the ceremony of the Raimi, if the augury from the sacrifice of the lamb did not turn out favourable, they made another sacrifice of a ram and if that too did not turn out lucky, they made another of a sterile ewe, and if this was unfortunate, they did not stop the festival but continued it with sadness and inner weeping, saying that the Sun, their father, was wrath with them for some fault or carelessness which, without knowing it, they had committed in his service. They feared cruel wars, barrenness of their crops, death of their livestock and other like misfortunes. But when the omens foretold good fortune, great was the joy with which they celebrated their Pasch for the hope of the good things to come.

After the sacrifice of the lamb they brought a great quantity of lambs, sheep and rams for the common sacrifice; and they did not perform it as the first, opening them alive, but by cutting their throats and flaying them; they kept the blood and the hearts and offered it to the Sun, as of the first, burning it all to ashes.

The fire for that sacrifice had to be new, given by the hand of the Sun, as they said. For the which they took a large bracelet, which they call *chipana* (similar to others which the Incas habitually wore on the left wrist), which the chief priest wore; it was larger than most; it had as medallion a concave stone like half an orange, very highly burnished; they held it against the sun and at a certain spot where the rays which came out from the stone joined they placed a little cotton very finely teased, as they did not know how to make tinder, which caught fire in a short time, for this is a natural thing. With the fire thus given by the hand of the Sun they burnt the sacrifice and cooked all the meat for that day. And they took of the fire to the temple of the Sun and the house of the virgins, where they preserved it all the year and it was a bad omen if it went out for whatever reason. If on the day before the festival, when they prepared what was necessary for the next day's sacrifice, there was no sun to make the new fire, they made it with two round sticks as thick as a finger and a yard long, boring one with the other; the sticks are cinnamon colour; they call both the sticks and making the fire *u'yaca*, the same word serving as noun and verb. The Indians use them instead of a flint and steel and carry them on journeys in order to raise fire when they have to sleep in unpopulated places, as I have often seen when travelling with them, and the shepherds use them for the same.

They regarded it as a bad omen to raise fire for the sacrifice of the festival with this instrument; they said that as the Sun refused his hand he was angry with them. They cooked all the flesh of that sacrifice in public in the two squares and shared it among all who were present at the festival, both Incas and curacas, as also the common people, by their rank. And both the one and the other were presented with the bread called *cancu*; and this was the first dish of their great fiesta and solemn banquet. Then they brought other great variety of eatables which they ate without drinking the while, for it was the universal custom of the Indians of Peru not to drink during their meals.

From what we have said may have arisen the assertion which some Spaniards like to make, that these Incas and their vassals celebrated a Eucharist like Christians. What their practice was we have stated simply; let each man make comparisons according to his inclination.

After the feast they brought drink in the utmost abundance, for this was one of the most notable vices of these Indians, although nowadays by the mercy of God and the good example which in this particular the Spanish have given them, there is not an Indian who gets drunk, and if the example had been such in every vice, they had been apostolic preachers of the Gospel.

The Inca, seated on his chair of solid gold placed upon a platform of the same, sent to the relations called Hanan Cozco and Hurin Cozco to drink the health in his name of the most notable Indians of other races who were present. . . . And when all the company had drunk each other's health and exchanged draughts, they all returned to their places. Then came on the dances and singers of different kinds, with the devices, blazons, masks and inventions which each nation had brought. And while they sang and danced they did not cease to drink, Incas drinking the health of Incas, captains and curacas drinking each other's health according to their private friendship, contiguity of their lands or other connections.

Nine days lasted the celebration of the Raimi with abundance of food and drink and with all the joy and happiness each one could show; but the sacrifices for taking the omens were performed only on the first day. After the ninth day the curacas returned to their homes with the permission of the King, well content and joyful to have celebrated the principal festival of their God the Sun. When the King was engaged in wars or visiting his kingdom, he celebrated the festival wherever he happened to be on the day of the festival but not with the solemnity of its celebration in Cuzco. And the Inca Governor and the high priest and the other Incas of royal blood took care to celebrate it in Cuzco and then the curacas and the ambassadors from the provinces each went to the celebration which was the nearest.

Chapter Six

UNDER SPANISH RULE

1. THE LAST OF THE INCAS

THE sudden collapse of the Inca power is an oft-told story, which will not be repeated here. In his *History of the Conquest of Peru*, Prescott has described in picturesque detail how Pizarro, after landing at Tumbez, struck inland from San Miguel on the 24th September, 1532, to meet Atahuallpa at Cajamarca, two hundred men adventuring into the heart of an empire of eight million with mobilized armies of some two or three hundred thousand in readiness. Prescott and many others have told of that terrible journey over the passes of the Andes by men ignorant of the country and unprepared for what lay ahead of them, have described the meeting between Spaniard and Inca with show of friendship on both sides, and the act of treachery by which Pizarro made himself master of the Inca's person with audacious contempt for his overwhelming superiority of forces. We shall not repeat the incredible history were it not so well authenticated of how the Spanish consolidated themselves at Cajamarca, with organized resistance paralysed before it had begun by the capture of the Inca, and of the subsequent advance to Cuzco. Instead of rehashing familiar facts we shall speak of the causes which contributed to so rapid and catastrophic a collapse of this grandiose empire to so small a force, since they must be expected to reveal some fundamental weakness in the structure of the vast empire that has been described.

It has become accepted as a historical commonplace that Pizarro was fortunate in that his arrival coincided with the defeat and capture of Huascar, the legitimate Inca, by the pretender Atahuallpa, so that he found the country weakened and unsettled by a long period of civil war. Now had the Spanish victory been won through protracted conflict between more or less equal forces, there might be some truth in this contention. But the Spanish numerical inferiority was so ludicrous that in any case their only hope of escaping extermination was to avoid a conflict in force.

And if the country was still in a somewhat unsettled state, at least large forces were already under arms—actually a great advantage to a country which depends upon mobilization of agrarian militia —and the troops under Atahuallpa's command were certainly adequate to wipe out or cut off Pizarro's small company, had their full force been deployed in time. We must look elsewhere therefore for the explanation of the Spanish success. Equally unlikely to be true is the explanation popularized by Garcilaso in order to excuse what might seem to be the supineness or even cowardice of his countrymen. Garcilaso says that the Indians did not effectively oppose the Spanish because they regarded them superstitiously as supernatural beings divinely sent. Unfortunately for the truth of this story they did oppose the Spanish with courage and devotion, but not soon enough for success. Certainly these tall, bearded white adventurers, with their horses, their firearms and their steel armour were something so entirely outside the experience of the Indians that they must have aroused a measure of superstitious awe. But the Incas were already regarded as divine and without any propaganda machine in their favour it is unlikely that the superior divinity of the Spanish would be automatically accepted; nor in fact is there any evidence that the Spanish ever stepped into the place of the Incas in this respect. Many of the chroniclers somewhat later tell of an Indian legend that in the distant past a race of tall bearded white invaders had ruled in the Titicaca basin. Cieza de León mentions a legend told to him by Chirihuana, the curaca of Chucuito, that 'in the island of Titicaca in centuries past there were bearded people white as ourselves and coming out from the valley of Coquimbo a captain, whose name was Cari, arrived at the place where Chucuito is now situated, whence, after having founded some new settlements, he crossed with his people to the island and made such war on the people there that he killed them all'.

But so far from the Spanish having been accepted as this legendary race miraculously returned, as many historians have maintained, there is every reason to believe that this legend was never genuine but was invented simply to flatter the vanity of the whites by Indians always well versed in the art of opportune and ingenuous dissimulation. This particular story appears only in accounts picked up by Spaniards and travellers, it is not told by the native or more knowledgeable writers of Indian lore; nor is there any hint in sculpture or ceramic portraiture that the Andean Indians ever knew or imagined a white and bearded race before the Spanish.

Of modern writers the Bolivian historian José Maria Camacho has spoken most sensibly about this so-called tradition. 'Another tradition transmitted by the earliest historians speaks to us of an immigration of white bearded men, who settled in Tihuanacu and by their power and industry were for long time lords of the land. This tradition has not even the merit of sincerity. The indigene invented it to flatter the vanity of his new masters the Spanish and they did not conceal their gratification when the Indian, with the sly cunning peculiar to him, introduced the white man as a supernatural and omnipotent being in Peruvian history. In this way the records of the New World appeared full of the marvels wrought by white bearded men, but to avoid error it must be made clear that they were no more than an invention of the natives to win favour with the conquerors and to excuse the shame of their defeat. Before the conquest they never had any idea of such people; no picture or sculpture, whether representing men or symbolising deities, anywhere in pre-Columban Peru reproduced a bearded man.'

Pizarro showed no astuteness or strategic capacity to plan the defeat of so powerful an empire. He certainly had no conception of what was before him when he started his adventure from San Miguel. As Prescott says: 'Had he faltered for a moment, had he stopped to calculate chances, he must inevitably have failed; for the odds were too great to be combated by sober reason. They were only to be met triumphantly by the spirit of the knight-errant.' His treacherous seizure of the Inca's person was an act of pure opportunism dictated by fear after he had rashly placed himself in an impossible position at Cajamarca. As an anonymous writer who was present on the occasion frankly confesses: 'Having seen and spied out the greatness of the [Inca's] army and the tents so fair to see, we returned to where the said captain was awaiting us, mightily affrighted at what we had seen, exchanging many opinions among ourselves at what should be done, being all much afeared that we were so few and embarked in a land where we could expect no succour.' Having obtained temporarily the upper hand by the capture of Atahuallpa, the Spanish did not wisely plan the consolidation of their hold but turned at once to the quest for gold and loot. Had Atahuallpa ordered a mass attack with disregard for his own life, they must surely have been eliminated.

That he did not adopt this heroic course was perhaps due to the political situation, since with himself out of the way the crown would have reverted to his rival Huascar or his successor. Instead, Atahuallpa ordered the death of Huascar, who was held prisoner by his generals, and himself adopted the hopeless policy of 'pacifying' his captors. From the first the Indians underestimated the ruthlessness of the Spanish.

There is no doubt that Atahuallpa was misinformed about the Spaniards in everything except their numbers. It is said, for example, that his intelligence led him to believe that the horses were useless at night and that the guns would fire no more than two shots. Had he wished to do so, he could certainly have destroyed them during their march across the Andes. That he allowed them to reach Cajamarca may have been partly due to curiosity, with the knowledge that every step took them further from their base on the coast. He certainly underestimated their power to receive sea-borne reinforcements. And it may be taken for granted that it never entered Atahuallpa's imagination that so few strangers would ever seriously pit themselves against his power or dare to initiate hostilities.

Where then was the weakness which enabled Pizarro's reckless coup to succeed? It is in the first place clear that the Inca regime had the weakness of excessive centralization. All authority was so thoroughly vested in the person of the Inca that so long as he remained alive, no independent initiative was possible. And this remained true even although Atahuallpa had but recently assumed the *llauto* by right of conquest from the legitimate heir. The Indian also has a nature fatalistic in adversity and submissive to constituted authority. The tendency to submit to authority as such, alien or national, proved stronger than the sentiment of national unity and the Spanish were never unable to find Indians to serve them against their countrymen. This weakness has persisted throughout Indian history until the present day, has prevented any really general Indian movement and enabled uprising after uprising to be suppressed by setting Indian against Indian. The superior striking power of the Spanish armour and their professional military tactics saved them in the later national rising under Manco; but at the beginning, if there had been unified and directed opposition, they must have been cut off and eventually destroyed. Atahuallpa's policy of pacification was in favour of their ruthlessness and later they met only scattered and disorganized resistance from the remnants of the Inca armies and from isolated military garrisons.

After the capture of Cuzco in 1533 Pizarro set on the throne of the Incas Manco Inca, a grandson of Huayna Capac, with the object of concentrating the loyalty of the local curacas and military commanders upon a sovereign who would be under his control. Manco learnt something of Spanish military methods from his association with them, and was also able to estimate their weakness. He was unwilling to remain content with the position of puppet king and organized a general revolt against the invaders. On the 18th April, 1536, Cuzco was besieged by an army 180,000 strong and the Spaniards with only 190 men, including 80 horse, and a few hundred Indians, passed through their severest test. 'For a season the fate of the Conquerors trembled in the balance.' They held out, however, until the following February, having endured a siege of ten months. Lima was simultaneously subjected to a ten days' siege and the position there too at one time looked hopeless. The revolt represented a final attempt to pit massed numbers of agrarian militia against a small band of trained soldiers with superior concentration of striking power. The Spanish were saved by the help they were able to obtain from the Indians who remained with them acting as spies and foragers and the Inca was hampered by the difficulty of victualling his numerous troops through a long and sustained campaign.

Upon the failure of the Cuzco siege Manco retired to the lower Urubamba valley and at Vitcos (Uiticos) or Vilcapampa set up the headquarters of a separatist Inca state. From his bases in the impenetrable mountain fastnesses he would cross the Apurimac on raiding expeditions and harry the road from Lima to Cuzco. The Spanish were unable to counter these guerrilla tactics. An expedition sent against him by Pizarro was annihilated. Gonzales Pizarro proceeded against him in person but was unable to penetrate the inaccessible mountain region. The post of Ayacucho was built to make the Cuzco road safe for travellers. So things remained until after the execution of Almagro in 1542 a small band of his followers fled to the Inca and were given refuge with him. In 1544 he accepted overtures from the new Viceroy Blasco Nuñez, who announced that he had come to enforce 'new laws' abolishing the *repartimiento*; but before any compromise could become effective he was murdered at a game of quoits by Gomez Peréz, the leader of the refugees. The Spanish refugees were all killed by Manco's followers before they could make good their escape. Whether the purpose of their senseless regicide was to secure their own pardon with the Viceroy can only be conjectured.

Manco was succeeded by his eldest son, Sayri Tupac, an unwarlike and pleasure-loving monarch, who reigned for ten years without clashes with the Spanish. In 1555 he was persuaded by the Viceroy Cañete to leave his retreat for a life of honourable ease under Spanish protection. He was actually visited in Lima by his kinsman Garcilaso as a boy, who has left an account of the occasion. He settled in the beautiful valley of Yucay outside Cuzco, where two years later he died—it was believed in Vitcos by poison.

He was succeeded in 1560 by Titu Cusi, a favourite son of Manco, who had been captured and taken to Cuzco on Manco's defeat in the Urubamba valley but had subsequently managed to return to Vitcos and had been present at his father's murder by Gomez Peréz. During Titu Cusi's reign he was visited by Don Diego Rodriguez de Figueroa, who was sent by the Viceroy to convert him to Christianity and persuade him to abandon his mountain fastness as his brother Sayri Tupac had done. Rodriguez has left a detailed account of his visit with a picturesque description of the ceremonial maintained in this last flowering of the fallen Inca state. He was unsuccessful in his mission but later Titu Cusi, perhaps for political reasons, had himself formally baptized by two Augustinian monks, Fray Marcos Garcia and Fray Diego Ortiz, who were also invited to visit Vitcos, the city of mystery. Their story is contained in the long *Corónica Moralizada del Orden de San Agustin en el Perú* by Father Antonio de la Calancha. Titu Cusi himself dictated to Fray Marcos and his *mestizo* secretary Martin Pando an account of the life and death of his father Manco Inca in the form of a memorial addressed to Philip II. The story of the last Incas is also written by a Spanish soldier Captain Baltasar de Ocampo, who visited the province of Vilcabamba somewhat later prospecting for gold and heard it from eyewitnesses. We therefore have good material for the history of this separatist Inca state—but very little of historical importance. The real continuation of the Quechua history is in the story of their survival in the Colony under Spanish rule.

In 1571 Titu Cusi died of pneumonia caught after a heavy party and was succeeded by Tupac Amaru, a younger son of Manco, who on the accession of Titu Cusi had been relegated 'into the House of the Sun with the Chosen Virgins and their Matrons'. He left this cloistered life unfitted for the duties of a ruler. At the same time the energetic Viceroy Toledo had determined to put an end to the embarrassment to Spanish prestige of the separatist Inca state. He first sent an ambassador, who was ambushed and killed, without the knowledge of Tupac Amaru, by his advisers. An expeditionary force followed under Captain Garcia, who was married to a niece of Tupac Amaru. Garcia pushed down the Urubamba valley, found the passes inadequately defended and captured the wellnigh impregnable Vitcos. Tupac Amaru had escaped into the tropical forest which begins further down the valley, was followed by Garcia and soon surrendered to the Spanish rather than endure the discomforts of the jungle. He was taken to Cuzco, where he was publicly beheaded after his wife and his chiefs had been tortured before his eyes. His young children soon followed his fate. 'So in 1572 perished the last of the Incas, descendants of some of the wisest rulers America has ever seen.'[1]

[1] Here is the moving description of the execution, written by the rough soldier Captain Baltasar de Ocampo in 1610 for the Viceroy, the Marquis of Montes Claros. 'The open spaces, roofs, and windows in the parishes of Carmenca and San Cristóval were so crowded with spectators that if an orange had been thrown down it could not have reached the ground anywhere, so closely were the people packed. The executioner, who was a Canari Indian, having brought out the knife with which he was to behead Tupac Amaru, a marvellous thing happened. The whole crowd of natives raised such a cry of grief that it seemed as if the day of judgement had come, and all those of the Spanish race did not fail to show their feelings by shedding tears of grief and pain. When the Inca beheld the scene, he only raised his right hand on high and let it fall. With a lordly mind he alone remained calm, and all the noise was followed by a silence so profound that no living soul moved, either among those who were in the square or among those at a distance. . . . The Inca then received consolation from the Fathers who were at his side, and, taking leave of all, he put his head on the block, like a lamb. The executioner then came forward and, taking the hair in his left hand, he severed the head with a knife at one blow, and held it on high for all to see. As the head was severed, the bells of the cathedral began to ring, and were followed by those of all the monasteries and parish churches in the city. The execution caused the greatest sorrow and brought tears to the eyes. . . . When the head was cut off, it was put on a spike, and set up on the same scaffold in the great square where the execution had taken place. There it became each day more beautiful, the Inca having had a plain face during life. The Indians came by night to worship the head of their Inca. At last, one night, towards dawn, Juan Sierra de Leguizamo came to his window and saw the idolatries practised by the people. He reported it to Don Francisco de Toledo, who then ordered the head to be taken down and buried with the body. This was done with no less solemnity than on the occasion of the interment of the body. Thus the inconvenience of the Inca's head being worshipped by the people was avoided.'

'The execution of Tupac Amaru', says Enrique Finot, 'stood revealed not as a just punishment but as an act of terrorization and the reputation of the Viceroy was blotted with the stigma of cruelty. From that time the descendants of the Inca family remained crushed and subdued. But the incident fomented the hatred of the native race, which waited patiently for an opportunity of manifesting itself.' Vitcos was abandoned and overgrown, the very memory of its site being lost. Three centuries later, in 1911, it was rediscovered by the expedition of Hiram Bingham and its ruins, now known as Machu Picchu, are one of the show pieces of Inca archaeology for tourists from Cuzco. Bingham's masterly description in *Lost City of the Incas* (1948) cannot afford to be neglected by those who are interested in the achievements of the Inca civilization. Bingham somewhat exaggerates its inaccessibility. It lies on the shoulder of the peak Machu Picchu, well down the Urubamba valley where the typical vegetation of the tropical jungle begins to appear, though its position two thousand feet above the valley assures for it a temperate climate. The valley of the Urubamba, known as 'the sacred valley of the Incas', becomes a precipitate and narrow gorge in its lower reaches, but no climbing is necessary until one reaches the foot of Machu Picchu itself. A modern railway has been carried to this point and a motor road is being taken further into the hot, moist valleys of Yungas, whose produce is transported to Cuzco. The river was also known in Inca times as Vilcamayu, or 'Huilca river', after the *huilca* shrub, which is found in the valleys below Picchu and from which was manufactured a narcotic snuff used to induce hypnotic intoxication. The name Vilcabamba is derived from this *huilca* shrub.

2. COLONIAL ADMINISTRATION

Following A. G. Keller[1], economists divide the colonies of the New World into *farm* colonies and *exploitation* colonies. Farm colonies were generally found in the temperate zones, which produced much the same range of commodities as Europe, while exploitation colonies were usually situated in the tropical zones and in regions rich in mineral resources. The farm colonies were established on a system of small holdings cleared and worked by the settlers themselves and their dependants. They produced

[1] *Colonization* (1908).

UNDER SPANISH RULE

enough for their own modest needs and their economy depended but slightly upon exploitation. Their trend was towards egalitarian forms of society, wage labour and democratic institutions. The aboriginal inhabitants of the land were not pressed into service but were either driven back or exterminated. The exploitation colonies on the contrary were founded by men who were induced to adventure abroad by the lure of wealth and who were unwilling or unable to toil in the land of their choice, where the climate was often unfavourable to European labour. Their economy was based upon the exportation of a small number of specialized products to Europe. They naturally tended to be organized on a capitalist model with highly specialized production, industrialization and latifundia instead of small freeholds. Their trend was towards an aristocratic type of society with extremes of luxury and indigence, a privileged immigrant minority exploiting suppressed native labour.

These economic tendencies were accentuated by the fact that while colonization of the temperate zones of the New World was largely in the hands of the English, the colonies of the tropical and semi-tropical zones and the regions rich in mineral ores fell mainly to the lot of Spain, where feudal institutions persisted longer than in some other European countries. The semi-feudal economy of Spain was translated to her colonies. The desire of the English colonist was to live and work on the land, free from hampering restrictions of the homeland; that of the Spanish colonist was to accumulate wealth from the proceeds of native labour, living in a town where he could reproduce the social conditions of Spain. Therefore in Spanish colonies towns were founded at the outset and the colonists were concentrated in them; in the farm colonies towns grew up gradually to meet the needs of the colony. The English emigrated with their wives and families and did not intermarry with the native populations. Very few Spanish women emigrated to the New World in the first century of colonization and a large *mestizo* class arose from admixture between the Spanish and the native women. The English eliminated the indigenes; the Spanish preserved them as a reservoir of exploited labour. Thus the farm colonies were extermination colonies, whereas the exploitation colony could continue only so long as there were subject peoples left to exploit.

With their long history of wars and crusades against the infidel the Spanish had developed a vigorous military and adventurous spirit and unrivalled powers of physical endurance, but with it a contempt for the more peaceful arts of agriculture and trade. Industry was little developed and Spain was deficient in skilled artisans. This created an attitude of mind which survives to the present day. The Spaniard is temperamentally an employer of labour but not himself a labourer. In frequent conversations with Bolivians of Spanish descent on the question of immigration I have always been told that Bolivia today requires not European immigrants but immigrants who will actually work on the land. And it is only in the last generation that Bolivian and Peruvian families of white blood have gone into foreign trade; the internal trade is still the province of the *mestizo* classes. Hence in the Spanish exploitation colonies the primary and persistent problem was to secure and maintain an adequate provision of common labour. As the native was unwilling to conform voluntarily with a system which offered him impoverishment and degradation for no return which he could appreciate, compulsion and disguised enslavement were inevitable. In Peru the conquerors found people who had been organized in a settled civilization economically self-sufficient and producing adequate surplus to maintain a ruling class in lavish resplendence; had they been willing to take over the position and methods of the Incas with the wisdom of the Incas for the care and preservation of their subjects, they might have achieved a prosperous and well-regulated colony with some sacrifice of immediate exportable wealth. But for many reasons this was impossible and exploitation was carried to an extreme of wastefulness. To the Indians the Spanish represented themselves as taking over the rights and functions of the Incas while bringing freedom in the place of slavery. But from the point of view of the Indians themselves the change meant the disappearance of a rule of known demands justly enforced and an administration adapted to their traditional culture and careful of their welfare, for the substitution of unlimited demands unjustly and oppressively exacted by an administration which disrupted the economic equilibrium of their traditional social pattern.

We shall write neither in condemnation nor in defence of the Spanish rule. We are not concerned to support or to controvert the 'black legend' of the colonial regime. Our concern is with the history of the native peoples. The Conquistadores and the colonists were men of their age and milieu; and if this history cannot be told without telling of oppression, cruelty, deception, economic disruption and human wastage, it will be told without moralization. Those who wish to moralize must always remember that oppression is not extermination and that successful exploitation ensures the preservation of the exploited.

The Spanish colonies were in principle possessions of the Crown, not dependencies of Spain, and were governed by royal decrees, or *cedulas*, put out by the Council of the Indies in the King's name and administered by officials appointed by the Crown and responsible to it. The interest of the Crown was to abstract the maximum revenue from the colonies while preserving them as sources of revenue for the future. Realizing that the wealth of the colony could be tapped only in proportion to its exploitable man-power, the Crown was interested to preserve the native peoples from excessive exploitation for private profit. It issued a perpetual stream of laws recognizing the rights of the Indian as subject of the Crown and protecting him from damaging oppression except in the interests of the Crown; it failed only to give him the practical means to enforce his theoretical rights and to safeguard himself from the oppression to which he was actually subjected. As Pereyra says of the Leyes de las Indias: 'All that was lacking to this compassionate corpus was one law which would have made possible the application of the rest.' The interests of the private colonist, whether in enriching himself and returning to Spain as rapidly as possible or in enriching himself as rapidly as possible and enjoying his riches in the Colony, were at variance with those of the Crown. He desired to exploit the native for his own benefit and had less forethought for the future, less concern for the maintenance of the reservoir of exploitable man-power. Hence there was constant conflict between the Viceroys and powerful private interests. Humane and enlightened legislation was consistently disregarded in practice. Throughout the colonial epoch principle and practice were continually at variance; one picture is given by the history of colonial legislation and quite a different picture by the history of colonial practice.

The legalistic mind of the sixteenth-century Spanish made it incumbent upon them to justify each stage of their occupation by a semblance of law. From the beginning of their adventure in the New World the leading theologians and jurists were exercised to establish to their own satisfaction the 'just title' of the Crown to dominion over the conquered territories and it was hotly debated whether the indigenous populations of America had a right to their lands, liberty and possessions or whether by their idolatry and degradation they had forfeited the natural rights of human beings. The political title of the Crown was held to be justified by the bulls of Pope Alexander VI given in 1492, which granted to the Crown of Castile all lands conquered south and west of a given meridian not already in the dominion of another Christian prince—the exact line of demarcation was established by the Treaty of Tordesillas between Castile and Portugal in 1494. This became the basis of the famous *Requerimiento* drawn up by Juan Lopez de Palacios Rubios, Chief Crown Jurist, which arguing from somewhat obscure doctrines of the Creation, the Redemption, the Temporal Authority of Rome and the Divine Right of Kings, required the confused natives under penalty of forfeiting their right to freedom and the confiscation of their lands and possessions to recognize the supremacy of a Pope of whom they had not heard and a king they did not know. The question of the natural rights of the Indians was decided in their favour at the Council of Valladolid subject to their voluntary recognition of the claims of the Spanish King. An ever-increasing body of *cedulas reales* defining and safeguarding these rights represented a series of uncertain compromises between the Colony's need for exploited labour and the Crown's desire to keep the despoliation of the natives within the limits of safety, an unsettled equilibrium between the interests of the Crown, the Church and the powerful private exploiters. Up to the present day the Indians have had no power in practice to insist upon the rights they were granted in law.

(a) Economic

The system of *encomiendas*, first established by Nicolas de Ovando (1502–1508) and transferred to Peru, is explained as a compromise designed to guarantee the supply of necessary labour while at the same time protecting the natives from indiscriminate despoliation. The *encomienda* was the fiduciary allocation to a colonist of a right to the services of a landed group of Indians, in return for which he had the responsibility of the 'patron' to arrange for their instruction in the Christian faith and the elements of civilized life and to protect their persons and property from abuse. Gaspar de Escalona says in the *Gazofilacio Real del Perú* (1647): 'This branch of fiscalization is connected with the tribute of the Indians entrusted [*encomendados*] to the Crown, and is called *encomienda* because they were entrusted [*se encomendaron*] to the possessors of the *encomienda* for the care which they had to take in indoctrinating and instructing them in our Holy Catholic Faith.' It was a kind of feudal serfdom which might have worked out in Peru with Indians accustomed to the absolutism of the Inca regime, had it been applied with moderation and humanity. In fact it became the open door to legitimized abuse. As Luis Peñaloza puts it in his *Historia Económica de Bolivia* (1946): 'In the Peruvian Altiplano there was no necessity to deal gently with the Indian and in fact the Spanish did not do so; the Indian was easily substitutable and cost nothing.' The *encomienda* changed his status from an Inca subject to a colonial slave. The obligations of the *encomendero* were limited in practice to the formality of the baptismal rite and his claims were unlimited. Exploitation of the *encomendados* was so ruthless that it threatened the survival of the race, which did survive only because effective colonization was for long limited to relatively small—even if the most choice—areas of the vast territories nominally occupied. Madariaga, who writes in defence of the Spanish colonial system, says of the *encomienda* and the importation of negro slaves: 'Both are compromises which the problem of labour in undeveloped lands inflicted on the economic and social side of life.'

In the early days of the Colony land had no value in itself, for the colonists had no desire to work the land. Even today any amount of unpopulated land away from the main lines of transportation may be bought in Bolivia for a song. Human labour upon the land was a source of revenue and wealth, but without any practical system of wage labour unoccupied land was worthless. The Indian economy had never relied on money as a medium of exchange and in the early years of the Colony coinage was almost non-existent among the Spanish colonists. The *encomienda* gave to its possessor the right to profit from the labour of Indians settled on the land but no title to the land itself. Owing to the movements of the Indians during the Civil Wars, the break-up of the communities and eastward migration to escape exactions and persecution, large areas were left waste. Towards the end of the sixteenth century, as a new source of revenue required to build Spanish sea-power, the Crown began to establish its right to all unclaimed land and to allow 'composition' whereby *de facto* enjoyment of the land could be converted to an established title in perpetuity. Indian communes were enabled to obtain recognition of their communal ownership of their lands under these provisions, which were often represented as a measure for the protection of the Indians. In fact they were more often the excuse for concealed expropriation. In the 'composition' of lands began the system of great latifundia which today cover the majority of Peru and Bolivia and have squeezed the free Indians into lands below subsistence level.

Repeated attempts were made by the Crown to abolish or mitigate the system of *encomiendas*, but without compulsory Indian labour industry and agriculture were crippled. All industry and all agriculture were carried on by means of unpaid Indian labour, commerce was dependent on it, and Indian labour was not to be had without compulsion. But the Crown never recognized the right to *encomienda* in perpetuity. Normally it was granted for two or three generations and was non-transferable. This uncertainty of tenure was an added cause for the more ruthless and inhuman exploitation of the Indian, encouraging a 'get-rich-quick' attitude. Early in the eighteenth century the system began to disappear, when half the revenue was exacted by the Crown and decrees were passed in 1717, 1720 and 1721 ruling that every *encomienda* vacated by the death of the owner or for any other reason should revert to the Crown. But the lot of the Indian was not bettered by its disappearance. The place of the *encomendero* was taken by the *corregidor*, an underpaid official whose duty was to collect the royal tribute and whose exactions were not less than those under the older system. The most iniquitous and oppressive feature of this system was the right of *repartimiento*, whereby the Indians of a district, in addition to the obligation to pay tribute and give personal service, in *mita* or otherwise, were compelled to purchase from the *corregidor* merchandise to a given value. The type of merchandise foisted upon them rested entirely with the *corregidor* and often included such arbitrarily ridiculous commodities as razors for a hairless race and French breviaries for Quechua-speaking illiterates. In a compulsory and monopoly trade the price required rested entirely with the *corregidor* and often exceeded the capacities of the Indians to pay. In their eagerness to extract the maximum profit from a distasteful post the *corregidors* would exact tribute two or three times over, demand payment from those who were exempt and raise the *repartimiento* beyond the legal amount. The Indians had in practice no remedy against such abuses, which were a main occasion of the insurrections of 1780. It is significant that in 1780 the *corregidor* of Chayanta raised the quota of merchandise the Indians were compelled to purchase from 150,000 pesos to 400,000 pesos and about the same time the *corregidor* of Tuita increased his quota from 120,000 pesos to 300,000 pesos.

The Spanish colonists of the New World were able to live in the manner to which they were accustomed, or which they regarded as their due, only by large-scale importation of consumer goods from Europe; and Spain, seeing in this trade a profitable source of revenue, fought to keep the monopoly. From 1503 all trade with the New World was monopolized by the Casa de Contratacion established in Seville and in 1720 moved to Cadiz. Spanish industry was unable to supply the demand and four-fifths of the merchandise shipped to the New World was bought outside Spain. The existence of the monopoly, the exorbitant customs duties and the long and dangerous passage increased the costs beyond measure; Potosi was renowned not only as one of the most luxurious but the most expensive town in the world. All this had to be paid for with exports, mainly of precious metals, and for this purpose Indian mine labour was required. The flow of gold and silver from the New World revolutionized European economy and laid the foundations of the capitalist monetary system of the modern world. And this achievement was made realizable only by the possibility of forced native labour.

Indian labour for the mines was obtained in Peru by means of the *mita*, an extension of the Inca precedent which was systematized by the Viceroy Francisco de Toledo. In conception a compromise with the inevitable necessity for labour and a reasonable imposition, it became in practice the most serious of all abuses. In principle the Spanish *mita* was a system of labour conscription for public works (which included building, mining and industrial workshops, although they were under private enterprise), whereby a proportion of each Indian community was impressed for a period of labour. While legal requirements were not always the same, in general one-seventh of the man-power of any community was liable to be on *mita* at one time. The most serious of the *mitas* were those for the silver mines of Potosi and the mercury mine of Huancavelica.[1] The Potosi *mita* largely depopulated the rich district of Chucuito and Indians were taken to Potosi from as far

---

[1] The Huancavelica *mita* is described by A. P. Whitaker in *The Huancavelica Mercury Mine*.

afield as Cuzco and Quito. Madariaga quotes the following personal account from Alonso Messia:

'They all go usually with their wives and children, and having seen them twice I am in a position to say that they amount altogether to more than seven thousand souls. Every Indian of these takes with him eight to ten sheep[1] and a few alpacas to eat; others who are wealthier take with them thirty to forty sheep; on which they carry their meals of Indian corn and potato flour, their covers for sleeping, mats to guard against the cold, which is sharp, for they always sleep in the open. All this cattle generally exceeds thirty thousand head, and nearly always amounts to about forty thousand. Now let us say that they are no more than thirty thousand, with the potato flour, the corn, quinoa flour and dried meat, and their new clothes; the whole is worth altogether more than three thousand pesos of eight reales. All this wealth in this manner takes the road to Potosi by stages and the distance of about one hundred leagues takes two months, since the cattle cannot travel quicker, nor their children of five and six years whom they take with them. Of all this mankind and common wealth which they take away from Chucuito, no more than two thousand souls ever return, and the remainder, about five thousand, in part they die, and in part they remain in Potosi. There are others who go to the valleys nearby, and the reason is that when they want to return they have neither cattle nor food for the road.'

In 1587 the *mita* for Potosi was fixed by Toledo at 1,430 men for work in the mines, 1,308 for the processing shops and 1,000 to replace those who were killed or injured. The number was later increased to 4,600 and in the period of its greatest production Potosi had 13,500 *mitayos*. According to the *Descripcion de Potosi*, in 1603 there were 4,780 Indians working in *mita* at 4 reales a day, 5,600 under contract (*mingados*) at 7 reales a day, 4,400 women and children at one real, and 13,220 engaged in the supply of food, fuel, wood, etc. for the mines. The normal 'day' of the *mitayos* was 36 hours, during which they remained uninterruptedly below the surface. They worked by the light of candles and extracted the ore by means of a small crowbar. Explosives were little used. The loosened ore was brought to the surface by *japiris* who carried it on their backs by rope ladders. Acosta says: 'A man moves a load of two arrobas [50 lb.] fastened to his back with a cloth and they go up in threes. The foremost carries a taper attached to his thumb

---

[1] *i.e.* llamas.

so that they can see, for there is no other light.' Little care was taken for the security of the workers or to shore up the shafts, and fatal collapses were frequent, for it was cheaper to replace the casualties.

The nominal period of a *mita* was a spell of four months. The recognized salary at Potosi was 4 reales a day[1], though in practice less. Jorge Juan and Sebastian de Ulloa say: 'For a spell of 300 days, 65 being discounted as festivals, a total nominal salary of 18 pesos is recognized. The sick and infirm do not lose their pay but their obligation is increased for the following year. Of the 18 pesos a year which they earn 8 are deducted to meet the fiscal capitation tax or tribute, $2\frac{1}{4}$ for the cost of clothes and the remaining $7\frac{3}{4}$ are devoted to their food and the ecclesiastical tenths. Before the end of the year the accounts are adjusted. Inevitably all the *mitayos* find themselves in debt. They are not allowed to pay in money but are made to work off their debt. Thus a perpetual enslavement is established. The sons follow their fathers to pay off their advances and so the Indians who are conscripted, on leaving for the mines, abandon their families in a transport of grief, all hope of rehabilitation and independence lost.'

Tribute was the foundation upon which rested the whole colonial system and tribute from the time of the Conquest became the most important influence in shaping the pattern of Indian life. The tribute, an obligation which derived from the Conquest itself, was fixed at eight pesos a year, of which five were to be rendered in cash and three in kind, by every Indian between the ages of fifteen and sixty. The Indians themselves had no monetary economy and their staple agricultural products ceased to have more than a nominal value in the new colonial economy. If they transmuted their obligations into personal service, they had no means of exacting real compensation for their labour, while their productive capacity was reduced by the time they were removed from the land. Their position was indeed desperate and they were compelled in large numbers to abandon the communes either to emigrate beyond the sphere of Spanish influence or to sell themselves into servitude on Spanish estates or *encomiendas* as *yanaconas* or serfs.

The Spanish colonists were slow in adapting their own subsistence pattern to the conditions of their new home, but introduced many European and sub-tropical animals and plants which

---

[1] Eight reales made one peso. The price of a hen was one to two reales, a llama cost four pesos and a mule forty-eight pesos in Potosi.

as they became acclimatized produced fundamental changes in the picture of Peruvian economy. The horse, the donkey and the mule (Spain at this time happened to be the leading mule-producing country of Europe), cattle and sheep, pigs, goats and poultry were introduced by the Conquest. Wheat and rice, barley and rye, among the cereals; a wide range of vegetables—among which the broad bean proved especially adaptable to the high altitudes; a great variety of new fruits were added to those already cultivated; and a number of specialized crops, such as grapes, olives, sugar cane and alfalfa, were transplanted. But none of these innovations exerted much influence upon the indigenous subsistence pattern. The new crops were grown in order to meet the demand for tribute in kind, to supply the needs of the *encomenderos* or to provide marketable products wherewith to obtain the requisite pesos for the monetary tribute. Maize, quinoa and the potato continued to be the Indian staples. The ox was incorporated into the Indian agricultural pattern fairly early because of its outstanding advantages as a short-distance beast of burden and agricultural accessory. Horses were bred on the Peruvian highlands and donkeys on the Bolivian Altiplano. Sheep were pastured in great numbers first by the *encomenderos* to supply the flourishing textile factories, or *obrajes*, which were worked by Indian unpaid labour of the *mita*. Thus a secondary agricultural pattern was imposed alongside the traditional Indian cultivation, but its purpose was solely to supply the needs of the dominant race and the Indian was slow to benefit. Even today Indians normally keep pigs and poultry but seldom or never consume them themselves.

Thus was the meticulous balance between population and productivity so carefully preserved by the Incas recklessly destroyed. The Indian economy was not organized to meet the demands made upon it and insufficient time and inducement were allowed for reorganization. The richest lands were pre-empted for *encomiendas*. Although they were debarred from the ownership of land, many *encomenderos* indulged in stock-raising and accumulated enormous herds which ousted the natives from their communal pasturages. Under the Incas towns and villages had not occupied arable lands, but the Spanish towns and monastic settlements were built upon the rich valley bottoms essential to the maintenance of Indian agricultural stability. The irrigation systems which had been the life-blood of Inca agriculture, and had controlled the density of the population the land could support, came largely under Spanish control and were either allowed to fall into decay or were diverted from Indian use. The legal prohibition against owning land weakened as time went on and the native communities were constantly deprived of their lands by purchase, expropriation or fraud. Thus they were gradually driven from the best of their land whilst new and impossible demands were made upon them. The native population in consequence tended to recede more and more from the centres of Spanish occupation and a new class of landless, vagabond Indians with no source of livelihood flooded the roads and proliferated in the towns, providing cheap domestic and workshop labour. The damage done to the Indian commune in the first era of colonization was such as to threaten the future of the Colony. It is estimated that in the first forty years between half and three-quarters of the native population disappeared and during the ensuing two centuries it was more than halved again. The brake was fortunately applied by the Viceroy Toledo, who saw the danger of so rapid a decline in the reservoir of labour and took measures to counteract the trend by re-establishing the communes. Their importance has never wholly been lost sight of again. As George Kubler says: 'It is difficult to imagine the disappearance of the *Quechua* commune otherwise than under conditions in which the institutions or groups both exploiting it and yet vitally interested in its preservation should also disappear. The age-long survival of the commune is, therefore, an attainment of successive governments, whether *Inca*, Colonial or Republican, which have exploited it. As long as it survives in its habitually depressed condition, new exploiters will be attracted to encouraging its continuation, and they will be favoured by its singular tenacity and stability.'

(b) *Social*

The stratification of society into social classes set in very early in Peru. The whites themselves were divided into *Peninsulares*, who were born in Spain and immigrated to the colony, and *Creoles*, who were born in Peru. There was rivalry and enmity between the two. The Creoles were excluded from high public employment and large commercial enterprise and were accused of arrogance and unreliability. The poorest adventurer arriving from Spain could be assured of marriage with a wealthy Creole heiress, for he brought that quality by which the Spanish set so much store and which could be assured in no other way, *limpieza de sangre*. The Spanish have always set great store by pedigree and purity of stock. Even today the Spanish families of eastern Bolivia, where admixture with the native Camba stock was small, openly vaunt their 'purity of blood' and speak with contempt of the families established in Quechua and Aymara territory, almost all of which are tainted with some admixture of native blood. As early as 1740 Jorge Juan and Sebastian de Ulloa had declared in the *Secret Reports* that there were few Creole families without taint of admixture.

Whereas in the English colonies of North America intermarriage with the native races was almost unknown, the Spanish showed no repugnance for the native women of Peru. Added to this, colonists from England in general took their wives and families with them but the proportion of women who went out from Spain was always very small. In consequence the rapid growth of a *mestizo* class was a typical symptom of the Spanish colonies.[1] Concubinage was the rule and the resultant mixed race began to take the place of a lower middle class in the towns. Though legally on an equality with the Peninsulares and the Creoles and recognized in principle as 'rational beings' (*gente de razon*), the *mestizos* were socially inferior. The fact of mestization exaggerated the inherent Spanish pride of race and the *mestizos* suffered the added taint of illegitimacy. They thus formed an indeterminate intermediate class, unwilling to unite themselves with the pure-blood Indians, whom they despised, and unaccepted by the Spaniards, who despised them. While receiving constant new accretions both from the Spanish and the Indian side, they have in the course of centuries tended by intermarriage to consolidate themselves into what is almost a separate racial group. While still excluded from the higher offices of government, the *mestizo* class, called cholos in Bolivia and Peru, have become in many ways the backbone of the social and economic life of these countries.

The cholos were despised by the Spanish as inferior and depraved in character and morality and this contempt survives to the present day. It is still universally believed and stated in Peru and Bolivia that whereas the pure Indian may have certain qualities which

---

[1] Again the moralizing historian must decide whether what took place in the Spanish colonies was not at least more humane than the efficient extermination of native populations in the Anglo-Saxon colonies of North America.

UNDER SPANISH RULE

can be respected, the cholo has none but combines the bad qualities of both races. He is described as vicious, immoral, unreliable, drunken, lazy and cowardly. I have still to hear a good word said in seriousness for the cholo as a class either in Bolivia or in Peru. At the beginning the cholos had all the disadvantages of despised inferiors and hangers-on of the whites, with no inherited traditional way of life or culture of their own. That they have succeeded not only in consolidating themselves into what is virtually a separate people, but in building up a distinct culture, traditions and way of living, separate from that of both Spanish and Indians, is evidence of vitality and energy. There is no real evidence at all that the cholo is congenitally inferior. As I have seen them, particularly in Bolivia, they are energetic, vital and hardworking, especially the women, tenacious of their own customs and way of life, which is a mixture of the Indian and the European but nearer the former than the latter. They are more prolific than either the Indians or the whites. They have a strong business sense and have taken over the bulk of the minor commerce in both countries. They have characteristics deriving from both their Indian and their European ancestry and have no peculiar respect for the characteristic virtues of either race. It is certain that they have important defects of character, but not more, I think, than can be accounted for by their intermediate social position and their exclusion from positions of responsibility and control in the administration of their countries. It is difficult to see by what standards a people which has shown the power to create and establish itself against every discouragement and disability, and which continues to show increasing vitality, energy and increase, can be regarded as intrinsically 'inferior'. The history of the Aymaras and the Quechuas must certainly include the sociology of the cholo race which has emerged from their intermixture with the Spanish blood. In fact there were two cholo peoples, that which arose from Spanish admixture with the Quechuas and that which arose from admixture with the Aymaras. But the cholos of each type have remained distinct to a far less degree than the pure-blood Aymaras and Quechuas.

As the cholos were despised by the whites, so they despised—and still continue to despise—the Indians. I have often heard a cholo who could have had only the smallest percentage of white blood speak with the most profound contempt of the 'aborigines'. Today, however, the distinction between cholo and Indian is considered to be social rather than racial. The cholo forms the commercial lower class in the towns and the exploiting upper class among the Indians. I remember once showing my chola maid in La Paz a coloured photograph of some Indian women in Santiago de Huata, a small *poblacion* on the shores of Lake Titicaca. She at once remarked with scorn '*indiacitas*'. When I pressed her to explain how she knew these women were Indians and not cholas, she pointed out that they were wearing clothes of handwoven and hand-dyed cloth, whereas cholas were rich enough to buy factory-made clothes. The Indians are the most impoverished of the population groups of Peru and Bolivia, either labouring in the mines or living on the land. From the first the *mestizos* were the principle instruments of the Spanish in the exploitation of the Indians. As Juan de Solorzano y Pereyra, Oidor of the *Audiencia* of Lima, says in his *Politica Indiana*: 'We see that the majority of the *mestizos* turn out to be of a vicious and depraved nature and it is they who usually inflict the greatest amount of injuries and vexations on the Indians themselves.' So the modern cholo has the name, and I think rightly, of being harsher and more overbearing in exploiting the Indians than the white master himself.

The Indian withdrew himself from the white invader and so far as he was allowed lived as a separate people avoiding contacts. Except in the neighbourhood of the towns he tried to retain his old settlements, his own system of government and administration, his traditional way of life and methods of building and agriculture. Except under compulsion he repudiated the white man's law and the innovations of the white civilization. It is only because this cultural independence was possible over wide areas of country little penetrated by the whites that the survival of the two races was possible. Symptomatic of the will to survival which these races have shown is the tenacity with which they have retained their languages. Although Spanish is the official language of both Peru and Bolivia, the language of the larger towns and of all major commerce, Aymara and Quechua have remained the natural languages of these peoples and have become the mother-tongue of the cholos with Spanish as a second language. In the country districts there are still large numbers of Indians who know no more Spanish than '*buenos dios*', while every white in the sierra of Bolivia and a large majority in Peru has learnt either Aymara or Quechua in his cradle. While in the larger towns

Spanish is habitually spoken except by the Indians or cholos speaking among themselves, in the smaller *pueblos* and *poblaciones* even the few whites in control habitually speak a native tongue. In costume also the Indians have remained distinct. Although their dress has received various modifications both at the first arrival of the Spanish and subsequently—which is an evidence that their conservatism does not arise from lack of ability to adapt but from the tenacious desire to retain their traditional way of life—the costume of both Indians and cholos, particularly that of the women, is entirely distinct and preserves many features from Inca times. In the colonial period the legal position of the Indians was that of minors subject to perpetual tutelage and protected by a stream of regulations from the excessive exploitation to which they were subjected in practice. Under the Republics their legal status has been somewhat equalized, though their economic depression has not altered. Yet the Indian continues to shun the white man's law except under compulsion and settles his own disputes himself.

The perpetual economic servitude of the Indian is to a minor extent due to his own character. The Indian passionately desires a reasonable betterment of his lot within the frame of his own life as he conceives it. He desires sufficient food rather than starvation diet, sufficient llama skins to keep out the biting cold of the sierra, he desires to celebrate his fiestas lavishly rather than meagrely. But he does not wish for different foods, different clothes, or a different way of life. He instinctively repudiates the refinements of the alien civilization around him which would bring in their train the disruption of his own culture. Not that he is by any means completely conservative. Every respectable Indian family possesses a chamber utensil which is for prestige and not for use. It is a sign of opulence among the mining communities—they alone are rich enough to afford this—to possess first a sewing machine and then a radio set. It is paradoxical that the only way in which the Indian could at least fight for his very modest requirements would be by developing the outlook of the 'economic man' which is foreign to his own life and tradition. It is a fascinating paradox of history that the Aymaras and the Quechuas have managed to survive retentive of a way of life which would seem to make survival impossible in the modern competitive and economic world. For the accumulation of wealth beyond his immediate needs is still foreign to Indian mentality.

Under Spanish colonial administration the elaborate Inca hierarchy disappeared. The old Inca nobility was decimated at the outset. Some few of the survivors were cultivated and honoured some little time by the Spanish as a means to attract Indian loyalty and obedience to themselves. But in their honour, be it said, they did not make very successful Quislings, and before the first century was out they had been systematically eliminated. If there were any survivors, they survived only by remaining in concealment and obscurity. Except within the short-lived separatist Inca state at Vitcos they exercised no influence upon the further history of their peoples after the Conquest.

The remaining Indian population fell into three groups. The bulk of the population who lived in the old communes, called the *hatunruna*, were liable to tribute and *mita*, forming the reservoir of labour exploited for the advantage of the Spanish. The Inca administrative machinery and personnel died with the overthrow of the Inca state, but the communes were still ruled by local curacas—usually called by the Spanish 'caciques'. The curaca was forced into the unenviable position of middle-man between the Spanish master and the Indian serf; he was obliged to collect and deliver the tribute due from his manor and to see that the required number of youths were forthcoming for the *mita*. It is often claimed that the curacas proved willing instruments in the hands of the Spanish for the oppression of the Indians and themselves increased the exactions in their own interests. And as it is true that until the system of *corregidores* became general they were freed from the control and supervision exercised by the Incas and left to their own devices so long as they satisfied the requirements of their Spanish masters, no doubt some took advantage of their position. But on the whole the demands of the Spanish were so far in excess of what could be reasonably supplied that little room was left for further impositions and there is not much evidence that the curacas did in general succeed in enriching themselves. Their position was invidious and difficult and no opprobrium survives in the minds of the Indians against them.

Finally there were the *yanaconas* who had been uprooted from their communes by economic pressure, by the civil wars or by the general scattering of population, and had entered the service of the Spanish on a feudal basis either in the towns or on the *encomiendas*. They were tacitly free from the obligations of tribute and *mita* and for this reason their ranks were continually being swelled from the *hatunruna*. With their freedom they had forsaken their cultural heritage and though their lot was somewhat easier, they constituted the greatest danger to the ultimate survival of their race.

And so despite much physical admixture the two races, white and red, continue side by side in the land, separate and distinct. The whites despise and fear the Indians and despite minority movements to educate and 'improve' them, while paying tribute to the antiquity of their culture, the white at heart regards the red as an economically passive element incapable of adaptation and useful only to supply the requirements of manual labour. Among the Indians the old racial resentment of the white usurper still smoulders below a superficial humility. The civilization which the white does not want to offer the red is unwilling to receive. And between the two stands the new cholo people racially more vital than either.

(c) *Evangelization*

Within the quickly growing volume of writing upon Latin America almost a special literature of its own has been devoted to interpreting the Spanish national character in the sixteenth and seventeenth centuries and explaining in terms of it their conquest and organization of their American colonies. But amid the fine generalizations of the historians, the hotly debated for and against, it is not unrefreshing sometimes to face the disillusioning reality of cold fact. The sober truth is that the majority of the first Conquistadores were the scum and the outcasts of Spain. Men who were the beggars and riff-raff of society, men with everything to gain because they had nothing to lose, joined the expeditions to the New World dazzled by the hope of wealth beyond their dreams and a life of ease in a land where they—who had always been underfoot—could strut and lord it supreme. Pizarro himself started life as an illegitimate swineherd and he was ennobled at the age of sixty and became Viceroy of Spain's largest and richest colony. Hernán Cortés said: 'And if all the Spaniards who are in these parts or who come to them were monks, or if their principal intention were the conversion of these peoples, I well believe that their conversation with them would be most profitable; but as it is the opposite, opposite must be the effect they produce; for it is notorious that the greater part of the Spanish people who cross here are of low quality, tough and vitiated with a multitude of vices and sins.' And Gómara paints a vivid picture of these first Conquistadores somewhat later when they assembled to greet the new Viceroy Blasco Núñez Vela at Trujillo. 'Their teeth worn out with eating toasted maize in the conquest of Peru; some covered with wounds and bruises from stones; others with the great sly mouths of lizards.' These were the pioneers who prepared the way for the merchants and gentry who were to come later. Their origin is, of course, nothing against them. But in estimating national character from what they were and what they did in Peru, it is wise to remember their origin.

Yet uncouth adventurers as they were, and blackguards in part, religion was a very real thing to them—the more vital as their situation became more fraught with danger. They were men of their time. Every Spaniard had the crusading tradition in his blood and even the lowest was not entirely unconscious of Spain as the defender of Europe against the Moorish infidel. It is not entirely untrue that they came with the sword in one hand and the Bible in the other and the steel-clad Santiago was their not unworthy symbol. Though inevitably ridiculed in individual cases, by and large the evangelization of the natives was accepted as both their duty and their justification. Las Casas said in 1546:[1] 'The unique and final cause why the Apostolic See granted the supreme principality and imperial overlordship of the Indies to the kings of Castile and Leon was the preaching of the Gospel and the propagation of the faith and the conversion of those native races of those lands, and not to make them greater lords or richer princes than they were.' Far as such extreme professions are from the hard reality of events, the obligation to further the ends of proselytization had always a general consensus of agreement. In some sense typical of the whole attitude was the action of Cortés, who received on his knees the first Franciscans to enter the city of Mexico and kissed the hems of their robes.

It is impossible to reach an impartial historical assessment of the value of the evangelization of the New World. Those who believe —as was then believed—that baptism into the Christian faith is the only gateway to salvation in the life to come must believe that the evangelizers brought the ultimate benefit to the Indians of Peru, in comparison with which all suffering in this world sinks into insignificance. Those who believe that the different races and peoples of the world have evolved as many different types of

[1] *Declaration of the Rights of the Indigenes.*

religion, each groping after a vanescent truth and none in final possession, will judge by a different and less precise touchstone. We shall make no attempt here to prejudge the theological standpoint but will try very briefly to present the facts of what happened.

If the rude military conquerors were firmly grounded in the faith, the Church had its material side too. It was supported by tithes and firstfruits, exacted payment for services and, despite the express prohibition of the Crown, the clergy and the ecclesiastical foundations became the greatest landowners in the Colony. In the year 1796 the revenues of the Church in Alto Peru were 1,239,000 pesos and those of the Crown only 1,255,760 pesos.[1] Ulloa y Juan spoke frankly in the *Noticias Secretas de América* about the greed of the parish priests and described among others a curé of Ecuador who exacted annually from his parish 200 sheep, 6,000 head of poultry, 4,000 *cuyes* (the Inca guinea-pig) and 50,000 eggs. Nor was his case exceptional. Certain it is that in the early period the teachers of the new faith seemed to preach the opposite of what they practised and later the parish priests were resented little less than the corregidors.

The successful evangelization of Spanish America was due to the energy and devoted initiative of the missionary societies almost entirely. Their work is one of the most complex, fascinating and astounding episodes of history which remains yet to be written. Throughout the new continent, from Mexico through Central America down to La Plata they drew their network of colleges, religious foundations and missionary outposts. They almost alone were responsible for bringing European learning and culture to America. And in this work they were helped by their cosmopolitan character. The Society of Jesus in particular included monks from almost every country of Europe—Germans, Hungarians, British and Poles. Nor did they follow behind after military conquest was consolidated. Where the military arm stopped the missionaries pushed ahead into the unknown.

After the first flush of conquest the great military adventurers began to organize expeditions into the vast tropical forests and plains to the east and north-east of the Altiplano, up the great affluents of the Amazon, in continued search of the fabulous land of gold, the Gran Paititi or El Dorado. The outcome of these expeditions was more calamitous but not ultimately different

[1] *Estadistica Boliviana* of José Maria Dalence.

from the experience of the Incas, who never succeeded in stabilizing their control over the Antis or the eastern jungles. The early expeditions were failures and soon ceased; it was long indeed before Spanish rule was surely established outside the boundaries of the old Inca Empire. The limit of Alto Peru in the south was at Tarija, founded on the edge of the Chaco against the untamed Chiriguanos. Ñuflo de Chávez pushed up through Paraguay and founded Santa Cruz at the site of the modern San José, but the colony lingered on in precarious isolation. It was the missionaries who first pushed on ahead of the military into this vast untouched area. From the Paraguay in the south, the Chaco and the whole extent of jungle and plain between the Cordillera and the Amazon northwards as far as Ecuador lay open to them. The Dominicans concentrated along the rivers Quetoto and Manique from Ayopaya, the Chaparé and Inquisivi northwards. The Franciscans penetrated the plains of Manzo in the huge triangle between the Bermejo and the Pilcomayo and at Apolobamba on the upper Beni. But the widest domain of all was the territory of the Jesuits, which became to all intents and purposes an independent Jesuit empire out of all contact with the official administration centred in the Viceroys of Lima and La Plata. From 1606 until their expulsion in 1767 what is now the modern state of Paraguay was their possession. From Santa Cruz they advanced into the eastern parts of Bolivia, the modern Department of the Beni, and from the river Beni and along the Mamoré to the Iteñéz or Guaporé and their affluents, they founded their missionary outposts, covering the provinces of Mojos and Chiquitos.

We know next to nothing about the peoples of these territories before the missionaries and all too little about the work of the missionaries themselves. By temperament and tradition the tribes of the interior were semi-nomadic in their habits, moving up and down the courses of the rivers, and they were naturally indolent in a land where Nature was profuse. The missionaries set out to change all this. They anchored their subjects to fixed settlements and compelled them to cultivate assiduously, where before they had been content to gather the fruits in season and pass elsewhere. They forced them to develop and employ their latent talents for craftsmanship and founded native industries which produced trade goods—many of which, like the hats of Mojos, acquired even a European fame. The founding of bronze and iron was introduced into Mojos. The beautiful work of wrought silver has remained famous until the present day. Weaving, carving, carpentry, feather-work and a host of other local crafts were encouraged under strict supervision and compulsion. The domains of the missions were colonies without colonists. One missionary might claim jurisdiction over ten or twenty thousand families. And peoples with so little talent for regular and sustained production could only be controlled by the sternest severity. Rule was enforced ruthlessly with the whip and because justice was impartial it was accepted. Humboldt, who travelled the unexplored valleys of the Orinoco, gives a surprisingly favourable over-all picture of the missions for so essentially impartial an observer. He criticizes the Jesuits who recruited souls by conquest. 'All who opposed any resistance were killed; huts were burnt, crops were destroyed, and old men, women and children were taken prisoner.' But he mentions that the Franciscans, Dominicans and Augustinians did not copy these militant methods of recruiting converts. Yet the Jesuit missions were economically the most successful. They established a compulsory and autocratic communism of goods. Nothing was possessed in private by the individual convert. All production was the common property of the mission and from it the missionary in charge sustained the needs of his flock, increased the wealth by trade and enriched his Order. The system undoubtedly worked. The Jesuit territories were flourishing and prosperous, Mojos in particular. Cattle were introduced into Mojos in 1690, proliferated there and still remain despite neglect and misuse the chief negotiable asset of the Beni. The depopulation and decline of the Beni dates from the expulsion of the Jesuits and the spoliation of the wealth they had fostered.

But this survey has carried us far from the matter of our book. For these tribes of the eastern forests were not of the highland stock and do not belong to the agglomerations which we call Aymara and Quechua. The enormous territories they covered had never formed a settled part of the Inca Empire. In the Spanish Colony of Peru the missionaries had less scope and freedom of action. They built colleges and churches, brought culture and learning to the land. But this meant little to the Indian, who remains an illiterate to this day.

It was the missionaries alone who brought any desire for understanding, and that psychological flexibility which makes understanding between different cultures possible, to their contact with the native peoples. Strange as it may seem, it is none the less true that they were the first to take what we should now call an ethnological interest in the Indians. They studied the native languages, produced grammars and dictionaries. Catechisms, confessionals and prayers were written in the native tongues. Even Puquina, the language of the Urus, was mastered by the monks of La Merced at Huarina. They investigated and recorded the myths and legends, the customs, rites and beliefs of the Indian communities. To the missionaries we owe not only such important works as the *Historia de Nueva España* by Padre Diego Durán, the works of Blas Valera, Guamán Poma de Ayala, Father Acosta and a host of others, but the widespread influence which made such study reputable. It is not too extravagant to say that they were the founders of the modern science of ethnology and had it not been for them, our material for reconstruction would be scarce indeed. If the works of the missionaries were taken away, such a book as the present could not have been written. Their contributions to the study of geography and naturalistic observation were by no means negligible either. To them we owe such works as *El Orinoco Ilustrado* by Padre José Gumilla, *Carta del territorio ecuatoriano* by Padre Vicente Maldonado, the *Historia de Reino de Quito* by Padre Juan de Velasco and the works of Padre Kino and the Chilean Juan Ignacio Molina. All this is a debt which cannot be forgotten.

This attitude of mind inevitably made for greater tolerance and a broader understanding in their contact with the Indian peoples. True, they treated adult peoples as children and never managed to distinguish between those who had developed a reasonably advanced civilization of their own and the tribes on the verge who were still living in a state of savagery. But their interest might have meant understanding and something almost approaching confidence between the two cultures. They encouraged the employment of Indian craftsmanship in the building and decoration of their churches and the Spanish colonial baroque was a veritable artistic mestization between the European and the Indian styles. The Indian ceremonies and fiestas were adapted into the new religion of Christ and a syncretistic ritualism resulted. The native music, dances and festivals were not suppressed but were given a Christian application, so that the fiesta of the sixteenth and seventeenth centuries became a perfect example of religious fusion. Nor was this difficult to reconcile with consciences on either side. Catholic orthodoxy was primarily concerned with dogmatic correctness of belief and idolatry was ultimately the incorrect ascription of deity to cult objects. Thus, granted correct profession, a large measure of toleration and latitude in ritual was easy. The Indian was not given to metaphysical analysis and dogmatic orthodoxy meant little to him one way or the other so long as his ritual and ceremonial were satisfactory. And a long tradition of religious syncretism made it easy and natural for him to fuse the new Christian ritual with his own. The ritual of the worship of saints has always exercised a strong appeal for the Indian temperament. Thus the Indian in general could confess formal orthodoxy with indifference and the practical compromise in cult and ritual gave rise to a true religious mestization which was satisfactory to both parties.

One of their happiest devices for spreading the knowledge of Christian belief was to encourage among the Indians religious plays rather in the manner of the old Mystery plays, appealing to the natural dramatic talent of the Indians. Garcilaso gives a most interesting account of this (Book II, chap. xxviii). 'They [the Indians] had little or no inventive talent, but are great imitators of what they see done. ... They show the same ability for the sciences, if they are taught, as is proved by the comedies which they have staged in various places. For some zealous friars of various denominations, but chiefly of the Company of Jesus, in order to recommend the mysteries of our redemption to the Indians, wrote plays for them to perform, for they knew that they used to perform plays in the times of their Inca kings and they saw that they had ability and talent for what they wished to teach them. And so a Father of the Company composed a play in praise of Our Lady the Virgin Mary in Aymara, which differs from the general language of Peru. And the theme was those words from the third chapter of Genesis: "And I will put enmity between thee and the woman . . . and it shall bruise thy head." It was played by Indian lads and youths in a *pueblo* named Sulli. And in Potosi a dialogue on the faith was recited in the presence of more than twelve thousand Indians. In Cuzco was staged another dialogue on the infant Jesus before all the nobility of that city. Another was staged in Lima before the Chancery, all the nobility and innumerable Indians; it was partly in Spanish and partly in the general language of Peru and its theme was the Holy Sacrament. The Indian youths played the dialogues in all four places with such grace and charm of speech, such fine gesture and movement, that they aroused the delight and satisfaction of the spectators; and such was their sweetness in the songs that many Spaniards shed tears of joy, seeing the grace and talent and good disposition of the poor Indians, and they were compelled to revise their former opinion that they were stupid, uncouth and without talent.' Thus a type of *mestizo* drama grew up both in Mexico and Peru. The schools of Cuzco and Potosi became famous. A number of the *autos* and *coloquios*, as they were called, have survived in the native languages and have recently been collected and translated. They are an interesting evidence of the psychological contact between the missionaries and the native peoples and some, as for example the *auto* of the Prodigal Son by a *mestizo* Espinosa Medrano, are not without literary merit.

3. INDIAN RESISTANCE

The tightening grip of oppression was punctuated throughout the seventeenth century by recurrent outbursts of retaliatory violence directed in the main against the corregidors. These localized riots were without any general plan or cohesion, sudden and spontaneous flashes of nervous hatred touched off by particular acts of abuse or injustice, or sometimes engineered by the Spanish themselves as incidental to the local conflicts between Peninsulares and Creoles. Their frequency over a wide area was, nevertheless, a symptom that the festering silent resentment of the Indians was nearing breaking point. No complete list of these local outbreaks will be attempted, but a few examples are given as an indication of the temper which prevailed among the natives.

In 1617 a long-drawn-out rivalry between the old Spanish Basques or *Vasgongados* on the one side and the Creoles, Andalucians and Estremenians on the other at Potosi had reached the pitch almost of a local civil war and the latter party had created armed bands of hot-headed youths, calling themselves *Vicuñas*, against the constituted authorities. Alonso de Ibañez, a rich Creole, was accused of having instigated a native insurrection in five neighbouring cantons, 'deceiving the unwary natives and promising them emancipation of the colonies', and was executed with other leaders of his party in the Plaza del Gato of Potosi.

In 1661 a cholo of La Paz, Antonio Gallardo, called 'Philinco', headed a popular riot, seized and killed the corregidor, set up a revolutionary administration and proclaimed the 'freedom of the Americans'. He lost his life in a heroic gesture during an attack upon Puno. A little later, during the governorship of the Viceroy Castellar, a rather similar riot among the urban Indians was suppressed in Lima.

In 1730 a serious riot was caused in Cochabamba by an attempt to institute a census for the purpose of tribute revision. Cochabamba was at that time the centre of one of the densest cholo concentrations in the Colony and the riot was strictly a riot of cholos rather than Indians proper. It is strange, considering the elaborate statistics of population instituted by the Incas, how resentfully both Indians and cholos have always reacted against a census. In this case it was connected rightly with an intention to increase tribute contributions. The riot was led by a cholo Alejo Calatayud, who massacred the local garrison, freed the prisoners and set up his own local government. He was betrayed by Rodriguez Carrasco, whom he himself had made corregidor, and was executed in 1731. Calatayud had no idea of organizing a revolution. His riot was a sudden impulse of anger and indignation and went no further than removing the immediate cause. A large number of very similar outbreaks, however, occurred here and there about this time, all with the murder of the local corregidors.

More clearly revolutionary in character was the attempt of Juan Belac de Cordova, who claimed to be of Inca descent and chose Oruro as the centre for a movement to restore the Inca regime. He had travelled much in Peru and Charcas and for fourteen years had prepared the overthrow of Spanish power. In 1739 he launched from Oruro his declaration of independence, in which he claimed that the Spanish 'maintain the poor natives in such a state of depression that in addition to paying outrageous annual tribute they compel more than ten thousand Indians a year to serve on the *mita* at each of the mining centres of Potosi and Guancavelica. In consequence these unfortunates are unable to enjoy their lives, their wives, their farms or their flocks, for they see themselves abused and forced to abandon all and most of them dying amid so harsh maltreatment, leave their poor children orphans, their unhappy wives widowed and their communities shattered.' The manifesto recommended that: 'There being now among us a person of royal blood of our Incas of Great Cuzco, who desires to restore the right and re-establish that monarchy, the Creoles and the caciques and all the natives are besought to give him their hand for this heroic action of restoring the right and liberating the country by purging it of the tyranny of the white foreigners who consume us.' He was denounced by one of his band and sentenced to the garrotte by the corregidor of Oruro. It is not clear that he had made any effective preparations for a movement of the magnitude which he envisaged.

The Tarma rebellion, which began in the eastern jungle or Montaña of Peru in 1742, led by Juan Santos, was the most serious precursor of the general insurrections which broke out forty years later. While planning to overthrow Spanish colonial rule, Santos remained loyal to the Church. Again in 1750 an Indian revolt in the province of Huarochiri was instigated by ringleaders in Lima, who were probably in touch with Santos.

While none of these actions reached the magnitude of a general insurrection, in the last quarter of the eighteenth century indigenous and for the most part spontaneous revolutions spread throughout the highlands from Cuzco to Tucuman, Aymaras and Quechuas acting in concert. Widespread as the movement was, there was no effective centralization of leadership or concerted tactics, but rather a number of separate revolts which flared up together from common sympathies and an underlying sentiment of solidarity but militarily very loosely linked together. The aims and motives of these revolts were differently formulated. In general the leaders professed loyalty to the Church, or even to the Spanish crown, and declared themselves in arms against bad colonial government and for the inauguration of a more equitable regime. At the same time they inconsistently proclaimed the revival of the Inca monarchy. The masses of the Indians certainly rose to arms solely with the purpose of ending the abuses which had become intolerable, beyond all the excessive tribute and the drain of the *mita* upon their effective man-power. They were ready to kill the whites who to them were the symbols of these abuses and they distrusted the cholos. To them the Incas were now only a vague memory of a past glory and the symbol of a good time of justice and reasonable demands which was gone. They had no positive or constructive policy to substitute for the colonial regime which they were to destroy and envisaged no more than continuing their lives traditionally upon their *ayllus* without abuse and exaction. Their leaders had no wider positive vision.

But this was no longer a purely racial conflict. It had become also a conflict between an oppressed and an exploiting class. In 1949 the communist historian Boleslao Lewin in a series of lectures and newspaper articles in La Paz represented the revolt of Tupac Amaru as a conflict of classes on the orthodox Marxist lines.[1] That interpretation is wrong. But it is equally wrong to represent it as purely racial odium. It was the outbreak of an oppressed race driven beyond the limits of endurance by extreme economic oppression. In this episode the cholos were in the main on the side of the Spanish, not again primarily for racial reasons but because they were as a class mainly tied to the towns and urban activities and this was primarily an agrarian uprising against exploiting urban classes. But many cholos played important or unimportant roles with the revolutionaries. The cholo wife of Tupaj Catari, Bartolina Sisa, was one of the leading spirits in organizing the siege of La Paz. Tupaj Catari's chief adviser, the scribe Bonifacio Chuquimamani, was a cholo. The revolt in Tupiza was headed by a cholo. And many more besides.

The fighting, which we shall now describe, was marked by sickening inhumanity and atrocities on both sides; prisoners were hanged, burnt, mutilated and tortured. Civilians were the objects of ruthless vengeance. The Indian massacre at Tiquina was more than balanced by the Spanish actions at Viacha and Laja. The atrocities wrought by the Spanish were in general more cruel and more coldly ruthless than those of the Indians. Although the Indians were reduced, the result of the movement was to increase the bitter and hopeless resentment on the one side and the silent fear on the other between these two races condemned to work out their future side by side without contact of sympathy or sentiment in the land once ruled by the Incas.

In 1779 revolt broke out in Chayanta, a Quechuan district of Potosi. The year before Tomas Catari, chief cacique of Macha, had travelled on foot to Buenos Aires to appeal to the Viceroy against an unjust increase in the exactions of the corregidor. Obtaining no satisfaction, he returned and raised the standard of revolt with his brothers Damaso and Nicolas. Tomas was seized and imprisoned in Chuquisaca (Sucre), but his brothers obtained possession of the person of the corregidor, Joaquin Alos, and effected an exchange. Tomas Catari entered into correspondence with Tupac Amaru, who was to lead the main revolt at Cuzco, and declared the liberty and sovereign power of the indigene in

[1] See also Boleslao Lewin, *Tupac Amaru, el Rebelde* (1943).

his district, with the abolition of the *mita* and tribute obligations. He was again captured by a detachment sent by the Audiencia and was taken to Charcas; but on the way his escort was attacked by the Indians and Catari lost his life in the fighting. The insurrection was continued by his two brothers, who laid siege to Chuquisaca with an ill-armed force of 7,000 men and were defeated with heavy carnage by Ignacio Flores, who later went on to the relief of La Paz. A heavy price was put on the lives of the two brothers and they were later betrayed to the Spanish and executed.

Meanwhile in February 1781 a riot broke out in Oruro, which originated in the rivalry between Creoles and Peninsulares. The Creole leader, Jacinto Rodriguez, attacked the corregidor Urrutia and through one Sebastian Pagador incited the Indians of the surrounding mining districts to come to his aid. Having been invited as allies, the Indians threw off restraint, murdering, looting and plundering. Some aid against them was received from the corregidor of Cochabamba, but the revolt of Rodriguez continued until the arrival of Reseguin, who had been sent by the Viceroy from La Plata to pacify the Province. This incident, while adding to the general confusion, stands apart from the main Indian insurrections.

In Peru the standard of revolt was raised by José Gabriel Tupac Amaru, the caudillo of Tungasuca, who claimed to be heir to the throne of the Incas. In January 1781 he laid siege to Cuzco, but displayed no outstanding powers of leadership or organization. He was defeated and captured by José del Valle and was executed in Cuzco in May of the same year. His brother, Diego Cristobal Tupac Amaru, continued the campaign briefly at Puno.

The most sustained and serious action in the whole revolt was the siege of La Paz, *de facto* capital of the modern Bolivia. In March 1781 a well-planned rising of the Aymara Indians of the Bolivian Altiplano, supported by detachments of Quechuas, broke out under the leadership of an Indian of Ayoayo named Julian Apasa, who took the name Tupaj Catari (combined from Tupac Amaru and Tomas Catari) and declared himself Viceroy of Charcas under the authority of the Inca Tupac Amaru. Although semiliterate (he could read but not write) and without broad political conceptions, Tupaj Catari was the most vigorous and energetic personality of the movement; he was a genuine embodiment of the Indian spirit which inspired the whole insurrection. His story has been written in novel form by the Bolivian writer Augusto Guzmán with truth to the spirit and accuracy of facts. The siege of La Paz by an army of 80,000 men was finely planned and executed with energy and skill. The city was completely ringed, despite the extreme difficulty of such a feat amid so many mountain exits. Feints and stratagems were used on both sides. The persistence with which the siege was maintained, reducing the city to the verge of starvation, shows the determination of the Indians and the quality of their leadership. They achieved everything except a direct storming by mass assault. Segurola thus described the state of the city: 'The enemy have used the assistance of many contrivances, engines and devices, casting against us arrows with tufts of burning wool, rockets carrying fires of sulphur matches, linen bundles enclosing fire and gunpowder discharged with slings and hand grenades shot from the mortars in the intelligence that they could be effective against some thatched houses adjoining our trenches, in such manner that, confident of the total destruction of the city, they have another built on the heights above; and by the mercy of God we have resisted in spite of hunger, pestilence and the enemy, including also those within, who have occasioned no less anxiety than those without, procuring their liberty and maintaining the most essential and best part of their services in the sacking, burning and other excesses, not only the horses, mules and asses having gone to provision the populace but after the dogs and cats were all consumed they used as sustenance even hides and the leather of small trunks.'

The memory of this siege still survives as a feeling of unconfessed insecurity among the white rulers of Bolivia.

In July a relieving army under Ignacio Flores forced its way into the city and joined the forces under Sebastian de Segurola, corregidor of Larecaja, who had been able to make provisions for the defence of the city before the siege was laid. But the siege continued and the circle was drawn again. Depredations by Flores upon the surrounding cantons made it more difficult to maintain the supplies of food for the besieging forces. But the fresh troops in La Paz meant more mouths to feed, and Flores retired to Oruro to await there reinforcements under Reseguin, who after pacifying Tupiza was advancing to the relief of La Paz with an army of 7,000 men. Meanwhile Tupaj Catari was joined by a young man who called himself Andres Tupac Amaru and claimed to be the son and heir of José Gabriel Tupac Amaru. He had recently taken Sorata by storm and put new life and spirit into the besieging army, but left the practical conduct of the siege to Tupaj Catari and retired to Peñas. After an unsuccessful attempt to flood the city by damming and then releasing the river, as had been done at Sorata, the siege was broken by the arrival of Reseguin in October. Some time later Tupaj Catari was taken by treachery and condemned by the *oidor* Tadeo Diez de Medina. The sentence was carried out on the 11th November, 1782, in Peñas. His wrists and ankles were bound to four horses by ropes of equal length and at a given signal the riders galloped the horses in four directions until pulled up by the body in the centre. Three times this was done before the dislocated limbs and the head were cut from the trunk.

With the death of Tupaj Catari the movement was virtually at an end, although a final episode of little importance was instigated in the province of Huarochiri in the name of José Gabriel Tupac Amaru in May, 1783 by one styling himself Felipe Velasco Tupac Inca Yupanqui.

Although Tupac Amaru has given his name in history to the whole movement and was generally recognized as the supreme leader and the future Inca, he exercised no effective central control. The resistance was most stubborn among the Aymaras and the Quechuas of the Bolivian Altiplano and Tupac Amaru's own contribution was not strong. The movement lacked concentration and was too diffused to be ultimately successful.

Tupac Amaru declared his aims to be administrative reform and it is doubtful whether he seriously planned an independent Indian state with himself as its reigning head in isolation from the Spanish crown. Young Andres Tupac Amaru, whose origin is something of a mystery, specifically claimed that his authority and that of his alleged father came legitimately from Philip III, by whom they were commissioned to overthrow the bad colonial administration. Tomas Catari went further and declared limited independence within his own district, while professing continued loyalty to the Church. Tupaj Amaru was not consistent or vocal but clearly intended, at first at any rate, the elimination of the white oppressors and all they stood for. Beyond this he did not see and even he was loyal to the religion in which he had been reared as boy sacristan of Ayoayo. Nowhere was there any clearly conceived positive programme to put in the place of the Spanish colonial regime and the invocation of the native Inca monarchy was no more than the empty trappings of a ceremonial pageantry. The

UNDER SPANISH RULE

concrete reality of the Inca regime had been forgotten and the day for its resuscitation was already past.

4. FROM COLONIES TO REPUBLICS

In an age when egalitarian and revolutionary ideas were in the air, when the intellectual aftermath of the French Revolution and the more recently won independence of the United States were stimulating to emulation free spirits throughout the world, it was the collapse of the Spanish monarchy before the armies of Napoleon which was decisive for the destiny of the Spanish colonies in America.

Metropolitan Spain was invaded by the French in 1807. In March 1808 Charles IV abdicated the throne and his son was proclaimed king in his stead as Ferdinand VII, only to renounce his title a month later. Widespread revolt followed the proclamation of Joseph Bonaparte to the throne in Madrid in July. Local Juntas were set up in the provincial towns of Spain, with a Central Junta at Seville. The accession of Ferdinand was acclaimed with enthusiasm throughout Spanish America and the first renunciation of obedience to the Council of the Indies took the form of loyalty to Ferdinand, king in captivity. It was only gradually and seemingly accidentally that what had started as a declaration of loyalty to the Spanish Crown against the French usurper took on the character of a secessionist movement. Thus the first outbreak of revolt took place in Sucre to the cry 'Vive Fernando VII!' and deposed the Governor, Ramón Garcia Pizarro, who also professed loyalty to the emissary of the Central Junta of Seville, José Manuel Goyeneche. By the very logic of events what had originated as a movement of loyalty to the crown led into the wars for independence from the crown. A Regency Council which was set up in Madrid under the protection of the British fleet drew up in 1810 a radical proclamation, beginning: 'From this moment, Spanish Americans, you are elevated to the dignity of free men.' But it was already too late. Events in the colonies had already taken on too clearly a secessionist character. And the ill-advised attempt of the restored Ferdinand between 1814 and 1820 to re-establish his authority in America was frustrated by the revolt of the army which had been assembled at Cadiz for reconquest.

The revolt at Sucre took place on the 25th May, 1808. On the 16th July the example of Sucre was followed in La Paz. The

Governor was deposed, a Defensive Junta was set up and Pedro Domingo Murillo, an energetic leader of mixed cholo blood, was nominated President. The proclamation of the La Paz Junta was unmistakable in its intention. 'Now is the time to shake off a yoke as disastrous to our welfare as it is favourable to the national arrogance of the Spaniard. Now is the time to organize a new system of government grounded on the interests of our country so seriously neglected by the bastard politics of Madrid.' This proclamation contains no mention of Ferdinand.

By a curious recurrence the 25th May was also the date, celebrated as the birthday of the Argentine Republic, when in 1810 a Junta was formed in Buenos Aires to take over the government of the province of La Plata. Yet so complicated was the origin of the secessionist movement that this Junta also was sworn 'to preserve this part of America for our August Sovereign Ferdinand VII'.

The progress of the Wars of Independence has been told in a number of formal histories and has little relevance to the story of this book. We shall therefore pass it over with the briefest of summaries and advance to matters more germane.

For some years after 1810 Alto Peru, or Bolivia as it now is, was alternately attacked by the Argentine armies of independence under Belgrano and defended by the royalist forces of Peru, which remained until the end the stronghold of royalism. A deadlock might have been reached but for the bold and ultimately successful project of the Argentine General San Martin to invade Chile across the Andes and from Chile to attack Peru by sea. After many vicissitudes San Martin entered Lima in 1821, and was there proclaimed 'Protector' of an independent Peru. Meanwhile Simon Bolívar, whose name more than any other has been associated with the movement of American independence, had established independent Republics in Venezuela, Columbia and Ecuador to the north of Peru. In 1822 Bolívar and San Martin held a secret meeting at Guayaquil, as a result of which San Martin resigned his office and retired into private life, leaving to Bolívar the task and the glory of completing the independence movement. In 1824 the royalist troops of Peru were defeated by Bolívar at Junín and again by his lieutenant Santa Cruz at Ayacucho on the 9th December. Ayacucho sealed the independence of Peru and indeed of all South America. Santa Cruz, left in command at La Paz, was responsible for constituting the independent republic of Bolivia, which as Alto Peru had formerly been included within the Viceroyalty of Peru and more recently attached to La Plata. His action was somewhat reluctantly confirmed by Bolívar, after whom the new state was named.

The motives which stimulated and maintained this widespread secessionist movement, so curiously displayed at the beginning as an affirmation of continued loyalty to the crown, are difficult to analyse. Since the French Revolution libertarian ideas were in the air. The example of the United States held a profound significance for the vigorous and progressive minds of the age. Despite the strict control of books and print in Spanish South America, revolutionary literature found its way into the homes of the Creoles. And many of the precursors and leaders of the separatist movement had travelled in Europe and there imbibed radical ideas and aspirations. Antonio Nariño, one of the genuine intellectual precursors of Spanish American liberation, suffered a long spell of imprisonment for issuing in Bogota a Spanish translation of the French revolutionary *Declaration of the Rights of Man*. Francisco Miranda, who spent many years trying to obtain support for a revolution in the Spanish colonies of America from England, France and the United States, had served in the war of North American independence and had held a command in the French revolutionary army. Simon Bolívar himself, one of the outstanding political minds in a century of political enlightenment, imbibed the radical ideas of Rousseau in his boyhood and served his apprenticeship amidst the ferment of European radicalism. Yet it would be a mistake to exaggerate the importance of these radical ideas from the 'enlightenment' without. While they were the stimulus of some few leading spirits, their influence upon the majority was not profound. In the movement as a whole immediate and practical interests were a more important spur than abstract ideals of liberty and independence. Indeed the disappearance of radical ideas in the internal organization of the new Republics once independence was achieved is conclusive proof of this. Nor was the desire for independence a nationalistic fervour to throw off an alien foreign yoke. Strong nationalistic sentiment has been a gradual and rather recent growth in most South American Republics and the spiritual link with Spain has been preserved to this day with surprising tenacity. At least as strong and probably more immediately important than the ideas of the Encyclopaedists were the legalistic principles which radiated out from the University of Sucre. From there were inspired such figures as Mariano Moreno, Secretary General of the Junta of Buenos Aires, Monteagudo, Castelli and Lemoine. In principle the Spanish colonies had always been regarded as private possessions of the Spanish crown, governed through the Council of the Indies, and not possessions of Spain. At Sucre was quoted the basic Law of the Indies, by which the King promised 'for Us and our successors they shall never be alienated or disjointed in whole or in part; and if We or our successors shall make any gift or transfer contrary to the above said, it shall be null and as such we declare it'. Hence, it was argued with the collapse of the legitimate monarchy the tie was broken. But this argument, influential as it was, was a legalization rather than a motive force of the separatist movement.

The economic factor has been given prominence by historians who, in the new way, delight in finding economic causes for all human vicissitudes. Certainly the Spanish trade monopoly was vexatious, especially to the River Plate and to Upper Peru which was economically dependent upon it. There can be no question that it aroused serious resentment. The 'Declaration of the Landowners', drawn up by Mariano Moreno, stated unequivocally: 'Justice demands that we enjoy the same commercial rights as the other cities which form part of the Spanish monarchy.' And: 'The sovereign did not confer upon your Excellency the high office of Viceroy to watch over the interests of the merchants of Cadiz, but our own.' Cisneros, who was appointed Viceroy in Buenos Aires by the Central Junta in 1809, after some vacillation found himself obliged to open up free trade with the British. Yet earlier the British attempts under Sir Home Popham and General Whitelocke, in 1806 and 1807, had been repelled with decisive vigour despite the incentive of a breach of the Spanish trade monopoly. This was a cause of discontent but must not be exaggerated out of its context. The wider cause was the resentment of the Creoles, or American-born Spanish, against 'privilege' in all its forms, which subordinated them to the Peninsular Spanish. The trade monopoly favoured the commerce of Spain at the expense of the wealthy and influential Creoles. But the highest dignities in Church and in government were also reserved for Spaniards appointed from home. This was the root cause of the secessionist movement. The acquisition of independence was the final victory in the long rivalry between the American-born

Creoles and the privileged metropolitan Spaniards from the home country. And I think it is not far from the truth to say that the majority of the Creoles would have preferred to maintain their allegiance to the Spanish crown if they could at the same time have done away with 'privilege' and achieved equality of opportunity in their own country with the Spaniards from home. There was no fervent majority desire to break with Spain for its own sake. Local patriotism was not yet born. The break was incidental to the long jockeying and resentment between the Spanish Spaniards and the American Spaniards—Spaniards both.

And what did all this mean to the Indian? We must avoid the temptation of facile romanticism so easy for the nationalistic historian who interprets earlier events in the light of later sentiment. In his *Blasón de Plata* the Argentine Ricardo Rojas describes the visit of Castelli to Tihuanacu on the 25th May, 1811, with his army of liberation. He imagines the Indians looking up to the General as 'a restorer of the ancient Indian life, since this and no less was the meaning of the revolution for them'. In fact the majority of the revolutionaries had no desire or intention to emancipate the Indians or to improve their social conditions. Nor were the Indians led away by their lofty professions. Indians fought in the revolutionary armies and in the royalist armies both. Indian communities were exploited by both sides. If Castelli's armies contained many pure Indians, we learn that the royalist army of 9,000 which opposed Santa Cruz at Ayacucho contained only 500 Spanish. The Indians had no enthusiasm for the Independence movement and did not regard it as their concern. They were in the right. Madariaga, the second part of whose *Cuadro Historico de las Indias* sets out to analyse the fundamental causes of the secession, writes: 'The wars of secession are the crisis between these two springs within the soul of the Indies: the longing for whiteness which tends to unify all the Indies and, through the Whites, to keep them attached to Spain; and the strength of the earth, which calls its peoples to itself and moulds them into a oneness to fit its own genius.' In a semi-mystical and philosophical sense this may well be the 'inner meaning' of the struggle for liberation. But the 'strength of the earth' was not an expression of the will of the Indian race. It was the pull of the land—and at most the influence of their tincture of native blood —in the white Creoles, in whom immediate self-interest was at war with their recognition of a spiritual link with Spain. The liberation from Spain was not a liberation of the Indians. The Indians in the new Republics remained 'under Spanish rule'—and a Spanish rule which in all essentials maintained its colonial character.

Simon Bolívar himself was certainly consistent to his creed of human equality and intended the emancipation of the Indians; but the forces of inertia were too strong for him. According to the colonial principle the Indian had no proprietary rights in his land. All lands were the property of the crown and the Indian was granted the usufruct only in return for a capitation tax or tribute. The Decrees of Trujillo in 1825 emancipated the Indian as a full citizen with equal rights and spread the burden of taxation over all, Indians and whites alike. By granting the Indians absolute possession of their lands, these Decrees turned them into free-holders instead of serfs. But opposition to the Decrees was strong both from the white Creoles and from the larger Indian land-holders, who now found themselves taxed in accordance with the size of their holdings. Nor indeed was the system of small individual freeholds one which held any strong appeal to the Indians, who still retained the old traditions of collective ownership of land by the *ayllu*. These measures were too radical for the Creoles who had fought for independence and their liberalism was quite foreign to the mentality of the Indian population. They were rescinded in the two following years and the position of the Indians remained as it had been in colonial times. For them the achievement of political independence from Spain brought no boon and held no meaning.

Chapter Seven

THE INDIAN TODAY AND TOMORROW

THE importance of the Indian populations in the modern states of Bolivia and Peru is seldom justly apprehended even within these countries themselves.

The Wars of American Independence, waged with the Indians and the cholos, left their circumstances unchanged and the breach with Spain brought them neither alleviation nor a kinder understanding. The revolutionarily humanitarian decrees of Simon Bolívar mirrored a stirring but still-born idealism, ineffectual for practical betterment, and the economic enslavement of the native peoples in the colonial epoch has been perpetuated by the rulers of the young Republics. As in *Bolivia y El Mundo* (1947) Jorge Pando Gutierrez restrainedly remarks: 'The conditions in which the agrarian indigene lives are frankly disastrous; he is without social security or medical care; he inhabits inhospitable regions; his alimentation is wretched and his hygienic conditions compare with those of the animals, for the latter share his house and his food.' Under the Republics contempt for the racial and genetic inferiority of the Indian was exaggerated to extremes beyond the utmost excesses of colonial days and the chasm of ignorance yawned wider between the red man and the white, who alone was vocal. Nineteenth-century writers such as Santiago Vaca Guzman, Gabriel René Moreno, Nataniel Aguirre, Eufronio Viscarra and Alcides Arguedas in Bolivia, who moulded and reflected opinion in a State built upon the toil and the sweat of the Indian, decried him unmet as one brutish and bestial, sub-human of intellect, impervious to education, resistant to progress, an economic liability, a drag on development and a disgrace to be glozed. 'Who will draw the Indian from his degradation? What is the social force that can lead him to a higher destiny?' asks Viscarra. While in *Juan de la Rosa* Aguirre speaks of Quechua as 'that most ugly jargon used by the brutalized children of the sun'.

Within the last thirty years or so the glimmering indeed of a new attitude has appeared with the theoretical realization that the existence of the Indian populations constitutes a national problem which cannot sensibly be shirked. Glorification of the past in the service of national pride has led to a revival of archaeological interest in the Indian races; the sudy of the Aymara and Quechua languages has become respectable, if still incipient; superficial interest in surviving Indian folklore, customs and institutions is becoming the order of the day and penetrates the national Press, where projects for the amelioration of the native peoples are a recurrent theme of discussion. In Bolivia a more profound, if disagreeable, realization of dependence upon Indian man-power was ruthlessly engendered by the shock of the Chaco war with Paraguay. Following in the wake of Protestant missionary bodies half-hearted projects for the state education of the indigene are drawn up on paper in the Government Departments. Laws for the protection and edification of the Indian are, as ever, passed and neglected with equal ease. And in both Bolivia and Peru a new school of sociologists is writing, which sees the future of those countries in increasing mestization on the lines of Mexico and points to the cholo—the 'New Indian' as he was glamorously dubbed by Uriel Garcia—as the heir to the future, the new shaper and repository of national history. As early as 1910 Franz Tamayo, the great *mestizo*, son of a Bolivian Spanish *hidalgo* and a woman of native blood, the only Bolivian writer to whom the epithet 'genius' can with surety be applied, published a flaming defence of the Indian, a daring attack upon the settled complacency of accepted opinion, in his *La Creación de la Pedagogia Nacional*, in which he maintains that: 'All that is strongest, all that is morally best, in Bolivia is the Indian.' And 'We must put an end once and for all to the Spanish spirit which still dominates our history'. Like all great forerunners and fighters of genius, Tamayo goes to extremes. But despite his constant exaggerations and frequent extravagances he writes with a profound and genuine insight into the Indian spirit and psychology which we may search the whole of literature vainly to discover elsewhere. From his work dates the new attitude which seeks, though it may fail, to understand.

But the traditional attitude is still dominant. Orthodox and general opinion still looks upon the Indian as degraded and degenerate, beyond the power to rescue, reactionary against progress and an economic nullity because, being sufficient unto himself, he is neither a producer nor a consumer of marketable

THE INDIAN TODAY AND TOMORROW

commodities. For the white minorities are still unconsciously controlled by fear of encroachment by the large coloured populations among whom they live and upon whom they depend.

For figures and facts give such an unmistakable picture of the predominance of colour and dependence of the white as cannot be dubious.

There is some reason to think that after a catastrophic decline during the colonial epoch the numbers of the Indians who inhabit the Andean highlands have shown a tendency to recover under the Republics. There is no doubt, of course, that the cholo class is increasing; but it is very difficult to determine with exactness the numbers of the Indians. For though there are three clearly distinct racial groups, there is no unambiguous criterion whereby to distinguish one from another and there exists a wide fringe at the margins where they merge. While a large proportion of the whites have some admixture of native blood, among Indians and cholos themselves the difference between them is thought of less as a racial matter than a matter of social status. Linguistically many Indians, especially in the urban neighbourhoods, have a modicum of Spanish, all professed cholos speak Spanish as a second language and the majority of whites learnt either Quechua or Aymara in the cradle. Hence the demological estimates of race-groups are at best only rough and ready.

In Bolivia there has been no recent population census.[1] The Directorate of Statistics in the Bolivian Ministry of Finance and Statistics estimates that of a total population of 3·8 million souls 50 per cent are Indians, 32 per cent are cholos and 15 per cent whites or near-whites. These figures may be more or less right, although the principles of discrimination used have not been stated. Other estimates, of which that given by Dr. Juan Manuel Balcazar in his excellent *Epidemiologia Boliviana* (1946) is typical, despair of a purely racial differentiation and are based upon occupational classification. On this basis is given: Indians (*i.e.* agricultural and mine labourers), 70 per cent; cholos (*i.e.* urban proletariat), 25 per cent; and educated classes 5 per cent. It is probable that in all Bolivia the Quechuas now rather outnumber the Aymaras. Frederico Avila in his *El Drama de la Sangre* (1944) puts the number of Quechuas and Quechuan cholos together at 50 per cent of the total population and the Aymaras at 30 per cent; the Quechuas are more readily susceptible to mestization than the Aymaras. On

[1] See note on page 251.

a linguistic division the figures officially recognized are: 43 per cent Spanish-speaking; 40 per cent Quechua; and 25 per cent Aymara. It is likely that these figures somewhat underestimate the proportion of the population which is bilingual.

In the Peruvian census of 1940, out of a total population of 7 million, 2·8 million, or about 40 per cent, were classified as Indians, 3·3 million as cholos. It is estimated that 1.5 million Indians in Peru are living in communes and so retaining as best may be their traditional modes of life and culture. Linguistically 63·4 per cent are given as Spanish-speaking, 46·8 as speaking Quechua and 4·4 as Aymara. In Peru the Quechuas very largely predominate over the Aymaras, the latter being found chiefly in the south around the borders of the lake.

Wendell C. Bennett has estimated in the *Handbook of South American Indians* that the population of the whole highland region of the Andes, including parts of Chile and Ecuador, is about 28 million, of which 6·5 million, or something less than a quarter, are Indians. Of these, roughly 5·5 million may be Quechuas and 600,000 Aymaras, according to a linguistic differentiation.

There is probably no other 'white' country in the world which has so high a proportion of non-white population so essentially integrated in its productive life as Bolivia. For indeed the country's life depends entirely upon the indigenous peoples and the very small white minority is not in any degree independent of them. The 60,000 or so Indians who are employed in the mines are responsible for more than 90 per cent in value of the country's exports and 50 per cent of the national revenue. Factory labour, the semi-skilled labour of the towns, mechanics and artisans, minor commerce and the lower administrative posts in the provincial townlets are supplied by the cholos. About 70 per cent of the population is agricultural and virtually all the agricultural labour, as well as the heavier manual labour of the towns, is performed by Indians. The white agriculturist in Bolivia and Peru is an employer or overseer of Indian labour but not himself a labourer. The small white minority controls the government, the administration and the higher grades of business, banking and commerce; but the productive life of the country depends upon the man-power supplied by the Indians, while the cholo is becoming ever more ubiquitous. The situation in Peru is similar, though less extreme. Neither country could continue to function without its Indian—or its cholo—population.

THE INDIAN TODAY AND TOMORROW

These are the hard facts which underlie all theorizations about the future and the destiny of the Indian races. And these are the facts which make his future no mere academic problem but the most vital and serious consideration for the future prosperity and continuance of the Republics which were carved out from the old Spanish Province of *Piru*.

PHYSICAL AND PSYCHOLOGICAL CHARACTERISTICS

Philip Means divides the races which have given stimulus to the great movements of human civilization into the nomadic peoples of the desert, the aquatic peoples of the sea-coasts and the peoples of mountains and highlands. The Aymaras and the Quechuas belong to the last group. Their development took place on the high mountain plateaux of the Andes roughly between 10,000 and 15,000 feet above sea level and at this altitude they remain most at home.

There prevails much popular misconception about the effects of altitude on human physiology and much has been written in the name of science which has scant justification in fact. Many writers have followed Alcides D'Orbigny in stating—without, I believe, a shadow of justification—that owing to their long sojourn upon the high Altiplano with its rarefied atmosphere the Aymaras have developed in compensation abnormal capacity of chest and lungs. Against all evidence it is commonly believed in Bolivia and Peru that the Indian peoples are unable to acclimatize themselves at a lower altitude and succumb to disease if removed from the heights. In fact physiological reactions are never a factor of altitude alone but of atmospheric pressure, or roughly the oxygen content of the atmosphere, which depends upon altitude in combination with latitude. Because the Peruvian and Bolivian Andes lie within the torrid zone, atmospheric pressure there is greater than it is at an equal altitude above sea level, in, say, the Alps. In the Alps the limit of forestation is reached at about 6,500 feet and the line of perpetual snow begins at 10,000 feet. In the Andes forestation extends up to 13,000 feet and the eucalyptus has recently been induced to flourish even higher; the perpetual snows begin not much lower than 16,000 feet. Contrary to the usual reports the notorious mountain sickness, or *sorojchi*, does not manifest itself much below the level at which the region of perpetual snows begins. The slight physiological discomforts often experienced by travellers to the Altiplano at 13,000 feet are mainly due to a combination of suggestibility and a too rapid change from the atmospheric conditions of the Pacific coast, where the air is denser than say on the coast of the Mediterranean, to conditions analogous to those which cause little discomfort to holiday-makers who visit Switzerland for winter sports. Physiologically La Paz at a height of 12,000 feet is equivalent to an altitude of about 5,500 feet in the Alps. It is therefore quite unjustified to regard the home of the Aymaras and Quechuas as physiologically abnormal, however exacting and inhospitable it may be.

The belief that the Indians are physiologically unable to adapt themselves to life at a lower altitude is equally mistaken. In Inca times work upon the coca plantations in the semi-tropical valleys was regarded as unhealthy and was used as a form of punishment. But this was because the Indians had not become immunized to tropical infirmities and because they were liable to attack from the untamed jungle tribes. The enormous quantities of Quechua remains discovered south of Lima and elsewhere conclusively prove that under the Inca very large Quechua colonies must have populated the coastal region and acclimatized themselves there. Aymaras similarly have become acclimatized on the coast further south, around Tacna and Atacama. The appalling mortality among the Indians forced by the Spanish to work upon the coca plantations of the Yungas of La Paz was due to the terrible working conditions imposed upon them there; so long as Indian labour cost nothing there was no inducement to economize upon it. But now both Aymaras and Quechuas have become fully acclimatized there. There has been noticed indeed recently in Peru a spontaneous Quechua tendency to migrate eastwards to the Yungas or warm valleys of the eastern slopes of the Cordillera. I have myself seen colonies of Aymaras from the Altiplano planted in the eastern lowlands of Bolivia, by the river Yapacani, on land little above sea level. But though physiologically the Indian is not less adaptable than other human types, psychologically he is very closely wedded to the harsh and unfriendly soil which has been for centuries his home. He is firmly established in his traditional ways of life and will not happily change his customary diet. It is owing to this psychological factor rather than to any physiological disability that attempts to colonize the Aymaras or the Quechuas artificially in the semi-tropical and low-lying interior of Bolivia have usually failed. Even in the Yungas, where they have now been acclima-

THE INDIAN TODAY AND TOMORROW

tized for more than two centuries, they maintain so far as conditions allow the same habits of dress, living and diet as they used on the Altiplano.

The Indian is of medium stature, inclined to be thickset, the trunk large, hands and feet small. Pigmentation varies from a deep chocolate bronze in the highest regions to xanthous ochroid hues in the warmer valleys. The head is large, the skull prolate with slightly flattened parietals. The face is broad and long with prominent cheekbones, fleshy aquiline nose and small almond eyes. In the women the face is often fuller than in the men, making it appear rounder, and the epicanthic fold is more pronounced, giving to the eyes the slanting Mongolian appearance so often remarked by travellers. The forehead flat and sloping slightly backwards. The mouth large and the lower lip fleshy, protrusive and sagging in the centre—one of the most characteristic features of the Aymara which has hitherto escaped notice. The hair is coarse, straight, black and strong, subject neither to baldness nor to calvities. The men are without facial hair. The teeth are strong and normally remain free from decay. Eyesight keen. Hearing is acute, though partial deafness not infrequently afflicts Indians dwelling on the Altiplano and may be due to the habit of wearing woollen ear-flaps as a protection against the biting winds. Longevity is normal and centenarians are not uncommon. In sharp distinction from the native races of the tropical interior, the Andean is not a devotee of bodily cleanliness. He washes face and hands not regularly but when necessity arises, never bathes and changes his clothes only a few times in the course of a lifetime, on the occasion of great fiestas. The conditions of his life render him liable to lice and other body parasites and from these he rids himself. From their habit of cracking them between the teeth has grown up the legend that the Urus feed on fleas and lice. Despite ill-balanced and often insufficient diet, the Indian belongs to the human type capable of exceptional physical endurance; his strength is not extraordinary, but his stamina is astonishing. A high degree of physical insensibility, which is artificially enhanced by masticating the natural anaesthetic coca, renders him impervious to the effects of hunger, cold, exhaustion and pain to an extent which is perhaps unequalled in another race.

The women share the same characteristics as the men and toil beside them. They are fertile, labour is normal and they resume their ordinary occupations within twenty-four hours of parturition. They suckle their children up to eighteen months or even longer and until the child is weaned it is carried on the mother's back in a pouch made from a strip of woven textile. Both men and women are affectionate to their children and an addition to the family is welcomed as good fortune. Grief at the loss of a child—and infant mortality is high—is sharp but short-lived. Sterility is rare and a barren woman may be repudiated by her husband. The women have some knowledge of aphrodisiacs, which they give to their husbands in the hope of obtaining children, and the belief in love-charms is universal. Birth-control techniques are not practised. Abortion is regarded with disapproval but is occasionally practised by unmarried women. There is a very high standard of conjugal fidelity in both sexes; infidelity or sterility in the wife may be an occasion of divorce. Before marriage greater laxness is permitted and no importance is attached to virginity. Children are regarded as an economic asset and a widow with children has little difficulty in marrying again. Children are rarely subjected to physical punishment.

The women convey an impression of robust energy and vigour. Warm blood courses beneath the brown skins of their faces, which are generally rounder and fuller, with broader cheekbones and a more distinctively 'Asiatic' appearance, than those of the men. There is nothing etiolated about their solid vitality. The men, though strong and resistant, seem less sturdy and somehow less vital, may even appear to wear a false air of frailty and as they pass patiently up and down the Altiplano foot-tracks in their tattered clothes of patched bayeta, with closed unsmiling faces, they sometimes seem like grey, bloodless ghosts flitting from an ageless past.

Even Tamayo, the greatest modern protagonist of the Indian, admits that intelligence is not his outstanding characteristic and that 'historically he must be judged a small intelligence and a powerful will'. His 'morbid concentration' and his 'mental sluggishness' stand in the way of his advancement. Those who are less favourably disposed describe his intelligence frankly as subnormal. This judgment will come as a surprise to anyone who has noticed the Indian children, whose vivacity, alertness, self-confidence and powers of observation betray an early quickness of intelligence which is almost precocious. It is a very usual thing to see a child of six or seven accompanying its parents, directing and instructing them, pushing and urging, like some guide and interpreter to a strange world. It is certainly true that this early vivacity soon disappears and the adult becomes sluggish, apathetic and stupid. The usual explanation that this is degeneration due to indulgence in coca, chicha and alcohol can hardly be true. For the Indian has consumed coca and chicha since the race was at the height of its glory and they cannot reasonably be supposed to have effects so different now from then; moreover the cholo's addiction to alcohol—and often to coca—is not less than that of the Indian, with more opportunities for indulgence, and does not produce in him such blunting of the intellect. It might be more reasonable to believe that the cause is the cumulative effects of undernourishment and overwork, combined with the dull hopelessness of a life which offers no consolation, no interests and no prospects of improvement. For the Indian has no interest in work unless it is the semi-ritualistic work of the land, no interest in the white man's world and no desire to understand it; if it is thrust upon him, he shuts his mind against it, walls himself off by complete mental apathy. But the Indians who live removed from the towns in their own world, with the old agricultural rhythm, or as fishermen by the lake, retain far greater mental alertness and are by no means stupid within their own circle of interest. Those who know the Indian in his own habitat, not merely as the despised urban serf or uprooted in the mining encampment, recognize that in natural and agricultural lore, in knowledge of racial traditions and superstitions, in the application of his own complicated principles of social organization, he has the slow but sure and practical intelligence of the typical countryman. But his interests are confined to the life which he instinctively recognizes to be his own, the life in which tradition can serve as his guide. Outside this he has no interest and no use for intelligence. For his attitude to intelligence is severely practical. When he is uninterested in his occupation and his environment he ceases to use his intelligence, abstracts his attention, becomes so completely impervious that nothing makes an impression upon him, until he seems of a stupidity that is little short of idiocy. His apparent stupidity when removed from the context of his traditional environment is thus rather a complete lapse of interest, a form of mental imperviousness which is an instinctive and unconscious protective measure against the encroachment of an alien influence. 'The Indian', says Tamayo, 'is a soul turned in upon itself. This shutting away of mind and feeling results in a kind of failure to assimilate things and ideas which come from outside. . . . His inverted and circumvallated nature, his inner solitude, are not disturbed by the fussy restlessness of the modern world; it is a kind of proud and silent determination to be and to remain what he is, and as he is. The Indian resists with the same tenacity with which he persists.'

The key to the Indian character is his traditionalism, a form of self-preservation which causes him to reject and repudiate everything alien to his traditional way of life. He is not a good subject for education because to him education in schools is an alien influence to be fought as for centuries he has fought all alien and disrupting influences. The children who have been subjected to education return if possible to the *ayllu* and forget what they have learnt, immersing themselves in the culture of their fathers. For centuries the Indian has been excluded from the world of the white man and he now accepts and welcomes the exclusion, defending his own individuality by the most irresistible of all weapons—complete lack of interest in everything outside. He lives enclosed in his own world and for him there is no other. He shuns contact with the local authorities of the State, preferring his own traditional forms of authority. He resents the obligation to pay taxes and military service as pretexts for persecution. The only foreigners who can approach his intimate life are the priest and the 'patron' of his hacienda who supervises in person and not through a cholo superintendent. The Indian seems to the outsider to be without ambition and initiative because he is without interest in the encompassing world of which he refuses to become a part; his ambitions are confined within the *ayllu* and constrained by the traditions which he cannot disrupt, for by them he lives. He has never become fully acclimatized to a monetary economy or to the principle of wage labour. Within Indian society labour is still largely communal or shared; trade is lively but remains three-quarters within the realm of barter. The Indian has not more tendency now than he had before the coming of the Incas to accumulate material or monetary wealth, which means nothing to him. The rich man is the man who has much land on which to labour and who eats well. The Indian who obtains money, perhaps by working a spell in the mines, dissipates it immediately by treating his friends to a drinking bout, by gambling, by a religious donation or by paying for an elaborate fiesta. The Indian—or for that matter the cholo—who is honoured by being chosen as

THE INDIAN TODAY AND TOMORROW

'patron' (or *alferez*) of an annual fiesta, and who is expected to bear the major part of the costs, will save for a year in advance and pledge himself for several years to come. Otherwise he has no motive to save and economize. He does not desire social insurance but only the security that he may continue to enjoy the fruits of his own labour and that he may not be deprived of adequate land to supply the necessities of his family.

The self-centred traditionalism of the Indian, whether you call it egotism, indifference or self-preservation, may also explain the conflicting opinions of his moral nature. One school of thought represents him as perfidious, cruel, egoistic, unsociable, venal, malicious, spiteful, suspicious, deceitful, without initiative or ambition, lazy, drunken, hypocritical, untrustworthy, cringing and cowardly. Balcazar says: 'Timid, mistrustful and hypocritical as a general rule, he becomes quarrelsome and cunning when he sees himself obliged to defend his heritage, his life or that of his family and his animals. Then he shows himself reckless, bold and cruel, carried in his frenzy to cannibalism. His vengeful spirit is beyond control. And when he attacks in mass, with the *ayllu* or ranch, he becomes so terrible that he can endanger the life of the neighbouring city, rendering the use of armed force urgent.[1] The Incaic virtues summarized in the classic adage "*amasua, ama llulla, ama ckella*" ("do not steal, do not lie, do not be lazy"), have been completely forgotten. The indigene is in general addicted to thieving, laziness and lying.' Others, who know him well, assert that the Indian morality is superior to that of the white and praise his high standards and strict performance of honesty, truthfulness, conjugal fidelity, respect for family ties, obedience to law, sobriety, frugality, patience, diligence and tenacity. The two views are not irreconcilable, for the Indian in his own environment is a different being from the Indian who has joined a mining camp or the urban rabble. Tamayo has said: 'The Indian becomes demoralized and corrupt through contact with the white.' The truth is that the Indian morality is a social morality and a morality of custom and tradition. It is part of the whole of life and not separable from it. I know from my own experience that among the Indians who are living in their own world on the land, removed from the influence of the towns, you may leave your possessions with entire confidence in the charge of the poorest hovel, you may confidently

---

[1] Since the insurrection of Tupaj Catari this fear, largely mythical, constantly gnaws at the Bolivian's sense of security.

expect hospitality, truthfulness and help. Such an Indian is laborious, sober, diligent, trustworthy and meticulous in the fulfilment of his given word. Family life is strict and vice virtually unknown. Poverty is no temptation to theft. Such an Indian gets drunk at the proper occasions—at the regular fiestas, marriages, deaths—but remains sober at other times. His whole life is ruled by convention. I remember that before I had been in Bolivia a week a compatriot told me a story against himself. He had been walking in the country and had asked an Indian the way. The Indian, who spoke Spanish, reproved him with the words: 'First one says "good-day" and then one asks questions.' It was only later that I appreciated the full significance of this story. Social convention and good manners are not for the Indian separate from morality; both are rigidly conventionalized and strictly maintained. Morality is not a matter of right or wrong, but is integrated in the totality of the traditional social convention by which the Indian lives. Remove him from his traditional world and you remove the props and principles of his moral code. The moral law is the law of tradition, the strongest law the Indian knows; take away tradition and you take away the moral code.

In the towns, in the mining settlements, along the railways, the Indian will cringe, beg and steal from the white man. In the Indian settlements there are no beggars and no man steals from another. In the towns of Bolivia and Peru locks and bolts, padlocks and bars, are a major item of commerce and there are shops which stock little else. When business premises are shut for the night, not one but four or five padlocks are affixed, each representing a pound or so of metal. In the Indian villages locks and bolts are unknown; a stick placed across the open door is still enough to repel intruders. The Indian is restrained in speech, inclined to be dignified and severe. He is in general kind to children and is never known to show cruelty to his animals. He has a strong sense of justice and is more often roused to anger by injustice than by genuine oppression. Family feeling is strong, for the whole Indian communal life is based upon the family. 'Mother' and 'father' are used as terms of respect and an Indian will address a white as '*tata*' or '*mamita*'. The oft-repeated accusation of oriental fatalism, passive acceptance of his lot, or apathetic resignation, need hardly perhaps be taken very seriously. Through centuries of repression, when protest has proved fruitless and armed resistance has brought reprisals without benefits,

THE INDIAN TODAY AND TOMORROW

experience has taught him endurance in preference to extermination. The oppressor cannot logically complain. Through its long and bitter experience the race has become tinged with a kind of despair which in the Aymara shows itself as latent rancour and in the Quechua as a more sentimental sadness. But it is a despondency of longing for his own world and not for entry into the white man's world, which seems to him the less admirable.

The Aymara is dour, austere, with little flexibility or adaptability. The Quechua has a milder and more sunny nature. You may see smiles and laughter among the Quechuas as they labour upon the land; the Aymara rarely smiles. The Quechua is less taciturn, quicker and more flexible; more imaginative, with certain poetic and aesthetic gifts. His character is more sentimental, milder, more sociable. Employers of native labour find the Quechua more easily manageable, more obedient and malleable. The Quechua is less resistant than the Aymara to symbiosis with the white and more apt for mestization. In Peru of recent years there has been a considerable migration of detribalized Quechuas, driven from their lands by economic pressure to the towns, and these uprooted Indians often adapt themselves to the life of the cholo. But fundamentally the Quechua has the same qualities as the Aymara, the same independence, the same self-sufficiency, the same traditionalism.

WAY OF LIFE

Both Quechuas and Aymaras remain basically agricultural and pastoral by choice and conviction; they are firmly wedded to the soil and are not easily induced to leave it either for other occupations or for more friendly and hospitable regions. Driven from the best lands of the Altiplano, they struggle patiently on what remains to them and rarely migrate to the rich and fertile territory of the interior. They are rooted to the soil and their natural habitat is the highlands. The private and communal ownership of land by Indians has diminished notably under the Republics and the large landed estates or latifundia cover the greater part of the territory. In both Peru and Bolivia enormous tracts lie waste and depopulated, nominally under private ownership, while the Indians are crowded upon holdings below subsistence level, which they are continually compelled to abandon by economic pressure. The majority of the agrarian Indians are now settled on the landed estates, where they usually succeed in establishing the semblance of a traditional commune or *ayllu* and are allowed their own plots to work in return for three or four days' work a week for the proprietor and personal service in his household. As a general rule the lands allotted to the Indians for their own use are poor and insufficient, while large parts of the estates remain undeveloped.

No general statistics are available for the Indians who own their own land. It is known, however, that they are continually being forced by indigence to abandon their lands for the towns, the mines or for service on the large estates. Agricultural yields in the highlands of the Andes are completely dependent upon the quantity and the timing of the annual rains, which are very irregular, and on the average there are two or three bad harvests in five. The Indian communities which are living at subsistence level no longer have an adequate margin to provide against the bad years and in times of drought are forced by starvation to seek subsistence elsewhere. Tschopik estimates that an Aymara Indian of Chucuito who is considered wealthy has 0·75 acre of good land, 1·45 acres of medium land, and the use of 0·75 acre of good land belonging to a cholo landlord. His average yield in a year is 5,125 lb. of potatoes, 4,750 lb. of barley, 1,875 lb. of quinoa, 405 lb. of beans and 650 lb. of wheat. A 'poor' Aymara of the same district supports a wife and two children on 0·11 acre of poor land and the use of 0·57 acre of medium land, which yields 625 lb. of potatoes, 750 lb. of barley, 250 lb. of beans and 270 lb. of quinoa. It has been estimated that the average crop of a Quechua family of the Cuzco district is five to six bushels of maize, forty to fifty bushels of potatoes, and under two bushels of wheat.

The ancient methods of cultivation persist with little change. The digging-stick, now sometimes with an iron tip, and the clodbreaker are still the main implements, although a primitive type of plough with a thin iron blade, drawn by a yoke of oxen, was adopted from the Spanish and is now also used, particularly by the Aymaras. The ancient method of communal shared labour by *aini* is still universal and the group working on a plot will move in unison to the rhythm of a chant or the music of flutes. The women join in the agricultural work with the men. The Indians still retain their old skill in irrigation and have an astonishing knowledge of the ways of water; they can bring a small canal over miles of irregular, hilly country with such surety that you could often

THE INDIAN TODAY AND TOMORROW

swear it was flowing uphill. But the lands which remain in their possession are now rarely adapted for ambitious irrigation projects and man-power is lacking. Terracing too is now little used, except where the ancient terraces are still cultivated. It is as much as the present population can do to keep the land free from stones year by year. Wheeled vehicles are not used in agriculture. The Indian is his own beast of burden, carrying everything upon his back. In the most typical picture which I carry away of the Andean Indian he is trotting along barefoot along the stony paths, bent double and clutching in front of his chest the ends of a rope by which an enormous burden is kept in position on his back, like some grotesque and gigantic hump. Donkeys and llamas are also used for transporting agricultural produce over longer distances. The llama will carry only 65 lb. and soon tires; but it is the most sure-footed of all animals on the precipitous and unsurfaced paths and is the only animal which can find its own food on the barren stretches of the Altiplano. Not even the donkey or the goat can graze on the tough dry *ichu* grass (*paja brava*), which is the characteristic vegetation. For the other livestock alfalfa and certain types of cactus are cultivated as fodder.

The main crops are the potato, of which very many varieties are cultivated, a similar tuber called oca (*oxalis tuberosa*), quinoa, cañahua, barley and a few vegetables among which beans, onions and garlic are the most important. Quinoa and cañahua, cereals which are indigenous to the highlands, have great nutritional value and are thought to have a higher vitamin content than any other known cereals. In the warmer and sheltered valleys are produced maize, a little wheat and many varieties of fruits and vegetables. The Indians also press into service such poor vegetation as grows wild on the Altiplano. The coarse *paja brava* (*ichu* grass or *stipa pungens*), edible only by the llama and the alpaca, is used for thatching and for packing. The *totora* rush which grows by the margins of Lake Titicaca and along the banks of the river Desaguadero is put to a large number of uses—from it are made the fishing boats or *balsas* in a style which has persisted from time immemorial, mats for roofing and for bedcovers, many ingenious articles of basketry, and the thick lower stalks serve as fodder for cattle. A low shrub called tthola (*lepidohyllum quadrangulare*), yareta (*asorella biloba*) and ckeuna (*polilepis incana*) are used for fuel, as also is the dried dung of the llama.

The houses and domestic technique have suffered no appreciable change since the times before the Incas. The houses consist of a single room about twelve feet by eight, with gabled thatched roof, without windows or smoke vents, and a single low door which usually faces east. They are usually built of field stones or adobe bricks and the floor is of pounded earth. They are grouped in disorderly and untidy fashion in family compounds which also include a storage shed and corrals. The kitchen is generally a separate small building adjacent to the main house. Niches to serve as cupboards are built into the walls and a few pegs are driven in on which to hang clothes, implements or musical instruments. There is no other furniture. The bed consists of llama pelts placed upon the floor or on a low earth platform and *lipichi* or sheepskin covers are sometimes used. Their houses are sometimes decorated for fiestas by strings of coloured papers such as children use at Christmas time but are otherwise severely practical without neatness or any concession to the aesthetic sense. There is generally no heating, but the houses are made as far as possible hermetically airtight against the bitter cold and the biting Altiplano winds, which cause great suffering when not tempered by the sun.

Kitchen utensils are limited to a few pottery cooking vessels and sometimes a plate or two. The Indians eat from the pot, sitting on the ground, and require no implements. They will relieve nature in public without pudicity but dislike eating publicly and when compelled to eat away from home will sit facing a wall, hunched up over their food to escape being overlooked. Their staple diet consists of potatoes or oca (usually taken in the dehydrated form of *chuño* or *tunta*) and cereals—quinoa, cañahua or barley in the uplands and maize in the valleys. Meat is very rarely eaten and fresh meat virtually never; on very rare occasions the richer Indian may partake of a little dried meat or *charqui* in a stew with *chuño* and quinoa. In the Chaco war, however, the Bolivian Indians developed a taste for both meat and sugar and in the mining settlements they are now able to demand these additions to their diet. A certain amount of fish from Lake Titicaca is commonly eaten by the Indians within reach, usually dried or salted. Cheeses of sheep's milk are made for commercial purposes and are sold to the towns but are sometimes eaten by those of the Indians who are better off. They eat two meals a day, one just after sunrise before beginning work and the second at sunset. Most of their food is taken in the form of soup highly seasoned with *aji*, a kind of

THE INDIAN TODAY AND TOMORROW 217

chilli or capsicum which is a prime article of commerce from the valleys to the uplands, or with certain 'piquante' berries, such as the *urupica*, which grow on the sierra. Balcazar estimates that the normal diet of the 'well-fed' Indian reaches between 1,500 and 2,000 calories a day, which may be increased by a further 500 calories from chicha and alcohol. There is a permanent deficiency of animal proteins.

Every Indian chews coca, the leaves of a shrub *eritroxylon coca*, which is cultivated in the warm and moist valleys of the eastern slopes of the Cordilleras, called Yungas, and from which the alkaloid cocaine is extracted. The Indian believes that the plant is of divine origin and has magical properties; by chewing the leaves he is able to become indifferent to hunger and pain, cold and weariness, and to perform feats of physical endurance which would be beyond his powers without it. The coca habit has been an object of controversy since the earliest days of the Conquest and has usually been condemned; but the habit has persisted and coca has remained a principal article of internal commerce and the only one which is derived solely from an indigenous demand. Modern medical opinion regards the mastication of coca as a mild form of drug-taking, leading to all the deleterious consequences of drug addiction, though a few scientists have claimed that the leaves also have a nutritive value. There is some evidence that in the old days coca was a luxury, used only on special occasions or when special physical effort was called for, as from the *chasquis*. But today every Indian chews coca and chews all day long. The leaves are chewed together with a charcoal ash, usually made from burnt quinoa stalks, to increase the effect by neutralizing the acid in the digestive juices, and every two or three hours ten minutes or so rest is taken while fresh leaves are added to the gob. An Indian normally purchases a pound of coca to last him a week, and if he is working for an employer expects free and supplementary gifts of coca in addition. Coca is ubiquitous. It is sold everywhere, and everywhere bought. The woven coca pouch is a universal feature of the Indian costume. Whatever the medical opinion may turn out to be if ever discussion is ended, coca is not only the one surviving luxury of the Indian race but has become a necessity of life, without which no Indian would believe himself able to work.[1]

The national drink from the time of the Incas is *chicha*, a fermented beverage manufactured from maize or less frequently

[1] For the history of coca see Appendix to this chapter.

from quinoa or cañahua. Fermentation is produced by means of *mucko*, balls of maize flour which have been held in the mouth and after prolonged insalivation dried in the sun. *Mucko* is a common article of commerce. The cereal is boiled slowly for a day or more with *mucko*—portions of stale chicha, junks of meat, water or sugar, or herbs are added to give the distinctive flavour on which each locality prides itself—and then the brew is allowed to ferment in clay vessels for a week or a fortnight. In the Urubamba valley, near Cuzco, you may see bunches of red flowers on the end of long canes displayed in front of this or that house as a sign that chicha has been brewed, and these chicha signs of unknown antiquity cheek by jowl with tin coca-cola signs startlingly represent the juxtaposition of two civilizations. Nowadays the Indians also drink cane alcohol, which is manufactured in Santa Cruz from the sugar cane there while Bolivia imports her sugar from Peru. In the mining camps the Indian is also able to afford beer. In his own environment the Indian drinks to excess only during fiestas and then he drinks and dances from beginning to end of the fiesta. Outside his proper environment he tends to use on drink any surplus cash which may remain to him after purchasing coca. There is no doubt that the consumption of drink does something to supplement the inadequate diet—Professor Escudo has estimated that a hundred grammes of chicha produce 416 calories. And there is no doubt that in the conditions of life normal to him the Indian regards drunkenness as a ritual necessity for appropriate occasions, remaining sober the rest of the time.

A word about the Indian miners, who are a main support of Bolivian economy and almost equally necessary to Peru. The vast majority of the mine labourers are Indian, some of the bosses and lower administrative staff are cholos and the technical and higher administrative staff mainly foreigners. The mines do little therefore to bring into direct contact the white and the coloured populations of Bolivia and Peru. Of the Indian workers the majority are seasonal, combining work in the mines with agriculture. The work is of necessity hard but the conditions of the miners are better than those of any other paid labourers in the country and with the larger mining companies equal to that of European miners. They are well paid and tolerably well housed, they obtain food and all necessities below market rates at the general stores, or *pulperias*, which the companies are compelled by law to provide for them; they have social insurance, medical attention and good recreational facilities. Mining is no novelty to the Indian. Minerals were exploited by the Incas and long before them, though never before to so great an extent. Yet the Indian has not yet succeeded in acclimatizing himself to the mining settlement. Most of them gravitate to the mines through necessity and remain through inertia. Though their life is now immeasurably better in the mines, they prefer the agricultural life on the land. Moral conditions are notoriously worse in the mining camps than among the agrarian Indians. Family life is weakened and irregular unions are the rule. The women work as *palliris* or sorters (it is considered unlucky for a woman to enter the mine) and the children are employed in lighter tasks as *chivatos*; both appear to suffer the same demoralization as the men. Drunkenness is common and loses its rhythm. The rules of the white administration are resented and the traditional native rules of life are weakened. Through strong miners' unions, often controlled by political agitators, the mining settlements become centres of discontent. An enormous enthusiasm for sport, and in particular football, is the one sign of saving grace. Even the smallest camp has its 'cancha' of 'futbol', though there be room for only one set of goal-posts.

The traditional picture of the drunken, vicious, deceitful and apathetic Indian is not a true picture of the Indian in his natural and traditional state. When integrated into his own communes he is sober, hard-working, honest and meticulous. But it is a picture which is most often true of the Indian who is uprooted from his traditional way of life. For the moral standards of Indian life are the traditions which govern his whole way of life. And when these traditions are stultified, he puts nothing else in their place and a general degeneration of character is common.

TRADE

Regional variation in agricultural production results inevitably from the geographical nature of the country, where differences of altitude favour diversity of crops within comparatively short distances, and has been supplemented from very early times by elementary local specialization in handicrafts. Trade has always been lively and the Indians have barter in their blood. Even under the Inca regime, when commerce was undertaken by the State and regional produce was distributed on a national basis, local fairs and markets did not completely disappear. Today every village has its weekly market and its annual fair, usually on the name-day of the patron saint. Many of the larger annual fairs still have a more than regional importance and are combined with religious fiestas adapted to the Church calendar. Copacabana, a famous centre of Indian pilgrimage to the Virgin there, is visited annually by forty or fifty thousand people. Great fairs are still held at Pucara, Tiobamba and elsewhere. But the importance of the fair has diminished from colonial days when it was fostered by the Spanish for the sale both of merchandise imported from Europe and of local products. In the fair at Jujuy 30,000 mules used to change hands. The greatest of the colonial fairs, that of Huari, was the most important economic factor in Peru after Potosi and when the output of Potosi began to diminish became the most significant medium for the exchange of merchandise and money. Products from as far afield as the Rio de la Plata, Salta, Santiago del Estero, Tucuman, from Mojos, Chiquitos and Cochabamba, as well as the output of central Peru, were all gathered together at Huari. In his *Historia de Belgrano y la Independencia Argentina* Bartolomé Mitre ascribes to Huari a capital function in the economic development not only of Peru but the whole of South America.

While the commerce of the towns has caused the importance of these great fairs somewhat to dwindle, the importance of the local market and fair in Indian life has perhaps increased. Trade is still conducted in the immemorial manner of barter and money as a medium of exchange plays no very significant function. Even the very ancient 'silent trade' which dispenses not only with a medium of exchange but with language, and which no doubt had its origin when the proliferation of local dialects made verbal communication difficult and unsure, survives in contemporary practice. The vendor squats on the ground in the market square and lays her goods before her on her cloth *aguayo*, arranged in a number of little piles. The buyer squats before her, opens her *aguayo* and displays goods in exchange. If the goods offered are not suited to the needs of the vendor, or if the amount seems inadequate, she sits unmoved, gazing ahead, apparently unaware of the bargainer. The latter either changes or increases her offer or passes elsewhere. When a satisfactory offer is made, the vendor takes the goods without words and the buyer takes her pile of the vendor's goods. Each party to the bargain asks and receives *japa*, or overweight, in token of good feeling, and the transaction is concluded.

THE INDIAN TODAY AND TOMORROW

Transactions are petty and profits minute. Indeed the whole business is not conceived on a profit basis. There is no eagerness to sell and an Indian woman will often remain happily a whole day without effecting a sale, or will refuse to sell rather than deplete her stock. If you offer to buy oranges from an Indian woman sitting before a dozen piles of two or three oranges each, she is as likely as not to reply '*Haniwa*'—'There aren't any'. The idea is not to sell, but to effect a 'trade', as they say in the States, that will be convenient to both parties. The only articles habitually sold for money are coca, salt, aji (which in the old days almost acquired the status of a medium of exchange) and specialized manufactures like felt hats, sandals, musical instruments, etc. Yet the typically Indian character of the native market, or *katu*, is beginning to recede before the influence of the cholos, who regularly visit them in their lorries to buy up market-garden produce, eggs, poultry, grain, skins, etc., for resale in the markets of the towns. In return they sell such europeanized products as kerosene, aniline dyes (which since before the last war are largely ousting the old vegetable dyes), matches, sugar, soft drinks, coca-cola, cane alcohol, and so on. The cholos deal in money to their own considerable profit and the character of the local markets is adapting itself accordingly.

COSTUME

It is the costume of the chola, ubiquitous in towns and villages, which renders Bolivia a country exciting and strange to the tourist and makes much that is sordid seem gay. The men are much less conservative of tradition in dress than the women and both the Aymara Indian and the cholo have europeanized their costume. But the women, both Indians and cholas, are tenacious of their *polleras*, as the native costume is called, and few cholas abandon it for European style (*vestidos*). The costume, basically the same for Indian and chola, lies somewhere between the ancient Indian dress and the europeanized dress as it was worn in Peru three centuries ago, with a few recent modifications.

The skirt, or *pollera*, which gives its name to the characteristic chola style, is a boneless crinoline, tight at the waist and flowing outwards in elaborate pleats to a wide bell at the base, half-way up the calf. It is made of heavy cotton material, lined, or for gala wear of thick silk or velvet. It is generally bright and flamboyant in colour, sometimes patterned but usually plain. A chola will wear five, six, or even ten *polleras* of different colours, one over the other, their number and richness being a sign of her wealth. She does not select from her wardrobe but wears all she has got. A good cotton *pollera* costs about 800 Bolivianos, which is the average monthly wage of a chola domestic servant in a European family in La Paz.[1]

On the bust she wears a blouse of rough cotton cloth for everyday wear, and of rich silk for fiestas. Doubled over the shoulders and hanging down behind, fastened in front with a gilt or silver pin (*topo*), is a bright woollen blanket, corresponding to the male poncho, or a shawl of golden-brown vicuña wool. Above the shawl is worn the characteristic *aguayo*, a square of brilliantly coloured native material four feet wide (the native loom weaves strips two feet wide and the *aguayo* is made by sewing two strips together), which is twisted into a pouch to hang behind the shoulders, the two ends being tied together in front of the chest. In her *aguayo* the chola or Indian carries her baby and anything else she wishes to take around with her—her shopping, her bedding, or the goods she is taking to market. A chola is never seen in public without her *aguayo* and very rarely without a baby on her back. She is completely without self-consciousness in relieving the needs of nature beside the public streets, her *polleras* flaring gaily around her like the great cup of some gaudy flower, or in suckling her child before the public eye. Along the main streets of the capital, on the steps of the public buildings and the banks, you may see a nightmarish phantasmagoria of warm brown breasts with their purple-violet areolae freely exposed to the greedy lips of children. When baby is satisfied he is wrapped again in the *aguayo* and with a twist and a heave hoisted onto his mother's back.

On her head the chola wears a felt 'bowler' hat, of light or dark brown, black, grey, blue or fawn, according to taste; red is rarely worn except by children. These hats are factory made and are manufactured locally in La Paz, although the better quality are imported from the Argentine. They are worn a little on one side and seem too small for the head, but a chola seldom removes her hat except in church or in her own house, and is remarkably adept at balancing it in place. Alcides D'Orbigny, who visited La Paz in 1830, says that the chola wore 'a man's hat, usually of white felt'. This was a 'pudding basin' hat, of native manufacture from

[1] These prices correspond to the year 1949.

THE INDIAN TODAY AND TOMORROW

natural-coloured felt, such as is still worn by the poorer Indian women. The bowler, which is now universal and one of the most distinctive adjuncts of the chola costume, was introduced about 1925. The thick, straight black hair is parted down the middle of the head and hangs behind to the waist in two plaits which are tied loosely together at the bottom by a tasselled cord of llama wool about a foot long. A chola whose plaits have been cut by a jealous rival in love has no option but to remain indoors until they grow again, leaving the field clear for her rival, or to take to European clothes—either alternative equally distasteful. The typical costume formerly included high-heeled boots coming half-way up the calf, but these have gone out of general use and are replaced by low-heeled shoes or sandals.

For gala occasions this costume is extremely rich and elaborate. The *polleras* are of heavy silk or satin and very numerous; the bodice is of finely embroidered silk and above it is worn a tightly fitting and intricately worked velvet waistcoat with a silk shawl in place of the blanket. A chola in gala array is a very proudly adorned creature.

The chola costume is a survival but not an anachronism. It is still currently worn by cholas everywhere and a chola 'in *polleras*' never wears anything else. In the capital of recent years, it is true, a few of the young girls are beginning to adopt European-style clothes, but this is not approved. The chola is proud of being a chola and proud of the distinctive dress of her class. There is indeed nothing funnier than to see little girls of five or six years old dressed in the complete chola costume and solemnly carrying a doll instead of a baby in the *aguayo*. The costume carries too a social distinction, for a woman in chola dress, however rich and fine, is not allowed into the clubs which are frequented by the white class, nor into the pit of the better cinemas, but is relegated to the gallery. The maintenance of the costume by the women is a voluntary asseverance of class.

D'Orbigny, judging as a Frenchman, said: 'The costume, adapted to the cold temperature of the country, has nothing seductive about it; it creates an impression owing to its originality but does not please; it does not permit of elegant or graceful gesture.' The chola is not seductive; solid and bulky in outline, she has nothing of French elegance. Yet she is not entirely devoid of grace. Her legs and ankles are usually slim, and particularly in the dance, when the many *polleras* flow in a wide circle around her, she has a definite charm of movement. Yet the main impression is of statuesque solidity and latent vitality of robust strength. Besides its picturesqueness and originality the chola costume is saved from banality by a very unusual sense of colour. She chooses bright and vivid colours, vigorous contrasts and abhors pastel shades or subtle blendings and gradations. She seeks neither the discreet uniformity dictated by Parisian fashions nor the crude contrasts of primary colours which delight the savage, but instinctively achieves an effect of heightened colourfulness by discords of adjacent hues, the kind of colour effect which was developed by Gauguin and a few other post-Impressionist painters. The colours are never subdued but bright and garish colours are so combined that each vivifies the other instead of cancelling with the clash. The chola's vibrant colour sense is inherited from the Aymara Indian, not from the Quechuas who have it in a much less pronounced degree, and has now surpassed the Aymara. It is a tribute to its vigour that the desired effect of a maximum colourfulness—which is by no means the same thing as simple brightness or gaudiness—is now achieved with factory-dyed materials. The impression of colour is aided by the extraordinary luminosity and clarity of the atmosphere on the Altiplano and could perhaps not be successfully achieved in other conditions. The chola radiates vitality and energy and the colourfulness of her costume is perfectly suited to enhance this impression.

The costume of the Aymara Indian is similar to that of the chola but less elaborate. Her *pollera* is less elaborately pleated, made of coarse but strong 'bayeta' cloth of native weave, usually red or deep orange, sometimes a bright blue. She sometimes wears the chola bowler hat, but more usually the dun 'pudding basin' type, which is a native industry. Over her shoulders she wears a woollen blanket, generally dark in colour, and the distinctive *aguayo*. The main difference between the Indian woman and the chola in working clothes is this, that the chola uses factory-made material and the Indian wears material of native weave and dye. As she walks along the bare highland flats, tending her flocks of sheep or llamas, she is invariably busy with a simple spindle, spinning thread from wool of sheep or llama, just as in the old Inca days travelling or tending the flocks the women would always spin. The bright dress of the Indian women is visible as a fleck of vivid colour miles away across the brown parched aridity of the Altiplano.

Until recently the men wore black bell-bottomed trousers slit up the sides of the ankles and thick white woollen socks showing through the slits. Above was a short tight jacket ending at the waist. This costume was outlawed by the Bolivian Government in the twenties and the Aymara Indian now dresses as a 'poor white', though from self-woven and much patched white or grey material known as bayeta—or, if he is very poor, from the stuff of old sugar bags. He wears on his head a battered 'trilby' and beneath this, as a defence against the cold and the winds, a knitted peaked cap with flaps coming down over the ears. Every Indian now wears a poncho, which wraps him round to the ankles. The poncho is a simple but very effective and useful garment. It is simply a large square of stuff made usually from llama wool, with a slit cut in the centre through which to thrust the head. On their feet both men and women wear home-made sandals (*ojota*) of untanned cowhide (or recently from the rubber of used tyres), with a strap which passes inside the big toe and behind the heel. When walking over particularly rough or stony ground the Indian will usually carry his sandals to avoid wear. Both men and women carry at the waist a small woven pouch in which they keep the daily ration of coca. It is sometimes covered on the outside with old silver coins—for the Indian still tends to regard metal coinage as an object intended for preservation and decorative use rather than as a medium of exchange.

The dress of the Quechua Indians has remained distinct from that of the Aymaras and retains many regional variations of style, despite the fact that the Incas are said to have attempted to introduce uniformity. The men as well as the women have retained a distinctive dress and have not in general adopted a modern European style like the Aymaras. The men wear short breeches which leave the knee exposed and below the knee their legs are bare. The hair is worn long, falling down to the shoulders. Over an open shirt made of cheap cotton material or bayeta they wear a sleeveless jacket and a poncho which is shorter than that of the Aymara. Suspended from the left shoulder by a woven strap they carry a large and beautifully patterned woven pouch. The women's costume is less vivid in colour than that of the Aymaras, though in some districts such as Cuzco the festive wear is colourful in a more subdued way. The Quechua woman wears a skirt (*aksu*) which is longer than the *pollera* of the Aymara and without the belling effect of the *pollera*. She does not, like the Aymara, wear a number of skirts. Above the *aksu* she wears an open shirt or bodice and over this a mantle fastened in front of the throat and hanging down to the knees, like the male poncho but covering the back only and not circling round to the front. Even the *aguayo* is less brightly coloured than that of the Aymaras.

The most varied feature of the Quechua costume is the hat, which shows regional differences everywhere. In Oruro and Cochabamba of Bolivia the Quechua women wear a hat of hard straw enamelled white, with a high crown like a Welsh milkmaid's hat. The base of the crown is ornamented with black ribbon with designs which vary from district to district. In Potosi the hat is similar in shape but black or dark green felt and looks like the traditional witch's hat. The women of Sucre wear no hat and are known for this reason as 'bare heads' (*cabeza pelada* or in Aymara *ccara-peke*). Elsewhere a kind of shovel hat of felt is worn and around Cuzco a wide-brimmed low-crowned hat covered with bayeta cloth. Cieza de León says of the headgear worn in the sixteenth century: 'On their heads they wear a kind of birettas like mortars, made of their wool, which they call chucos. And their heads are all very long without occiput, for in childhood they crush them and mould them to the shape they wish. The women put on their heads a kind of biggin, almost the same shape as those of the friars.'

RELIGION

The Indian temperament inclines deeply to reverence for both human and divine superiors. His submissiveness to constituted authority which facilitated the political organization of the Incas and the domination of the Spanish explains also his ready piety within the Catholic faith. But it is a Catholicism which has been combined with traditional beliefs and superstitions and converted from a religion of salvation to a religion of this life. For the religious outlook of the Indian remains strictly practical and his religious acts are intended to exert a favourable influence upon the affairs of this world. Since the Dominican friar Vicente de Valverde, chaplain to Pizarro, propounded the articles of Christian faith to Atahuallpa at Cajamarca through the interpreter Felipillo, who—according to Garcilaso—explained that the Christians believed in 'three Gods and one God and that made four', Christian doctrine has made rather little progress among the

THE INDIAN TODAY AND TOMORROW

native population, which is not inclined to metaphysical clarification. The Christian doctrines of the after-life—heaven and hell, salvation, punishment and reward after death—are verbally accepted where they are taught, but have little real meaning and less influence among a practical people who are concerned only with the needs of this life and are interested in the souls of the dead only in so far as they may have power to affect living society. Christian ritual and hagiology have, on the other hand, a much stronger appeal, worship of the saints alongside traditional deities is universal and the sale of religious candles is one of the most flourishing branches of commerce to the native population.

In the very early years of the Conquest the natives were compulsorily subjected to mass baptism, but Christianity made slow headway against strong passive opposition. A religion which was inculcated by violence and the sword, whose accredited exponents were among the instruments of a savage oppression, made little appeal to a simple and upright race. The national State religion of the Incas disappeared with the fall of Inca power and the collapse of the Inca priesthood, for it had been a religion whose main content was its ceremonial worship of the divine Sun-dynasty; but the bulk of the immemorial religious tradition, the beliefs, superstitions, ritual and cults, survived and survive, though the plasticity of the Indian mind soon proved amenable to the Christian teachings which were at first repudiated. In the seventeenth century the Church initiated an extensive campaign for the extirpation of idolatry and in 1667 it was announced that the conversion of the Quechuas was completed and genuine idolatry no longer existed in Peru. Such an optimistic verdict was possible only because the Church itself made its standards somewhat more lenient and introduced the old scholastic distinction between idolatry and harmless superstition. For while many Indians now accepted Christianity—or such parts of it as they understood—with genuine belief, and many more from motives of opportunism, the old *huaca* religion and the old superstitious rituals persisted. But the Church decided that the worship of the *huacas* and the traditional rituals were not idolatry, were not heretical and did not involve infidelity in a convert, so long as they did not involve the attribution of divine essence to the objects of worship. And as the Indian has never thought of divine essence in the abstract but has worshipped many deities without bothering to define their relation to Huirajocha or Pachacamac in a metaphysical sense, it was not difficult for him to meet the Church authorities in this without conscious insincerity. Thus after 1650 many native practices which had before been the object of militant missionary repression came to be tolerated as harmless, if deplorable, superstitions and the way lay open for the advance of syncretic Christianity. Since that time it has not looked back.

Despite resolutions in 1697 and 1725 and a Papal brief in 1766 declaring that the Indians should be educated and admitted to religious orders, they were successfully excluded by means of the institution of royal patronage and Christianity has remained, like the Inca State religion before it, a religion imposed and administered from above. It has not been less effective for that reason. Since the middle of the seventeenth century syncretization has proceeded and it has become a functional part of native life. In the great insurrections directed against colonial administration loyalty to the Church was professed. And now Christian belief and cult, its meaning and intention often distorted out of all recognition, is incongruously welded in an ineluctable fusion with native practice. God and Christ are two deities living in amity together; often Christ is regarded as supreme. God is sometimes identified with Inti, the Sun, and curious results follow when this identification is combined with the old belief that the Sun is liable to fall ill and his illness, indicated by the rainbow, may contaminate the drinking water and bring disease upon the community. The Virgin is mainly worshipped in identification with Pachamama, Mother Earth, both fertility powers, and certain figures of the Virgin are centres of pilgrimage, working miracles of healing, bringing fertility to the childless and good luck to all. But the lesser deities, the *aukis* or mountain spirits, the *apus* or place spirits and the local saint are thought to be more directly and regularly concerned with human affairs, and therefore more necessary to be propitiated. The annual mass on the local saint's day, for which the whole Indian community saves remorselessly and pays most gladly, is made the occasion of the most important regional fiesta and upon its punctilious and lavish celebration the prosperity of the year's work is believed to depend. All public ceremonies are now co-ordinated with the Church calendar. Today no more than in pre-Columban days does the Indian try to systematize his pantheon. His religion remains a thing of uncoordinated bits and pieces. As Mishkin rightly says, 'the modern Quechua have not developed a highly integrated religion. The

THE INDIAN TODAY AND TOMORROW

elements often do not jibe; there is no attempt to relate one element to another. In distinction to Mexican, or let us say, Guatemalan examples, Quechua religion appears to be a loose jumble of beliefs, ideas, and practices, disconnected and unsystematized.' The common feature running through the whole is its practical nature and its orientation to the affairs of this life. Doctrine is rudimentary, mysticism is absent, ritual is performed to ensure that the results of toil will be blessed and defended from the evil powers here and now.

The composite nature of contemporary Indian religion leaps most strikingly to the eye in the fiestas of the saints' days and the processions of the Virgin. The ceremony begins with a celebration of Mass in the village church, during which the whole of the silver wealth of the community—large and small silver salvers, ceremonial silver staffs of office, silver ornaments and decorations, *topos* or dress pins, goblets and chalices, plates and masks—is displayed upon a large board raised above the main door of the church. After the conclusion of the Mass the image of the Virgin is walked in procession around the streets, followed by a band of pious women and attended with demonstrations of deep devotion. The procession is followed by two or three Indian musical bands, each with its groups of costume dancers. The traditional native music is played on the traditional instruments, percussion and a large variety of woodwinds, which have survived from pre-colonial days with very little European influence. As in Inca days when representatives of all the peoples of the empire assembled together in their typical costumes for the great festivals of Raimi, so today at these local celebrations the dancers imitate by their costumes a wide variety of different peoples and characters. Many dress as the various savage jungle tribes of the interior. Some in white 'judge's' wigs and enormous feathered head-dresses appear to represent high officials. Some wear devil masks; others wear the mask and costume of the lion, the tiger and the bear. The Indian has an instinctive gift for caricature, and mimics the Spanish Conquistador, priest and nobleman to very humorous effect. A more recent arrival is the long-nosed mask caricaturing the Jew. Most of the costumes and gestures are traditional and stereotyped and the modern dancers are often no longer aware what it is they are mimicking. There are round dances and trooped dances, all with a rather solid, rolling rhythm of movement, and dancing is always accompanied by drinking. Men and women can continue dancing as long as they can stand and stop only when they fall down and are unable to rise. It is impossible to convey in words the immense incongruity between these ageless native ritual dances and costumes and the Christian ceremonial which accompanies them. During the fiestas to the Virgin you will feel like a wave the utter whole-hearted sincerity of native piety and you will see the natives too in the ultimate abandonment of intoxication. For the Indian of the Andes intoxication has always had a ceremonial meaning; by ancestral custom and present conviction it is an essential part of religious performance, not an indulgence but a ritual.

It is impossible to draw any line between religion and superstition or to separate either from secular life. Every activity, every action, is conventionalized and stereotyped by tradition, and the Indian himself recognizes no distinction between religious and secular tradition. It is as necessary to bury a dried llama embryo in the ground on which a house is built as to lay the foundations well. Dried llama foetuses are sold in every Indian market and always for magical purposes. It is as necessary in time of drought that the children and dogs should howl for rain in the traditional way as it is to recite the *Misericordia* and pray to the saint. Offerings of coca or alcohol, purificatory ceremonies, are as essential as the work of agriculture and building. Baptism is important to prevent the spirit of a child which should die unbaptized returning to injure the community and keep away the rains. Christian marriage is regarded as lucky and most couples try during the first two or three years companionate marriage (*sirvinacuy*) to save enough to pay for the Church ceremony. It would be impossible to root out superstition without uprooting the very bases of native society and building society anew.

THE FUTURE

The tendency to glorify the lost greatness of the Incas and to deplore the deterioration of that high level of social organization which was achieved before the Spanish Conquest is not limited to sentimental historians of the past. Francis Violich, who wrote a survey of contemporary urban problems in ten Latin-American countries, gives the following verdict. 'With the inspiration and the challenge of the Andes behind them, the Incas built a great and prosperous civilization, rich in art and high social standards, in a

THE INDIAN TODAY AND TOMORROW

little more than 400 years. In the same amount of time—400 years—our European culture has humiliated man before these mountains and lowered the descendants of the Incas to a condition scarcely better than that of its native animals. There is much to be learned and much to accomplish before we can justify bringing the benefits of our civilization to the Incas. Even down along the dry desert coast of Peru the remains of Chan-Chan and other pre-Inca towns indicate the high civilization of peoples who lived thousands of years ago. The most significant fact to consider in studying these cities is that, completely lacking our technical development, they were able to plan and provide for living facilities of a high order, and for a remarkable use of natural resources. They planned and provided in the interest of the community. Such accomplishments put us on the spot: if they were able to achieve a fairly high standard of living with their limited means, we, today, with miraculous techniques on every hand, are left without a single excuse for poverty, bad housing, or poorly equipped cities, whether in South America or in North America.'
In the examination of social problems it is necessary beyond all to keep our feet firmly planted upon solid ground and to avoid sentimentality. There is no doubt that Bolivia and Peru are 'backward' countries in the accepted sense of the term, that the standard of life of their native populations, which preponderate, is notably lower than that of the general run of working communities. There is no doubt that this depressed standard of life represents a deterioration from the relatively happy and flourishing social life of Inca days. But there is equally no doubt that the introduction of European technical culture represents enormously increased potentialities for raising the standard of life above the level which was possible with the facilities available to the Incas; that these potentialities have been realized for the minority at the expense of a worsening in the conditions of the majority results from the pattern of social organization.

It is a mistake to picture the social problem of Bolivia and Peru as a class problem on the orthodox Marxist lines. The depressed class is an 'inferior' race and a race which has no longer a strong consciousness of racial unity. Of the Quechuas Mishkin says, 'There seems to be absent among the Quechua of today any strong intercommunity feeling. Certainly, no current of a national consciousness exists.' And Tschopik gives the same judgment about the Aymaras. 'Today, the Aymara have no feeling of national unity in spite of a common language and similar customs.' My own observations agree with these verdicts. The Indian consciousness of being an Indian is an awareness of belonging to a depressed social class but does not involve a positive feeling of cohesion or racial loyalty. Nor is there even an incipient conflict of classes in the Marxist economic sense. The Indians do not even secretly aspire to class dominance within the economic structure of the modern states but vigorously resist any closer integration into the existing social organization. They aspire to a renewal of their traditional agricultural community life and passive racial consciousness restrains them from any collective desire for economic domination within the State. They desire rather to remove themselves from the State and to live outside it, both economically and politically. In these countries you not only have a ruling race and a depressed race, but you have two races and two cultures existing side by side. The Indians, as has been said, still survive virtually in their Bronze Age and still refuse to adapt themselves to the modern invention of the Economic State.

The future of the Indian peoples will henceforward be decided by the future of the countries in which they are numerically dominant. While sentimental and moral considerations are seldom perhaps entirely without influence in the course of social affairs, in this case the solutions proposed by the sentimentalist and the moralist, who have usually failed to understand the peculiar outlook of the Andean Indian, have been no less opposed to the aspirations of the Indian than to the interests of the whites. The future of the Indians will, then, whether we like it sentimentally or not, whether we approve it morally or not, be decided by the practical needs of the white states of which they form an unwilling but necessary part. And the problems which both Bolivia and Peru are facing are fundamentally the same. Both countries are impeded by inadequate man-power; both countries are economically dependent upon the man-power supplied by the Indians; and both countries are aware that even the available man-power is being very inadequately used. Three opposed solutions are commonly propounded within these countries themselves. (1) The Indian peoples can and should be rescued and regenerated by education and social reform so that they may exercise an active and positive function, economically and socially, in the countries in which they preponderate. (2) The Indian races are doomed to slow extinction; they are finished and the solution of the countries' problems must

THE INDIAN TODAY AND TOMORROW

be sought elsewhere. (3) The future of the Indian races, as the future of their countries, lies in increasing mestization, in the cholo class, as with Mexico.

1. The education of the Indians is continually projected and constantly discussed but is very unlikely to be put into effect. The Indians themselves have often shown an eagerness for village schools where they could learn Spanish, but still show stubborn resistance to those forms of education which would lead them away from their traditional ways of life towards a closer integration with the alien forms of modern culture around them. Indian children who have received education in schools return to the community and forget what has been learnt. At heart the Indian people desire beyond anything else to perpetuate their traditional communal life. The white ruling minorities are at heart no more anxious to educate the native majorities for real social responsibility, which would logically lead to the termination of the white supremacy and a shift of political power to the coloured majorities; for both Bolivia and Peru are nominal democracies where every citizen who can read and write his name has the right to vote. By producing an overwhelming majority of politically conscious Indians, even if it could be done in face of the Indian's own lack of political interest, the ruling white minorities would risk losing their control. Against resistance on both sides this is unlikely to happen.

While the political results of education, if it could be achieved, are always realized, its practical significance in the economic life of the country has not been thought out. The regeneration, if not the ultimate future, of the Indian races could be practically assured by granting to them adequate lands for their needs and in both countries this could be done without encroaching upon land in profitable use. Education of peoples subject to such economic depression as the present-day Indians is putting the cart before the horse. Their economic condition could be improved without cost by distribution of unused (not unowned) lands and an increase in their numbers would follow automatically. As their own economic condition was kept above bare subsistence level, their economic contribution to the country might become more positive. It must be recognized, however, that the probability of this solution being adopted is also very remote.

2. The view that the Indian is without the inherent ability to adapt himself to European civilization is almost certainly false.

Under the Colony the Indians showed themselves not only skilled craftsmen but able under Spanish guidance to achieve high competence in pictorial and sculptural art. They have shown themselves competent to deal with modern machinery and since the Conquest they have proved capable of adopting many European agricultural techniques which did not seem to conflict with their traditional modes of life. But by and large the attitude of repudiation towards the European culture and the modern State persists.

If, then, the Indian races are gradually to die out, as seems perhaps the most probable on all accounts, the problem of man-power will become ever increasingly acute. The future prosperity of Peru and Bolivia is bound up with their success in taking measures to increase the available labour force. If the alternative of the immigration of a white labouring class is adopted, it will mean in the long run the extinction of the Indian peoples. But it would also be contrary to the whole tradition of Latin America, where the white man controls and regulates but does not supply common labour. Moreover, large parts of both Bolivia and Peru are probably unsuitable, either because of altitude or because of the tropical climate, for the proliferation of a white labouring population.

3. The most recent school of sociological thought, which is gaining steadily in strength, looks to increasing mestization to create a new national culture that shall be neither a mere reflection of European cultures nor a mere survival of indigenous culture but a fertile spirit born of the amalgamation of the two through the new creative cholo race. Tamayo spoke of mestization as 'the fulfilment of the historical fatality which is our destiny and the most solid basis of the national consciousness'. Frederico Avilo says of Bolivia, 'we are advancing slowly but surely to the minting of a new racial type, the American biological synthesis: the *New Indian*. It is the indubitable depository of our present national energy, the *mestizo*, who will produce, as he is already producing, this new subject of our history, this new creator of a national culture.' Yet even the most enthusiastic protagonists of the 'new Indian' and the new national *mestizo* cultures are driven to admit that the new race, the new nationalisms and the new cultures are still ideals which the historical cholo of actuality does little to fulfil. As the Peruvian writer Frederico Bolanos says: 'The process of mestization has still to manifest its most perfect florescence in quality, stamp and vigour',

Ideals and aspirations are useful to energize our efforts, but it is good too sometimes to test them against the more solid if less inspiring bedrock of fact. Yet the facts about the cholo race are not easy to determine. There are cholo families which, having reached the upper levels of society, have intermarried with white families and become almost indistinguishable from the whites. At the other end of the scale are cholo families living within the Indian environment and distinguished from them only by a superior economic position. The great bulk of the cholo class is outwardly more close to the Indian than to the white—the native blood appears to predominate at least up to the third or fifth generation. In appearance the typical cholo—if one can yet speak of a type—is somewhat less pigmented than the Indian, more pigmented than the white; is sturdier and more thick-set than the Indian in build; he is more vivacious than Indian or white; he has a lively though undisciplined intelligence; and he usually has social and economic ambitions which act as a driving force. Unlike the Indian, the cholo often has a strong sense of patriotism. It is certain that many of the outstanding Republican leaders have been cholos—men like Santa Cruz, Murillo, Tamayo, Melgarejo and Belzu—and it is certain that the cholo class is assuming an ever more important position in the economy of the countries. It is impossible to doubt its energy and vigour and there is no reason to suppose that the racial mixture carries with it any inherent defects of character or intelligence. But the cholo lacks as a race the inherited cultural tradition of the European and has torn up those roots in the soil which feed the best moral tradition of the Indian. While the cholo has energy and capacity, I have found no evidence that he has the creative power to evolve the new culture which is desired.

If we forsake idealistic speculation for sober fact, it is very doubtful too whether increased mestization is a possible remedy even for the narrow problem of deficient man-power—whether in fact it is anything more than words. In the early years of the Conquest admixture between the Spanish and the Indian women was the rule. Some of the soldier conquerors celebrated regular marriages with ladies of the Inca nobility and all sated their desires in irregular unions, giving early rise to the large cholo class. And there is some reason to believe that this free racial mixture to some extent saved the situation in Peru, for in the eastern departments of Bolivia, the Beni and Santa Cruz, where admixture did not take place, the indigenous races have practically disappeared and some of the finest lands in South America are languishing of inanition owing to the utter inadequacy of the population. But the facts are that direct mestization has virtually ceased everywhere. For more than two centuries there has been no intermarriage of white with red and contact between the two races has become an unthinkable social solecism except perhaps if the young white in the 'teen years cares to sow his wild oats among the Indians of the family estate. At the bottom of the social scale cholos who have sunk economically to the level of the Indians will intermarry without racial repugnance with richer Indian families; and at the top of the scale cholo families which have assimilated themselves with the whites may be able to marry into near-white families. But apart from these two extremes the cholos now intermarry among themselves and the racial gap between white and red has become so firmly established as to be virtually absolute. Brazil may be a racial melting-pot but for more than two centuries Bolivia and Peru have been the reverse. Not only is there no sign of an increase of mestization but the mestization of the early days of the colonial epoch has long ceased.

I have attempted to tell of the history of the Aymara and Quechua Indians, of their present conditions and culture, and of the problems which they constitute for the states which have grown up around them. I have mentioned the several solutions which have suggested themselves of their future, from extermination to incorporation, but I do not care to venture a prediction as to what solution, if any, is likely to be attempted. Whatever is done will be done from economic necessity and not for the benefit of the Indians—though their survival may, of course, prove an economic necessity which has to be secured. My own view is that their economic status could be raised at little cost by increasing their lands from the unused lands of Bolivia and Peru and that this would have a beneficial effect on the economies of those countries, though it probably would not be a final solution of their labour problems. I realize that it is unlikely in the extreme that this course will be adopted in either country.

Appendix

COCA: THE GREEN GOLD OF THE YUNGAS

Long long ago in the remote ages of the Collasuyu, says an Aymara legend, Indians from the Altiplano found their way over the crest of the mountains, what the Spanish call the brow or *ceja*, into the tropical rain forests of the Yungas, those deep canyon-like valleys which thrust their long fingers into the eastern slopes of the Cordillera. Here they found rich and fertile land, good earth for their farmsteads and a nature prodigal of vegetation. But the forest was lord of all and there was no free land upon which to farm. In this predicament they set fire to the undergrowth in order to clear a little space for their needs. But the fire they had set blazed and spread through the forest until it was seen like a roaring inferno below by Khuno, the god of snow and storm, from his palaces on the snow-clad peaks of Illimani and Illampu. And the smoke rose up from the valleys and filled the horizon and polluted his pure mansions of ice. Angered thereat Khuno assembled his weapons of lightning and thunderbolt and hurled down hail and storm upon the valleys, wounding and rending the earth. The conflagration was extinguished but all living vegetation was destroyed with it and even the trees which had survived the fire were denuded by the force of the hail. Coming out from the caves in which they had taken refuge from the storm, the guilty Indians found nothing but desolation around them, nor was there any longer a path back to the highlands. Wandering desolate and famished, at last they found in a little clearing surrounded by leafless trees an unknown plant of bright and brilliant green, which the wrath of the storm-god had been unable to destroy. Gathering the leaves of this plant they placed them in their mouths to stay the pangs of hunger, and immediately they were invaded by a sense of supreme well-being. They no longer felt the hunger, the weariness or the cold. Refreshed with new energy they returned to Tihuanacu, where they revealed the secret of this marvellous plant to the *auquis*[1] and the *amautas* and thus the knowledge of coca spread throughout the sierra.

[1] Elders.

Coca, or *cuca* as it is pronounced in the native tongues, *erythroxylum coca*, the 'divine plant' of the Incas or the 'green gold' of the Yungas, has been cultivated for how many centuries we know not in the deep valleys of the eastern Cordillera, prized and revered by the Indians of the highlands. There is no way we can know how far back its use dates into the past. But coca leaves have been discovered in the early tombs and burial grounds of the Pacific coast which must date from near the beginning of the Christian era. They are contained in small woven bags attached to the desiccated bodies of the dead, exactly like the pouches, or *chuspa*, in which the modern Indian carries his coca. Some of these leaves, still well preserved by the dry, hot sandy soil in which they had lain buried, were brought to England and investigated by C. Olive Griffiths in 1930 for the Pharmaceutical Society of Great Britain. In the museums too one may see many evidences that coca was an indulgence of very great antiquity in the Andes. I myself possess a portrait jar from Tihuanacu in which the characteristic bulge of the coca quid in the cheek is clearly marked.

About the way of life of the people in the very early times our knowledge is of the slightest. But in Inca times we know that coca was the object of semi-religious mystery and reverence. Coca leaves were used by the wise men, or *amautas*, for divination and were burnt as a sacred fumigant before religious ceremonies and to purify suspected places from evil spirits and the spirits of disease. They were offered in ritual sacrifice to the gods, to propitiate the earth-goddess Pachamama, and to ward off ill luck. A tincture of coca is thought to have been one of the ingredients in the process of mummification which is still imperfectly understood. Plasters and poultices of coca leaves were applied, then as now, to wounds and contusions, and infusions of coca were given then, as they are today, as a remedy for stomach and intestinal afflictions. And among the modern Indians coca has lost nothing of its former medical and magical importance. It is still used by the diviner (*yatiri*) to foretell the future and by the magician (*pako*) and the doctor (*kollasiri*) to diagnose the cause of disease. Coca is still offered to Pachamama to ensure her favour for the crops and is burnt to bring good luck to a new house that is built. Coca leaves are offered to the dead and to all supernatural powers. A simple offering consists of six perfect leaves placed green side up one above the other (*aita*). A more elaborate offering consists of 144 *aita* in twelve rows of twelve. And the most effective offering of all is to burn a block of llama fat with coca at midnight inside a ring of dried llama dung and to throw the ashes into a stream. Today as heretofore coca is no less essential a part of the ritual life of the Indian than it is a daily necessity and indulgence.

Garcilaso says that in Inca times coca was less abundant than in his own day, for it was eaten only by the Inca and his relations and by certain curacas to whom the King as a great favour sent a few bales a year. If its use was so limited under the Incas, Prescott pungently remarks, 'the people gained one luxury by the Conquest'. But the bulk of evidence goes to show that its use was fairly general before the Spanish reached Peru and indeed the habit was so universal and so firmly established so soon after the Conquest that it is impossible reasonably to doubt that the common people had indulged it before.

For hear what the earliest chroniclers have to say. In 1555, only twenty years after the Conquest, the explorer Augustín de Zárate, who visited the silver mines of Potosi, reported: 'In certain valleys among the mountains grows a shrub called coca, which the Indians value above gold or silver. . . . This plant possesses the virtue, well known to the indigenes, that by keeping its leaves in the mouth one does not feel hunger or thirst.'

Writing in 1550, the alert and inquisitive soldier-traveller Cieza de León tells us: 'In Peru, in all its extent, it was the custom, and is, to carry this coca in the mouth and from morning until they retire to sleep they carry it without emptying it from their mouths. And when I enquired of certain Indians why they keep their mouths ever filled with that herb (the which they eat not nor do they more than carry it between their teeth), they say that they have little sense of hunger and feel great vigour and strength. For my part I believe that it must have some effect, though rather indeed it seems a vicious custom and the sort to be expected of a people such as these Indians are. In the Andes from Guamanga to the town of Plata this coca is cultivated and it grows on small trees which much they tend and cherish that they shall produce the leaf they call coca, which is a form of myrtle, and they dry it in the sun and then pack it in certain long and narrow bales, each one a little over one arroba.[1] And in 1548, 1549 and 1551 this coca or herb was so prized in Peru that it is beyond imagination that there can have been in the world herb or root or produce of a tree which produces every year like this—except spices, which

[1] Arroba: a Spanish measure, about 25 lb.

are a different matter—so highly valued. . . . This coca was taken to be sold to the mines of Potosi and so many gave themselves to planting it and gathering the leaves that it is now worth much less; but it will never cease to be prized. There are some in Spain now rich with the profits they have made from this coca, buying it up and selling it to the markets of the Indians.'

And Garcilaso de la Vega, himself a descendant of the Incas, writing somewhat later but with a very thorough knowledge of the Indian habits which he had remembered from the days of his youth, tells the same story of the great store which the Indians set by coca and the astonishing commercial importance which it acquired almost from the beginning of the Spanish dominion. 'Nor shall there be cause to forget the herb which the Indians call *cuca* and the Spaniards *coca*, which has been and is the principal wealth of Peru for those who have done commerce therein; rather will it be just that it be described at length in accordance with the great estimation in which the Indians hold it, for the many and great virtues which they knew of it before and the many more since the Spanish have experimented here in matters of medicine. Father Blas Valera, a man diligent and attentive and one who lived many years in Peru and left it more than thirty years after me, writes of both as one who has seen their proof. I shall repeat without embellishment what he says and then I shall add the little which he omitted to say, and to avoid prolixity abbreviating much.

'He says, then: "Cuca is a shrub of the height and thickness of the vine; it has few branches and on them many delicate leaves, the width of the thumb and in length about half the length of the thumb, of agreeable odour but not very sweet, which leaves the Indians and the Spanish call *cuca*. So pleasant is cuca to the Indians that they prefer it to gold and silver and precious stones. They plant it with great care and sedulity and gather it with more. For they pick the leaves one by one by hand and dry them in the sun and when dry they eat them, but do not swallow; they merely savour the fragrance and swallow the juice. The value and vigour which the labourers derive from cuca may be gathered from the fact that the Indians who eat it show themselves stronger and more apt for labour; and often, satisfied with it, they work the whole day long without eating. Cuca preserves the body from many infirmities and our doctors use it in powdered form to arrest and placate the swelling of wounds; to strengthen broken bones; to draw out cold from the body and prevent it from entering in; to treat festering sores when they are full of worms. And if with such singular virtue it does such notable benefits for external maladies, shall it not have even greater virtue and power in the bowels of those who eat of it?

"It hath too yet another great profit and this is that the greater portion of the income of the Bishop and canons and other clergy of the Cathedral Church of Cuzco derives from tithes upon the cuca leaves; and many Spaniards have grown rich and are still growing rich from the commerce of this herb. But some, ignorant of all these things, have spoken and written much against this shrub, influenced only by the fact that in ancient times the gentiles, and now certain sorcerers and diviners, offered and offer cuca to the idols; for the which, they say, it should be banished and prohibited entirely. Certainly this had been passing good counsel had the Indians been accustomed to offer only this herb to the devil. But whereas the ancient gentiles and the modern idolators sacrificed and sacrifice crops, vegetables and fruits, those which grow above and those which grow below the earth, and offer their beverage and cold water and wool and their clothes and herds and many other things, everything in fact which they possess, and as they should not be deprived of all, so should not they be deprived of that herb. They should be taught, abhorring superstitions, to serve one only God in truth and to use all those things in Christian fashion."

'Thus far Father Blas Valera. Adding what is lacking, for greater plenitude, we shall say that those shrubs are of the height of a man. To cultivate them they plant seed in a nursery, as with green vegetables; they make trenches for them, as for vines; they transplant the seedlings, as the vine; they take great care that no root, however small it be, shall be bent, for that is enough to cause the plant to wither. They gather the leaves, taking each branch separately between the fingers and running up it by touch until they reach the bud, and they must stop short of it or the whole branch withers. In verdancy and structure the leaf, back and front, is like to the arbute, save that three or four of those leaves, so delicate they are, make in thickness one leaf of the arbute. It delighteth me much to find in Spain things so suitable to which to compare those of my land and which are found not there, in order that there and here they may understand and know the one by the other. When the leaf is gathered they dry it in the sun. It must not be completely dried, for it loses much of its verdancy which is much prized and crumbles to dust, so delicate it is; nor must it retain much humidity or in the bales into which it is packed to be transported from place to place it grows mouldy and rots. It must be left at a certain point between moist and dry. The bales are made of split canes, of which there are many and good, both thin and thick, in those provinces of the Antis (*i.e.* the tropical valleys). And with the leaves of the thick canes, which are more than a third of a yard broad and half a yard long, they cover the bales outside, that the cuca shall not get wet, for water damages it much. And they tie up the bales with a special kind of hemp, which also grows in that district. When you consider the quantity of each of these things which is used in the service of cuca, it behoves rather to give thanks to God, who thus provides all where its necessity arises, than to write of it, being beyond belief. If all these things, or any one of them, had to be brought from elsewhere, the labour and the cost would be greater than the profit. That herb is gathered every four months, three times in the year, and if the many weeds which continuously grow among it are well and frequently rooted out, for the earth of that region is very damp and very hot, each harvest may be brought forward more than fifteen days and thus may be obtained nearly four harvests in a year. For the which reason a greedy proctor of tithes, who lived in my time, suborned the foremen of the principal and richest demesnes in the district of Cuzco that with much assiduity they should have them weeded frequently and with this diligence he deprived the proctor for the following year of two-thirds of the tithe on the first gathering. For the which there arose a bitter lawsuit between them but its result I, as a boy, did not learn.

'Among the other virtues of cuca it is said to be good for the teeth. Of the strength it gives to those who carry it in the mouth I remember a story which I heard in my country from a cavalier of blood and quality named Rodrigo Pantoja, and it happened that travelling from Cuzco to Rimac he came upon a poor Spaniard (for there are poor there as here), who was going on foot and was carrying on his back his little daughter two years of age. He was an acquaintance of Pantoja and thus they spoke together.

'Said the cavalier: "Wherefore is it that you walk thus laden?"

'The peon replied: "I am without the means to hire an Indian to carry this child for me and therefore I am carrying her myself".

'As the soldier spoke, Pantoja looked at his mouth and saw

THE INDIAN TODAY AND TOMORROW

that it was full of cuca. And as at that time the Spaniards held abominable all that the Indians ate and drank, for that it seemed to them a thing vile and degraded, he said: "Though it be true what you say of your need, why are you eating cuca, as the Indians do, a thing loathsome and abominable to the Spanish?"

'Replied the soldier: "Verily, sir, I too abominated it nothing less than those others, but my necessity forced me to imitate the Indians and carry it in my mouth; for I assure you that if I carried it not, I could not support my load. But by its means I feel such strength and vigour that I can suffer the toil I bear."

'Pantoja was astonished to hear him and recounted the story in many parts, and from that time forward they gave some credit to the Indians, who said that they ate it of necessity and not from greed. And so one must believe; for the herb has not a good taste.'

Thus in the first generation of the Colony the coca myth began and for a time nothing was too fabulous to be stated and believed, while successive chroniclers rivalled one another in their praises of the magic plant which enabled the Indians to sustain incredible feats of endurance without food, drink or sleep. At the same time more cautious voices made themselves heard and there were some who averred that this indulgence in coca was a cause of the misery and degradation of the Andean Indian, for which in fact the Spanish oppression was mainly responsible. The blunt Spanish soldiers simply regarded it as the sort of filthy habit which might well be expected of a race they assumed to be inferior and debased; the religious authorities, as Blas Valera said, set up in opposition against it because of its connection with many native superstitions which they regarded as idolatrous. Even in the second half of the sixteenth century one can observe the seeds of the great controversy about coca which is not yet ended. Its value was repudiated by the Council of Lima and in 1569 a Royal Cedula stated that the belief that coca does away with hunger and gives added vigour for toil was an illusion of the devil. In 1572 the Viceroy Francisco de Toledo, influenced partly by unfavourable propaganda in Europe and partly by the abuses of Indian labour on the coca plantations, forbade the payment of tribute in coca and prohibited its cultivation and use. But the demand continued. Toledo's prohibition was cancelled by Royal Cedula in 1573, and the practical necessity to maintain the supply of coca for the Indian labour employed in the mines became ever more firmly established, while the revenues derived by the Spanish from its commerce grew from day to day. When the city of La Paz was founded in the basin of the river Choqueyapu in 1548, it was intended that it should serve as a half-way house for the rich convoys bringing silver from Potosi to the coast. But much of its prosperity derived too from the traffic of coca passing through it in the other direction from the Yungas to Potosi for the use of the mine labourers. And to this day the coca industry of the Yungas is an important source of revenue to the capital. For the Indians today ascribe to coca the same virtues as their ancestors and through centuries of economic suppression have succeeded in maintaining recognition for it as the one remaining article of necessity in their daily lives, so that the cultivation of coca has always been of economic importance as a rich source of revenue both for the private exploiters and for the State.

Coca was first exported to Europe in 1544, but it was not until after the emancipation, and two centuries after its discovery, that it began to be of general interest to medical science. The young doctor Angelo Mariani put on the market the 'Elixir Mariani', which he manufactured from imported coca leaves after a vain attempt to grow the plant in Paris, and this was hailed by leading doctors from all parts of the world as the virtual panacea for every illness. For a time coca was used as a cure for the addiction to morphine and alcoholism, while only the Germans pointed a note of warning that the drug was itself habit-forming. In 1860 Albert Niemann succeeded in isolating the alkaloid of coca, which was named cocaine, and noticed its properties as a local anaesthetic. Tomas Moreno y Maiz, Surgeon in Chief of the Peruvian Army, conducted detailed experiments on the anaesthetizing properties of cocaine and proved that animals fed with coca leaves died of hunger as soon as others. Finally in 1884 Carl Koller, a young investigator working with Sigmund Freud, made the dramatic practical discovery of the value of cocaine as a local anaesthetic in ophthalmic surgery. Though it has now been to some extent superseded, coca played a leading role in the evolution of anaesthetics.

Coca is now cultivated in Ceylon, Java and Peru for the industrial extraction of cocaine. In Peru it is also cultivated for native consumption and in Bolivia solely for this purpose.

Coca is a shrub which grows to a height of some six feet, although in cultivation it is kept pruned to not more than two or two-and-a-half feet. It has alternating leaves of an ovoid shape, from two to four centimetres broad and four to eight centimetres

THE INDIAN TODAY AND TOMORROW

long. The upper surface is deep emerald green and lustrous, the under surface lighter green. On the under surface the midrib is pronounced and two slighter lines run from base to apex of the leaf forming a narrower ellipse on either side of the midrib. The plant requires a warm and moist climate similar to that in which tea is grown and flourishes best at an altitude between one thousand and fifteen hundred metres above sea level. In Bolivia it is cultivated mainly in the Yungas, an Aymara word which is now used as a general term for the humid and fertile sub-tropical valleys which run down from the eastern slopes of the Cordillera Real towards the vast pampas of eastern Bolivia.

The methods of cultivating the coca have not changed materially in the last six hundred years and though generally credited to the agricultural skill for which the Inca Empire is renowned, may go back much earlier than this.

The plant is cultivated from seeds, which grow in small clusters of two or three oval red pods with a hard black kernel. The seeds are gathered between December and March, usually in the evening or when the sky is overcast in order that they may not be damaged by the strong rays of the sun. The young plants are grown in special nurseries, moist and shaded, for six months or a year until they reach a height of about a foot together with the root. They are then transplanted into the open. For the first two years after transplantation the plant needs careful attention and must be kept free of parasites and destructive insects. After two years the first harvest is made (*jinchuncha*), but only a small number of leaves are picked so as not to overstrain the plant. Three or four months later a true harvest (*khichi*) is possible and all the leaves are gathered. The plant has a life of forty or fifty years and the leaves are harvested three or four times a year. Every five years or so it is pruned back to the central stem in order to maintain the quality of the leaves.

The *cocal* or coca plantation is usually prepared shortly before the transplantation of the young plants. It is situated on steeply sloping ground on the side of a hill. The ground is first cleared of weeds and undergrowth and then formed into a series of steps beaten hard with a special short, heavy stick called *chunta*. The steps (*tackhana, huachu*) are about 60 centimetres wide and 60 centimetres deep, leaving furrows of about 30 centimetres between, in which the plants are set. A well-made *cocal* will last some fifty years. It is said that the system of steps serves to prevent erosion on the sloping ground, retains the moisture in the furrows and lessens the growth of weeds—which in this climate are very luxuriant and quick growing—in the hard pounded soil. The *cocales* have a characteristic appearance owing to this system of stepping and stand out as bare ribbed patches on the exuberantly clad mountain sides, visible from great distances.

The leaves are harvested (*mita*) three or four times a year when they are 'ripe'—well developed and a rich, dark green—and before they begin to drop. After each gathering the *cocal* is cleared of weeds (*tirar masi*). The leaves are picked carefully by hand and placed into aprons which hang from the waists of the pickers, folded into the form of bags. The day's crop of leaves (*matu*) is kept overnight in a covered shed called *matu-huasi*, and next day is dried in the sun.

The drying is a delicate process attended by many risks. Special drying-floors are used, made of slate or tiles and surrounded by covered sheds into which the leaves are swept at night. A thin layer of leaves is spread on the drying-floor (*cachi*) and is continually moved by the Indian attendant (*camani*) with a broom. If owing to unexpected rain the leaves are left more than three days in the *matu-huasi* before drying, if they are gathered too moist and too speedy evaporation takes place in the hot sun, or if they are moistened by rain or dew when only partially dry, they blacken (*chojta*) and their value is diminished. While the large estates have their own properly constructed drying-floors, the small Indian cultivators have to make do with the yards of their huts or, as I have often observed, the floors of the churches are used for this purpose without implied disrespect.

When fully dried the leaves are taken to the presses and packed in cubical bales of coarse cloth and banana leaves, called *tambores*, a measure used only in the commerce of coca. The *tambor* comprises two *cestos* and the weight of the *cesto* is variable. The small Indian cultivator, who has no press of his own, sells his dried leaves to an entrepreneur at the rate of 32 lb. to the *cesto*. The latter sells to the public presses at the rate of 30 lb. to the *cesto*. The packer, finally, reduces the weight of the *cesto* to just under 25 lb., the *tambor* of two *cestos* weighing 50 lb. with packing. A special measure is also used in the Yungas for determining the size of the *cocal*. The Indian uses as his unit of measurement a pole called *brazada*, of twice the arm's length of a man; the white man's unit is four *varas* of 2·78 feet. A square of twelve *brazadas*,

THE INDIAN TODAY AND TOMORROW

on an average about 42 metres a side, is called a *cato* and is the unit of square measurement of the *cocal*. The *cocal* is measured by *catos* and its yield in *cestos* of 32 lb. An average yield in each harvesting is five *cestos* of dried coca a *cato*.

The present retail price of coca in La Paz is 35 Bolivianos a pound and a recognized normal consumption is a pound a week, which the Indian buys on Sunday for the ensuing week.

The mastication of coca is a universal habit among the Aymara and Quechua Indians of the Altiplano and Cochabamba, and is fairly common among the *mestizos* or cholos. The habit is contracted early in life and is common to both sexes. Only in parts of the northern Province of Caupolican, where the difficulties of transport render coca more costly and where the Indians, who are pastoral and have little outlet for their produce, are almost without resources, coca is an expensive luxury. Elsewhere it is a daily necessity. The use of coca is chiefly confined to the highland Indians and among the tribes of the tropical interior the habit is rarely seen. Under the influence of the Incas, however, it spread to some of the tribes of the Amazon basin, and in his *Jungle Paths and Inca Ruins*, W. McGovern says that he observed its use among the Tucano tribes of the Amazon, although instead of chewing the leaves they take it in the form of powder.

Mastication (*coquear, acullicar*) is an art that must be learnt. The *coqueador, acullicador* or *picchador*, takes a handful of leaves from his pouch (*chuspa*), selects for preference those which are well grown and bright green in colour, rejects the stalks, and places the leaves in his mouth with all the slow deliberation of a tobacco smoker filling a favourite pipe. Together with the coca leaves he puts in his mouth small pieces of an alkaline paste made from the ashes of quinoa stalks or other plants (*llijta, llucta* or *elipta*), the effect of which is to increase the extraction of alkaloids from the coca. An interesting parallel may be traced with the habit of mixing betel leaf in India with lime for chewing. The masticated leaves with the *llucta* are formed into a ball (*jacchu*) which is kept in the cheek and to which fresh leaves (*acullicos*) are added every hour or so. The process may continue for eight or ten hours or more before the *jacchu* is finally ejected. The habit of coca chewing is not to be recommended aesthetically, but it is not less obnoxious than the formerly popular habit of chewing tobacco among Europeans and is less disgusting than the modern habit of chewing elastic gum, in which the children delight. The discoloration of teeth and lips which many observers have noted in coca chewers and quoted in proof of the deleterious effects of coca, is in fact produced by the black *llucta* and not by the coca. It may be compared with the yellow discoloration suffered by heavy cigarette smokers.

The coca leaf contains several alkaloidal derivatives of ecgonine, the most important of which is cocaine. According to Noel L. Allport, analyst to the British Drug Houses, Ltd. (in *The Chemistry and Pharmacy of Vegetable Drugs*): 'The percentage of total alkaloids present in the commercial leaves varies from 0·1 to 2·4, Java coca containing the highest amount, consisting largely of cinnamyl-cocaine. Truxillo (*i.e.* Peruvian) leaves generally contain more alkaloid than the Bolivian drug, but only about one-half is cocaine, whereas this alkaloid may constitute three-fourths of the total bases yielded by the material from Bolivia.' The amount of cocaine in Bolivian coca is still very variously estimated and investigation tends to be influenced by active controversy concerning the alleged deleterious effects of the coca habit on the indigene. In *Epidemologia Boliviana* (1946), Dr. Juan Manuel Balcazar, Professor of Hygiene in the University of La Paz, stated that the cocaine content of Bolivian coca leaves is 7·8 grammes per kilogramme and estimated that if the Indian consumes fifty grammes of coca a day, his daily consumption of cocaine will be 39 centigrammes. Even if it is assumed that the *coqueador* extracts only a third of this quantity (though according to Dr. Balcazar the *acullicu* with *llijta* enables the extraction of twice the quantity which would be extracted by masticating the leaves without *llijta*), the Indian would consume 13 centigrammes of cocaine a day. In a study of coca published in Santiago Dr. Mendoza Catacora put the cocaine content at 0·2 per cent. In the *Gaceta de Quimica y Farmacia*, recently published in La Paz, Dr. H. Carvajal, an assiduous investigator, claims that Bolivian coca contains 2·4 per cent of alkaloids of the ecgonine group and 1·2 per cent of cocaine. Other scientists, such as Dr. G. Mortimer in the U.S.A., have belittled the toxic effects of coca and claimed for it a high nutritional and vitamin value. The last view is frequently maintained in Bolivia, not entirely from disinterested motives.

The old controversy about the practical effects of coca upon the native races is still alive, although practical steps are not suggested. The traditional view, which is still supported by probably the great majority of practical men, is that without coca the native could not support the difficult conditions of his life and the rigours of the climate, and in particular the exacting labour in mines often at great altitudes. The opposite view that the redemption of the race is impossible so long as the pernicious indulgence in coca is allowed to continue is advanced mainly by doctors and scientists, whose opinions obtain considerable publicity in the daily Press. An intermediate view is held that the abolition of the coca habit, though desirable, is not feasible while the faulty nutrition and undernourishment of the native races continue. The conference of La Haye in 1912 and in 1933 the League of Nations proposed rigorous control of the consumption of coca and the gradual abolition of its cultivation. In 1927 Bolivia in the League of Nations signed the Protocol of the Convention of opium and other narcotics, including coca. The uncontrolled use of coca was condemned by the Fourth Pan-American Conference of the Red Cross and in 1939 by the First Bolivian Medical Congress in La Paz. In 1948 the World Health Organization of the United Nations Organization undertook the study of coca and in 1949 a small investigatory commission visited Peru and Bolivia, to decide in a fortnight the problem which has been the hub of controversy since men of the white race came to South America until today.

It has been frequently stated in medical treatises that the coca addict betrays the characteristic symptoms of cocainism—he is abulic, apathetic, lazy, lacking in moral sense, of clouded intelligence, lethargic in his reactions but liable to sudden bursts of violent passion from inadequate causes—and it is assumed that owing to the amount of coca they consume all the Indians of Bolivia must be addicts. These statements are completely logical, but are lacking in scientific verification. I have indeed on occasion seen an Indian who appeared to be in a state approaching stupor from coca or from cold or from the combined effects of the two. But from my own observation I am convinced that those Indians —and they are the vast majority—who take coca as an adjunct to the rigorous toil of the mines or of agriculture, or to sustain them in their long treks across the Altiplano, do not visibly display these symptoms of addiction. And it is certain fact that the Aymara and Quechua races, condemned to exceptionally rigorous climatic conditions on an arid and unfriendly soil, exploited mercilessly in the severest of physical labours through centuries of imposed economic impoverishment, have shown a racial vitality and a capacity for survival that is rare among coloured peoples who have come under the domination of the white races and which has not been shown by the indigenous races of the interior of Bolivia. Whether this proved power of resistance has been in spite of coca or because of it, may still be argued. It is true also, and must have some significance, that the same qualities are claimed for coca by the Indian today as were claimed in the early days of the Spanish Conquest and that its use is still limited to the races which are indigenous to the higher altitudes. In whatever direction, however, the controversy about coca may be decided, in a country where it is regarded as a traditional and basic necessity of life and the nearest known approach to a gift from heaven by Indians constituting some 70 per cent of the total population, as an accepted indulgence by *mestizos* constituting some further 10 per cent, and in which it is an important source of revenue to the State, its suppression would involve practical problems of no easy solution.

For the cultivation and the economic importance of coca in Bolivia persists in despite of controversy. At least since the foundation of the Republic production seems to have remained remarkably stable at around ten million pounds a year, of which four-fifths come from the Yungas. D'Orbigny quotes an anonymous pamphlet published in La Paz in 1832 under the title *Descripción del aspecto, cultivo, trafico y virtudes de la Coca*, in which the annual production is estimated at 400,000 *cestos* and the production of the Yungas at 300,000 *cestos*. According to the figures of the Directorate of Statistics, the total production of recent years has been about 5,500 tons and that of the Yungas 4,500 tons. Of this production, some 85 per cent is consumed in the country and 15 per cent is exported. The two main export markets for Bolivian coca were the Argentine and Chile until in 1926 Chile prohibited its importation. And although this prohibition was subsequently lifted, the importation has dwindled to almost nothing. Consumption of coca in the Argentine during the last ten years or so (mainly among the native labourers of the north) was reckoned at about 800,000 kilogrammes a year, of which about half entered the country as contraband. In 1946 the Argentine Government fixed an import quota of 410,000 kilos a year and took steps to check the contraband traffic. The result was a severe drop in the price of coca in Bolivia.

The cultivation and traffic of coca is no less lucrative today than it was to the early Spanish adventurers. Many of the small Indian cultivators of the Yungas achieve a modest opulence to which

THE INDIAN TODAY AND TOMORROW

their brothers of the Altiplano cannot aspire. The largest fortune in Bolivia, outside mining, has probably been made by Don José Maria Gamarra, a large proprietor of coca plantations and founder in 1945 of the Sociedad Agricola Industrial José Maria Gamarra, S.A., the most important of the coca businesses of Bolivia. Born in Coripata in 1869, Don José Maria is still active despite his eighty years, a vigorous and humorous personality, who despite his great wealth prefers the life of the people. I have been largely indebted to his kindness and to the hospitality of Colonel Angel Telleria, then Superintendent of the Gamarra haciendas, and his charming Scottish wife, for the opportunity to discover what little I have been able to learn about the Yungas of La Paz.

NOTE ON BOLIVIAN CENSUS.—*See page* 203.

A census of population was held in Bolivia in September, 1950, and preliminary results were made public after this book had gone to press. The total population was found to be 3,019,031, three-quarters of a million less than the official estimate made in 1947. Of these about two and a half million belong to the highland Departments. The urban population is quoted as 1,013,350 and the rural population as 2,005,681. No racial breakdown has yet been published. Owing to the demographic difficulties which arise with the native populations of the Andes it is certain that official statistics of population must be less than the actual population numbers, particularly in the rural areas, though how much less it is obviously impossible to guess. It would not be outrageous to suppose that the official estimate of 3.8 million may be pretty near the actual population figure nor is it at all unreasonable to assume that some three-quarters of a million escaped the census net.

BIBLIOGRAPHY

The following select bibliography is designed to cover fairly evenly all the matters dealt with in this book. A very full ethnological bibliography, with references to articles in scientific journals, will be found in the second volume of the *Handbook of South American Indians* and a fairly extensive bibliography for the Inca period is given in Louis Baudin's *L'Empire Socialiste des Inka*. An annotated bibliography for the whole history of Peru has been produced by Father Ruben Vargas Ugarte—*Historia del Perú: Fuentes* (Lima, 1939).

For convenience of reference the following bibliography is divided into 'Chroniclers' and 'Historians', a necessarily rough and ready division justified by usage and convenience. The 'Chroniclers' are those writers who in the colonial epoch wrote of contemporary events or of the pre-Columban period from contemporary sources.

Many of the works of the 'Chroniclers' remained in manuscript until recently, and some are still unpublished. The most valuable editions of their works are the *Colección de Documentos Inéditos del Archivo de Indias*, published in Madrid, and the *Colección de Libros y Documentos Referentes a la Historia del Perú*, edited by H. H. Urteaga and C. A. Romero and published in Lima. Those marked with an asterisk are available in English translation among the publications of the Hakluyt Society. An annotated list of 'Chroniclers' with short biographical notices was published by P. A. Means under the title *Biblioteca Andina* (Connecticut Academy of Arts and Sciences, Transactions (New Haven, Conn., 1928)). A brief assessment of historical importance is made by John Howland Rowe in his article 'Inca Culture at the time of the Spanish Conquest', in the second volume of the *Handbook of South American Indians*, and a fuller chronological discussion will be found in the first chapter of Louis Baudin's *L'Empire Socialiste des Inka*.

1. Chroniclers

ANONYMOUS, *Tres relaciones de antigüedades peruanas*, ed. Marcos Jiménez de la Espada (Madrid, 1879).

BIBLIOGRAPHY

Anonymous, *The conquest of Peru as related by a member of the Pizarro Expedition*, ed. and trans. Joseph H. Sinclair (New York Public Library, 1929).
*José de Acosta, *Historia natural y moral de las Indias* (Mexico, 1940).
Pablo José de Arriaga, *La extirpación de la idolatría en el Perú* (Lima, 1920).
Augustinians, *Relación de la religión y ritos del Perú hecha por los primeros religiosos agustinos que alli pasaron para la conversión de los naturales* (Madrid, 1865).
Alvaro Alfonso Barba, *Arte de los metales* (1642).
Ludovico Bertonio, *Arte y gramatica de la lengua Aymara* (Leipzig, 1879).
—— *Vocabulario de la lengua Aymara* (Leipzig, 1879).
Juan de Betanzos, *Suma y Narración de los Incas que los indios llamaron Capaccuna, que fueron Señores de la Ciudad del Cuzco y de todo a ella sujeto* (Madrid, 1880).
Antonio de la Calancha, *Corónica moralizada del orden de San Agustín en el Perú con sucesos egenplares vistos en esta monarquía* (Barcelona, 1638. Selections republished La Paz, 1939).
*Pedro Cieza de León, *Parte primera de la Crónica del Perú* (Buenos Aires. Colección Austral, 1945).
—— *Segunda parte de la Crónica del Perú* (Madrid, 1880).
Bernabé Cobo, *Historia del Nuevo Mundo* (Seville, 1890–95).
Gaspar de Escalona y Agüero, *Gazofilacia Real del Perú* (1647).
Miguel de Estete, *Noticia del Perú* (Lima, 1924).
Francisco Falcón, *Representación sobre los daños y molestias que se hacen a los Indios* (Madrid, 1867; Lima, 1918).
Diego Fernández, *Prima y segunda parte de la historia del Perú* (Seville, 1571; Lima, 1876; Madrid, 1914).
*Garcilaso Inca de la Vega, *Comentarios Reales de los Incas* (Buenos Aires, 1943).
—— *Historia general del Perú. Segunda parte de los comentarios reales de los Incas* (Buenos Aires, 1943).
Diego Gonzales Holguin, *Gramatica y arte nueva dela lengua general de todo el Perú* (Lima, 1607).
—— *Vocabulario dela lengua general de todo el Perú* (Lima, 1608).
Bartolomé de Las Casas, *Apologética historia sumaria* (Madrid, 1909).
—— *De las antiguas gentes del Perú* (Madrid, 1892).

Reginaldo de Lizárraga, *La descripción y población de las Indias* (Madrid, 1909).
―― *Descripción breve de toda la tierra del Perú* (Madrid, 1909).
―― *Descripción colonial* (Buenos Aires, 1916).
Bartolomé Martínez y Vela, *Anales de la Villa Imperial de Potosí* (La Paz, 1939).
Nicolas de Martínez Arzanz y Vela, *Historia de la Villa Imperial de Potosí* (Buenos Aires, 1943).
*Fernando Montesinos, *Memorias antiguas historiales y politicas del Perú* (Madrid, 1882).
―― *Anales del Perú* (Madrid, 1906).
Cristóbal Molina de Santiago, *Relación de la conquista y población del Perú* (Lima, 1916).
Cristóbal de Molina de Cuzco, *Relación de las fábulas y ritos de los Incas* (Lima, 1916).
Martín de Morúa, *Historia del orígen y genealogía real de los reyes Incas del Perú* (Lima, 1922–5).
Honorio Mossi de Cambiano, *Gramatica de la Lengua general del Perú* (Sucre, 1860).
―― *Diccionario de la Lengua general del Perú* (Sucre, 1860).
*Baltasar de Ocampo, *Execution of the Inca Tupac Amaru* (Hakluyt Society, 1907).
Gonzalo Fernández de Oviedo y Valdés, *Historia general y natural de las Indias* (Madrid, 1851–5).
*Juan Polo de Ondegardo, *Del linage de los ingas y como conquistaron* (Lima, 1917).
―― *Los errores y supersticiones de los Indios* (Lima, 1916).
*Joan de Santacruz Pachacuti Yamqui Salcamayhua, *Relación de antigüedades deste reyno del Perú* (Lima, 1927).
Pedro Pizarro, *Relación del descubrimiento y conquista de los reinos del Perú* (Madrid, 1844. English trans. by P. A. Means, New York, 1921).
Felipe Guaman Poma de Ayala, *Nueva corónica y buen gobierno* (Lima, 1948).
Pedro Sancho de la Hoz, *Relación para S.M. de lo sucedido en la conquista y pacificación de estas provincias de la Nueva Castilla* (Lima, 1917. English trans. by P. A. Means, New York, 1917).
Fernando de Santillán, *Relación del orígen, descendencia, política y gobierno de los Incas* (Madrid, 1879).
*Pedro Sarmiento de Gamboa, *Historia de los Incas* (Buenos Aires, 1942).

BIBLIOGRAPHY

JUAN DE SOLÓRZANO Y PEREYRA, *Politica Indiana* (Madrid, 1736-9).
ANTONIO DE ULLOA Y JORGE JUAN Y SANTACILIA, *Noticias secretas de América* (London, 1826).
—— *Relación histórica del viaje a la América meridional* (Madrid, 1748).
*FRANCISCO DE XÉRES, *Verdadera relación de la conquista del Perú* (Lima, 1917).
AGUSTÍN DE ZÁRATE, *Historia del descubrimiento y conquista de la Provincia del Perú* (Madrid, 1853).

2. HISTORIANS

DIEGO FRANCISCO ALTAMIRANO, *Historia de la mision de los Mojos* (La Paz, 1891).
LEANDRO ALVIÑA, *La Musica Incaica* (Cuzco, 1919).
FLORENTINO AMEGHINO, *La antigüedad del hombre en el Plata* (Paris, 1880).
MIGUEL LUIS AMUNÁTEGUI, *Los precursores de la Indepencia de Chile* (Buenos Aires, 1925).
FREDERICO AVILA, *El Drama de la Sangre* (La Paz, 1944).
JUAN MANUEL BALCAZAR, *Epidemología Boliviana* (La Paz, 1946).
ADOLPH FRANCIS ALPHONSE BANDELIER, *The Islands of Titicaca and Koati* (New York, 1910).
LOUIS BAUDIN, *L'Empire socialiste des Inka* (Paris, 1928. Spanish trans. José Antonio Arze, Santiago, 1945).
LUIS M. BAUDIZZONE, *Poesía, Música y Danza Inca* (Buenos Aires, 1943).
HIRAM BINGHAM, *Lost City of the Incas* (New York, 1948).
—— *Inca Land* (Boston, 1922).
JOSÉ MARIA CAMACHO, *Historia de Bolivia* (La Paz, 1904).
—— *Estudio sobre Tihuanacu* (La Paz, 1938).
ROMAN D. CARBIA, *Historia de la Leyenda Negra Hispano-Americana* (Buenos Aires, n.d.).
JOSEPH CASTILLO, *Relación de la Provincia de Mojos* (La Paz, 1908).
HILDEBRANDO CASTRO POZO, *Nuestra comunedad indígena* (Lima, 1924).
ALFONSO CRESPO, *Santa Cruz* (Mexico, 1944).
BELISARIO DIAZ ROMERO, *Tihuanacu. Prehistoria americana* (La Paz, 1919).
FERNANDO DIEZ DE MEDINA, *Franz Tamayo* (La Paz, 1944).

J. M. B. Farfán, *Poesía folklórica quechua* (Tucuman, 1942).
Enrique Finot, *Historia de la conquista del oriente boliviano* (Buenos Aires, 1939).
—— *Nueva Historia de Bolivia* (Buenos Aires, 1946).
Enrique de Gandía, *Historia del Gran Chaco* (Buenos Aires, 1929).
—— *Historia de Santa Cruz de la Sierra* (Buenos Aires, 1935).
Uriel García, *El Nuevo Indio* (Cuzco, 1930).
Ventura García Calderón, *Literatura Inca* (Paris, 1938).
Angel M. Garibay, *Poesía indígena de la altiplanicie* (Mexico, 1940).
C. C. Griffin, *Concerning Latin-American Culture* (New York, 1940).
Angel Guido, *Fusión hispano-indígena en la Arquitectura colonial* (Rosario, 1925).
Augusto Guzmán, *Tupac Amaru* (Mexico, 1944).
Jorge Pando Gutierrez, *Bolivia y el Mundo* (La Paz, 1947).
Earl J. Hamilton, *American Treasure and the Price Revolution in Spain, 1501–1640* (Cambridge, Mass., 1934).
Raoul and Marie D'Harcourt, *La Musique des Incas et ses survivances* (Paris, 1925).
Seymour E. Harris, *Economic Problems of Latin America* (New York, 1944).
Edgar Lee Hewett, *Ancient Andean Life* (New York, 1939).
Th. Hornberger, *Acosta's Historia Natural* (University of Texas, 1930).
A. von Humboldt, *Travels to the Equinoctial Regions of the New Continent* (London, 1852).
R. A. Humphreys, *The Evolution of Modern Latin America* (Oxford, 1946).
Augusto Iglesias, *Bolívar el Hombre del Destino* (Santiago, 1942).
T. A. Joyce, *South American Archaeology* (London, 1916).
F. A. Kirkpatrick, *The Spanish Conquistadores* (London, 1934).
—— *Latin America* (Cambridge, 1938).
W. H. Kobel, *In Jesuitland* (London, 1912).
Jesus Lara, *La Poesía Quechua* (Mexico, 1947).
H. C. Lea, *The Inquisition in the Spanish Dependencies* (New York, 1908).
Walter Lehman and Heinrich Doering, *The Art of Old Peru* (London, 1924).
Boleslao Lewin, *Tupac Amaru* (Buenos Aires, 1943).
Francisco A. Loayza, *Chinos Llegaron antes que Colon* (Lima, 1948).

BIBLIOGRAPHY

L. Leland Locke, *The ancient Quipu, a Peruvian knot-record* (New York, 1923).

Emil Ludwig, *Bolívar, the Life of an Idealist* (New York, 1942).

George McCutchen McBride, *The Agrarian Indian Communities of Highland Bolivia* (New York, 1921).

W. McGovern, *Jungle Paths and Inca Ruins*.

Salvador de Madariaga, *Cuadro Historico de las Indias* (Buenos Aires, 1945. English trans. *The Rise of the Spanish Empire* and *The Fall of the Spanish Empire* (London, 1947)).

Clements Robert Markham, *The Incas of Peru* (London, 1910).

—— *A History of Peru* (Chicago, 1892).

Philip Ainsworth Means, *Ancient Civilisations of the Andes* (New York, 1931).

—— *Fall of the Inca Empire and Spanish Rule in Peru, 1530–1780* (New York, 1932).

José Toribio Medina, *Historia del Tribuno del Santo Oficio de la Inquisición en Lima* (Santiago, 1887).

M. Menéndez y Pelayo, *Historia de la Poesía hispano-americana* (Madrid, 1912).

Carlos Monge, *Acclimatization in the Andes* (John Hopkins Press, 1948).

Bernard Moses, *South America on the Eve of Emancipation* (New York, 1908).

J. F. Mugaburu, *Diario de Lima, 1640–94* (Lima, 1917).

William A. Neiswanger and James R. Nelson, *Problemas Económicos de Bolivia* (La Paz, 1947).

Erland Nordenskiöld, *Origin of the Indian Civilizations in South America* (Comparative Ethnographical Studies, vol. 9, Göteberg, 1931).

Manuel de Odriozola, *Documentos históricos del Perú* (Lima, 1863–7).

O'Leary, *Bolivar y la Emancipación de Sur-América* (Caracas, 1883 and 1915).

Modesto Omiste, *Crónicas Potosinas* (La Paz, 1919).

Alcides d'Orbigny, *L'Homme Américain* (Paris, 1839).

—— *Voyage dans L'Amérique Méridionale* (Paris, 1844).

—— *Descripción geográfica, histórica y estadística de Bolivia* (Paris, 1845. Reprinted La Paz, 1946).

Gustavo Adolfo Otero, *La vida social del coloniaje* (La Paz, 1942).

Luis Peñaloza, *Historia Económica de Bolivia* (La Paz, 1946).

Carlos Pereyra, *Historia de América española* (Madrid, 1920-6).
E. L. Petre, *Simón Bolívar* (London, 1909).
Mariano Picon-Salas, *De la Conquista a la Independencia* (Mexico, 1944).
Carlos Ponce Sanginés, *Ceramica Tiwanacota* (Buenos Aires, n.d.).
Arturo Posnansky, *Tihuanacu. La Cuna del Hombre Americano* (New York. Published with English trans. opposite the Spanish).
W. H. Prescott, *History of the Conquest of Peru* (London).
Gabriel René-Moreno, *Biblioteca boliviana. Catalogo del archivo de Mojos y Chiquitos* (Santiago, 1888).
—— *Ultimas días coloniales en el Alto Perú* (Santiago, 1896).
Jose de la Riva Agüero, *El Perú histórico y artístico* (Santander, 1921).
—— *Los cronistas de convento* (Paris, 1938).
Paul Rivet, *Los orígenes del hombre américano* (Mexico, 1943).
Ricardo Rojas, *Himnos Quichuas* (Buenos Aires, 1937).
José Rojas Garcidueñas, *Autos y Coloquios del siglo xvi* (Mexico).
W. S. Robertson, *Rise of the Spanish-American Republics* (New York, 1919).
Emilio Romero, *Geografía económica del Perú* (Lima, 1939).
Bautista Saavedra, *El Ayllu* (La Paz, 1903).
Luis Alberto Sánchez, *La Literatura de Perú* (Buenos Aires, 1939).
Victor Santa Cruz, *Historia Colonial de La Paz* (La Paz, 1941).
—— *Historia de Copacabana* (La Paz, 1948).
Manuel Limpias Saucedo, *Los Gobernadores de Mojos* (La Paz, 1942).
E. W. Shanahan, *South America* (London, 1927).
W. Smyth and F. Lowe, *Narrative of a Journey from Lima to Para* (London, 1836).
E. George Squier, *Peru, Incidents of travel and exploration in the land of the Incas* (New York, 1877).
Franz Tamayo, *La Creación de la Pedagogía Nacional* (La Paz, 1910).
Julio C. Tello, *Antiguo Perú* (Lima, 1929).
—— *Orígen y desarrollo de las civilisaciones prehistóricas andinas* (Lima, 1942).
J. B. Trend, *Bolívar and the Independence of Spanish America* (London, 1946).
Bernado Trigo, *Las Tejas de mi Techo* (La Paz, 1939).

E. TORRES SALMANDO, *Los antiguos jesuitas del Perú* (Lima, 1882).
JAVIER PRADO UGARTECHE, *Estado social del Perú bajo la dominación española* (Lima, 1941).
HORACIO H. URTEAGA, *El Perú* (Lima, 1928).
JORGE RICARDO VEJARANO, *Orígenes de la independencia suramericana* (Bogota, 1925).
FRANCIS VIOLICH, *The Cities of Latin America* (New York, 1944).
ELIZABETH WAUGH, *Simón Bolívar* (London, 1944).
A. CURTIS WILGUS, *Native Background in Latin-American History* (Washington, 1936).
SILVIO ARTURO ZÁVALA, *La encomienda Indiana* (Madrid, 1935).
S. ZAVALA, *New Viewpoints on the Spanish Colonization of America* (University of Pennsylvania, 1943).
Four-volume *monograph* published for the Quatercentenary of La Paz (La Paz, 1949).
Five-volume *Handbook of South American Indians*, published for the Smithsonian Institution Bureau of American Ethnology. Articles by leading ethnologists. The second volume is the most completely relevant.

INDEX

Acosta, José, 11, 23, 24, 39, 43, 55, 95, 172, 186
agriculture, 120-2, 130, 132-3, 137, 140-2, 174-5, 204, 209, 213-15, 218, 219, 230, 232, 234, 245-6, 249
aguayo, 220, 222, 223, 224, 226
Agüero, José de la Riva, 62, 82
Aguirre, Nataniel, 201
ají, 7, 97, 103, 118, 216, 221
Alexander VI (Pope), 168
Allport, Noel L., 248
Almagro, Diego de, 20, 161
Almagro, Diego (El Mozo), 111
Alos, Joachin, 191
alpaca, xi, 8, 93, 103, 172, 215
Alvarado, Pedro de, 24
amauta, 34, 40, 72, 73, 74, 84, 93, 98, 114, 237, 238
Ameghino, Florentino, 3
ancestor worship, 133, 141, 143
Ancon, 52
Antevs, E., 4
Antis, 4, 203, 234
Apasa, Julian, see Tupaj Catari
Apo Mayta, 86
Apurimac, 50, 78, 83, 87, 161
Arawak, 11, 57
Arguedas, Alcides, 201
Arequipa, 52, 103
Arica, 103
Arius Montanus, 1
Arriaga, José, 15, 36
astronomy, 76
Atacama, 103, 206
Atahuallpa (Inca), 20, 21, 41, 49, 72, 84, 85, 87-8, 90-2, 99, 106, 157, 158, 159, 160, 226
Atlantis, 1
Augustinians, 185
auqui, 237
Avila, Frederico, 3, 203, 234
Ayacucho, 161, 196, 199
Ayar Aucca, 81, 82
Ayar Cachi, 35, 81, 82, 111, 112, 113
Ayar Manco, 111, 113, see also Manco Capac

Ayar Tacco Capac, 73, 74
Ayar Uchu, 81, 82, 111
ayllu, 43, 45, 81, 84, 93-4, 96, 98, 104, 110, 123, 124, 126, 133, 137, 190, 200, 210, 211, 214
ayni, 93, 214
aynoka, 93
Ayoayo, 192, 194

Balcazar, Juan Manuel, 203, 211, 217, 248
Basadre, Jorge, 19
Baudin, Louis, 26, 28, 100, 101, 119, 123, 252
Belgrano, Manuel, 196
Belzu, 235
Benalcazar, 21
Beni, 184, 185, 235
Bennett, Wendell C., 42, 50, 54, 66, 204
Betanzos, Juan de, 21, 27, 41, 45, 81, 136
Biblia Poliglota, 1
Bingham, Hiram, 82, 164
Blasco, Nuñez Vela, 161, 182
Blas Valera, 72-3, 114, 186, 240, 241, 243
Bolanos, Frederico, 234
Bolívar, Simón, 196-200, 201
borla, 90, see *llauta*
Buenos Aires, 191, 195, 198, see also La Plata

cacique, 90, 94, 180, 189, 191, see also *curaca*
Cadiz, 72, 171, 195, 198
Cajamarca, 20, 72, 88, 97, 102, 157, 159, 160, 226
Calancha, Antonio de la, 28, 162
Calatayud, Alejo, 189
Camacho, José Maria, 19, 55, 159
Camba, 4, 176
cañahua, xi, 7, 93, 117, 215, 216, 218
Cañete (Viceroy), 162
cannibalism, 22, 107, 113, 211

260

INDEX

Capac Raymi Amauta, 76
Capac Yupanqui (Inca), 84
Carbia, Romulo D. 23 n.
Cari, 13
Carrasco, Rodriguez, 189
Carvajal, H., 248
Casa de Contratacion, 171
Castelli, 198, 199
Castelnau, Francis de, 56
Catacora, Mendoza, 248
Catari, Tomas, 191, 194
catu, 93, 94
Cayo Manco Amauta, 75
Chaco, 69, 83, 103, 184, 202, 216
Challchuchima, 87, 90
Chanca, 86, 132
Chan-Chan, 51, 231
Charles IV, 195
charqui, 97, 216
chasqui, 56, 103, 119, 217
Chavin, 53-4, 56, 61, 62, 63, 66, 134, 135, 136, 137
Chayanta, 171, 191
Chibchas, 103
chicha, 119, 209, 217, 218
Chimborazo, 87
Chimbote, 51
Chimnes, 103
Chimu, 51-2, 75, 80, 86, 93, 138
Chincha, 52
Chinese, 1, 5-6, 39, 53
Chipayas, 11, 67, 69
Chiquitos, 184, 220
Chiriguani, 75, 136, 184
cholo, 32, 176-8, 203-4, 234-6 and *passim*
Christianity, 11, 15, 119, 131, 133, 138, 142, 143, 156, 162, 168, 169, 181-8, 226-30
Chucahua, 56
Chucuito, 85, 94, 158, 171, 172, 214
chullpas, 67
chumpi, 116
chuño, 97, 117-18, 216
Chuquiapu (Choqueyapo), see La Paz
Chuquimamani, Bonifacio, 191
Chuquisaca, 191, 192, see Sucre
Church, 168, 183, 189, 190, 194, 198, 220, 227, 228, 230
chusma, 116
Cieza de León, Pedro de, 13, 21, 23, 27, 34, 35, 41, 43, 45, 61, 65, 81, 111, 126, 136, 158, 226, 239

Cisneros, 198
citua, 140, 151
climate, 51, 52-3, 63, 117, 137-8, 141
Cobo Bernabé, 23, 26-7, 28, 56, 61, 81, 95, 97, 120, 121
coca, xi, 8, 31, 119, 142, 206, 207, 209, 217, 221, 225, 230, 237-51
Cochabamba, 10, 69, 102 n., 189, 220, 226, 247
Collao, 9, 43, 44, 45, 76, 78, 100, 118, 237, see Kollasuyu
commerce, 97, 118, 219-21, 243-4, 250
commune, 95-6, 120, 122, 123, 132, 140, 173-5, 180, 204, 214, 219, 228, 229, 233
communism, 88, 94-5, 121-2, 124, 213, 214
condor, 150
confession, 142
Conquistadores, xi, 15, 166, 181, 182
Constitución, 87, 88
Copacabana, 72, 104, 220
Coquimbo, 158
Cordova, Juan Belac de, 189
Corpus Christi, 141
corregidor, 170, 171, 180, 188, 189, 190
Cortés, Hernán, 23, 181, 182
cosmological myth, 43 ff.
costume, see dress
cotton, 8, 116
Council of the Indies, 16, 167, 195, 198
courier, 130, see *chasqui*
coya, 89, 109, 149
creation, 44-5, 73
Creole, 175-6, 188, 189, 197, 198-9, 200
Crown, 167, 168, 169, 170, 183, 190, 194, 195, 197, 198, 199
curaca, 90, 94, 98, 120, 121, 122, 124, 149, 150, 151, 152, 153, 155, 156, 180, 239
curinquingue, 92
cuy, 183, see guinea-pig
Cuzco, 13, 20, 23, 24, 26, 28, 34, 55, 56, 59, 61, 70, 72, 74, 78, 81, 82, 84, 85-7, 98, 101, 102, 103, 104, 106, 109, 110, 112, 113, 125, 126, 128, 129, 130, 132, 139, 140, 149, 156, 157, 161, 162, 163, 164, 172, 187, 188, 189, 190, 191, 192, 214, 218, 226, 241, 242

Dalence, José Maria, 183 n.
del Valle, José, 192
Desguadero, 12, 86, 215
Diaz de Castillo, Bernal, 136
Diaz Romero, Belisario, 3
Diez de Medina, Frederico, 56
Diez de Medina, Tadeo, 194
divination, 141, 142-3, 153-5, 238
Dominicans, 184, 185, 226
D'Orbigny, Alcides, 135, 136, 205, 222, 223, 250
dress, 116-17, 221-6, 229
drunkenness, 18, 124, 156, 209, 211, 212, 218-19, 230
Durán, Diego, 186

education, 98-9, 121
El Dorado, 183
encomienda, 168-70, 173, 174, 180
Escalona, Gaspar de, 168
Escoma, 50, 67
eucharist, 156, 187, 228, 229

Falcón, Francisco, 94
fast, 150
feline motif, 54, 135
Ferdinand VII, 195, 196
Figueroa, Diego Rodriguez de, 162
Finot, Enrique, 65, 164
flood, 2, 44, 73, 109
Flores, Ignacio, 192, 193
Franciscans, 182, 184, 185
Freud, Sigmund, 244

Gallardo, Antonio, 188
Gamarra, José Maria, 251
Garcia, Gregorio, 5
Garcia, Marcos, 162
Garcia, Uriel, 202
Garcilaso Inca de la Vega, 19, 24-5, 27, 28, 48, 56, 61, 72, 85, 96, 97, 109, 113, 118, 121, 122, 126, 135, 139 n., 141 n., 149-56, 158, 162, 187, 226, 239, 240
Gasca, Pedro de la, 21
geography, 50-2
Giannecchini, Doroteo, 136
Gómara, Francisco López de, 23, 27, 182
Gomez, Peréz, 161, 162
Goyeneche, José Manuel, 195
Gran Paititi, 183
Griffiths, C. Olive, 237

Guaman Poma, see Poma de Ayala, Felipe Guaman
guanaco, 8, 56
Guaqui, 55, 86
Guarani, 4, 75
Guzmán, Augusto, 192
Guzmán, Santiago Vaca, 201
guinea-pig, xi, 8, 118, 183
Gumilla, José, 186
Gutierrez, Jorge Pando, 201

hailli, 122, 146-7
Haring, C. H. 18
Hatuncolla, 85, 113
hatunruna, 93, 98, 99, 180, 181
Herrera, Antonio de, 124
Holguin, Diego Gonzales, 139
housing, 115-16, 216
huaca, 60, 82, 93, 131-4, 140, 142, 227
Huallaga, 50
Huancaure, 109, 112, 113, 132
Huancavelica, 171, 189
Huanuco, 75, 202
Huari, 220
Huarina, 186
Huascar (Inca), 74, 85, 87-8, 91, 157, 160
Huayna Capac (Inca), 24, 72, 84, 85, 87, 111, 161
Huayna Potosi, 57
huilca, 164
Huillcanota Amauta, 76-7
Huiracocha; see Virajocha
Humboldt, A. von, 31, 155
Humboldt current, 52

Ibañez, Alonso de, 188
Ica, 52
Illapu, 47, 140
Inca Roca, 84, 114
Inquisition, 17, 23
insurrection, 170, 188-95
Inti, 139, 140, 228, see Sun worship
intihuatana, 76
irrigation, 7, 51, 52, 63, 93, 96, 103, 109, 120, 137, 174-5, 214-15

jaguar, 52
Jaguar worship, 134-8, 141
Jaguarogui, 136
Jesuits, 13, 72, 114, 183-8
jilakata, 93
Jujuy, 220
Junín, 86

INDEX

Keller, A. G., 164
Kenko, 127
Khuno, 237
Kolla, 4, 9, 59, 85-6, 110
Kollana, 57
Kollasuyu, 9, 100, 109, 110, 237, see Collao
Koller, Carl, 244
Kubler, George, 175

La Barre, Weston, 12
language, 3, 6, 10, 11, 56, 84, 99-100, 104, 178-9, 186, 202, 203-4
La Paz, 12, 55, 57, 58, 67, 72, 73, 102 n., 123, 135, 137, 188, 191, 192-4, 195, 196, 206, 222, 244, 248, 249, 250
La Plata, 23, 183, 184, 192, 195, 197, 220
Las Casas, Bartolomé de 16, 17, 19, 23, 27, 182
Leguizamo, Juan Sierra de, 163 n.
Leguizamo, Mancio Sierra de, 123
Lewin, Boleslao, 191
lihua, 93
Lima, 26, 51, 52, 72, 75, 86, 102 n., 103, 161, 162, 178, 184, 187, 189, 190, 196, 206, 252
Llasca (also Laja), 12, 191
llama, xi, xii, 8, 74, 93, 103, 116, 153-5, 173 n., 179, 215, 216, 223, 224, 225, 230, 239
llauto, 90, 160
lliclla, 116
Lloque Ticac Amauta, 75
Lloque Yupanqui (Inca), 84
Loayza, Francisco A., 5, 27
Locke, L. Leland, 30
Lund, P. W., 3
Lupaca, 85, 86
Lurin, 86

McGovern, W., 247
Macha, 191
Machu Picchu, 61, 82, 127, 128, 129, 164
Madariaga, Salvador de, 16, 18, 31, 32, 169, 172, 199
Madre de Dios, 86
magic, 124, 141, 143, 230
magician, 134, 235
maize, xi, xii, 7, 97, 103, 117, 118, 119, 125, 140, 141, 150, 151, 174, 182, 214, 215, 216, 217

Maldonado, Vicente, 186
mallcu, 84, 93
Mama Cora (or Mama Cura), 111, 114
Mama Guaco (or Mama Ciuiaco) 35, 81, 111, 114
Mama Ipacura, 81
Mama Ojllo (or Mama Occllo) 81, 106-13, 149
Mama Raua, 81, 111
Manco Capac (Inca), 28, 34, 81, 84, 106-9, 110, 132, 149
Manco Inca, 160-2
Manta, 86
Marañon, 50, 54
Marasco Pachacuti, 65
marca, 84, 94, 103, 126
Mariani, Angelo, 244
Markham C. R., 20, 35, 62
Maukallacta, 82
Maule, 87
Mayta Capac (Inca), 84
Means, P. A., 20, 55, 71, 73, 205, 252
Medrano, Espinosa, 188
Melanesia, 5
Melgarejo, 235
Messia, Alonso, 172
mestizo, xiii, 162, 165, 166, 176, 178, 187, 213, 233, 234-6, 247, 250
Mexico, xi, 23, 38, 39, 182, 183, 188, 202, 229, 233
Mindendorff, E. W. 64
Miranda, Francisco, 197
Mishkin, Bernard, 228, 231
missionaries, 99-100, 101, 131, 183-8, 228
mit'a (mita), 94, 96, 119, 130, 140, 170, 171-5, 180, 189, 190, 191
mitmac, 13, 103-4
Mitre, Bartolomé, 220
Mochica, 51
Mocomoco, 10
Mojos, 184, 185, 220
Molina, Cristóbal de, 20, 26
Molina, Juan Ignacio, 186
Monteagudo, 198
Montesinos, Fernando, 26, 27, 34, 47, 63 n., 71-9, 80, 83, 113, 139 n.
Moon, worship of, 140
morality, 123-5, 208-13
Moreno, Gabriel René, 201
Moreno, Mariano, 198
Moreno y Maiz, Tomas, 244
Mortimer, G., 248

Morúa, Martín de, 26, 27, 28, 29, 81, 98, 113, 123
Mossi, de Cambiano, Honorio, 27
mummies, 51, 133, 238
Murillo, Pedro Domingo, 196, 235

Napoleon, 195
Nariño, Antonio, 197
Nazca, 52, 86, 102
Nelson, N. C., 5
Niemann, Albert, 244
nobility (Inca), 91–2, 97, 98–9, 119, 120, 121
Nordenskiöld, Erland, 5, 30
Ñuflo de Chavez, 184
ñusta, 99, 139
nutrition, 117, 201, 216, 249

obrajes, 174
oca, 7, 93, 117, 215, 216
Ocampo, Baltasar de, 162, 163 *n.*
Ollantaytambo, 125, 127, 128
Ondegardo, Juan Polo de, see Polo Ondegardo, Juan
oracles, 142
orejones, 92, 98, 111, 112
Orinoco, 185
Ortiz, Diego, 162
Oruro, 10, 12, 189, 190, 192, 193
Ovando, Nicolas de, 168
Oviedo y Valdés, Gonzalo Fernández de, 23
ox, 174, 214

Pacasa, 86
Paccarictampu, 81, 82, 109, 111
Pachacamac, 52, 76, 102, 140, 227
Pachacuti Inca Yupanqui, 28, 30, 80, 84, 85, 86, 126, 127, 129, 130, 132, 140
Pachacuti Yamqui Salcamaywa, Joan de Santacruz, 19, 25, 27
Pachamama, 133, 141, 228, 238
Pagador, Sebastian, 192
Palacios Rubios, Juan Lopez de, 168
Pando, Martin, 162
Pantoja, Rodrigo, 242
Paracas, 52, 54
Pardo, Luis A., 82
Paullu Ticac Pirua, 75
Paypicala, 56
penal code (Inca), 122–5
Peñaloza, Luis, 169
Peninsulares, 175–6, 188, 192, 198–9

Pereyra, Carlos, 167
Perry, W. J., xii
pharalaya, 93
Philinco, 188
Philip II, 162
Philip III, 194
Pinelo, Antonio de Leon, 2
Pirua, 47, 68–79, 83–4, 110, 113, 114
Pirua Pacari Manco, 73, 74
Pisac, 127
Pizarro, Francisco, xi, xii, 20, 21, 27, 38, 72, 85, 87, 157, 158, 159, 160, 161, 181, 226
Pizarro, Gonzales, 161
Pizarro, Hernando, 90, 111
Pizarro, Pedro, 90
Pizarro, Ramón Garcia, 195
plough, 8, 120, 214
Polo de Ondegardo, Juan, 23, 26, 55, 94, 95, 99, 104, 117, 136
polygamy, 89, 98
Poma de Ayala, Felipe Guaman, 19, 25–6, 27, 42, 81, 136, 186
Poopo, 12
Popham, Sir Home, 198
potato, xi, xiii, 7, 8, 93, 117–18, 172, 174, 214, 215, 216
Potosi, 10, 128, 132, 171, 172, 173, 187, 188, 189, 191, 220, 226, 239, 240, 244
Poznansky, Arturo, 6, 55, 57–60, 63, 64, 65
Prescott, W. H., 25, 67, 157, 159
Pucara, 61, 78, 83, 86, 220
Pucher, Leo, 3, 136
Pumaorcco, 82, 83
Puna, 87
Puno, 189, 192
Puquina, 11, 186

quinoa, xi, xii, 93, 97, 117, 118, 119, 172, 174, 214, 215, 216, 217, 218, 247
quipu, 28–30, 35–41, 98
Quisquis, 87
Quito, 69, 86, 87, 102, 103, 104, 136, 172

raimi, 149–56, 229
religion, 131–43, 226–30, see also Christianity, Sun worship, ancestor worship, ritual, *huaca*
repartimiento, 161, 170
Reseguin, 192, 193, 194

INDEX

Rimac, 52, 75, 242
ritual, 119, 120, 121–2, 124, 132–3, 138–42, 187, 227, 229–30, 238–9
roads, 55, 102–3, 105, 130
Robledo, Jorge de, 21
Rocha, Diego Andres, 5
Rojas, Ricardo, 49, 199
Romero, C. A., 20, 252
Rowe, J. H., 25, 26, 85, 104, 129, 252
Rycaut, Sir Paul, 25

Sacsahuaman, 126, 129, 130
Salcamaywa, see Pachacuti Yamqui Salcamaywa, Joan de Santacruz
Sanchez, Luis Alberto, 19
Sancho de la Hoz, Pedro, 20
San José, 184
San Martin, 196
Santa Cruz, Andres de, 196–7, 199, 235
Santa Cruz de la Sierra, 184, 218, 235
Santiago de Huata, 178
Santos, Juan, 190
Sarmiento de Gamboa, Pedro, 1, 2, 6 n., 17, 23–4, 27, 28, 29, 34, 44, 47, 81, 98, 113
Sayri Tupac, 162
Segurola, Sebastian de, 193
Seville, 171, 195
Sinchi Rocca (Inca), 82, 84
Sisa, Bartolina, 191
socialism, 18, 88, 95–7, 110
Solorzano y Pereyra, Juan de, 178
Sorata, 3, 193, 194
sorcery, 124, 142–3, see magic and magician
Squire, G. E., 66
Sucre, 28, 55, 102, 191, 195, 198, 226, see also Chuquisaca
sucres, see terraces (agricultural)
Sun worship, xii, 89, 95, 97, 99, 101, 107–8, 112, 113, 114, 120–2, 130, 133, 134, 135, 137, 138–42, 149–56, 227, 228

Tamayo, Franz, 202, 208, 209, 211, 234, 235
Tamputtocco, 78, 81, 82, 110, 113
Tampu Quiru, 112
Tarija, 3, 184
Tarma, 190
Tawantinsuyu, 88, 100, 110
Tello, Julio C., 62, 63, 136, 137
terraces (agricultural), 51, 63, 94, 96, 120, 137, 215

Thunupa, 140, 141
Tihuanacu, 4, 6, 11, 13, 44, 45, 46, 47, 48, 49, 50, 52, 54, 55–67, 68–79, 83–4, 110, 113, 114, 128, 129, 134, 135, 137, 138, 159, 199, 237, 238
Tiquina, 191
Titicaca, 10, 12, 13, 26, 43, 44, 55, 58, 62, 63, 67, 81, 85, 86, 102, 106, 108, 132, 135, 158, 178, 215, 216
Titu Cusi, 162
Titu Yupanqui Pachacuti, 77–8
Toco Cozque, 113
Toledo, Francisco de (Viceroy), 17, 23, 24, 163, 171, 172, 175, 243
Topa Inca, 52, 86–7
Tordesillas, Treaty of, 168
totora, 12, 215
town planning, 125–6
tribute, 96–7, 168, 170, 173–4, 180, 189, 190, 191, 199, 243
Trujillo, 51, 52, 72, 182, 200, 248
Tschopik, Harry, 214, 231
tucricuc, 97, 100
Tucuman, 75, 77, 87, 102, 190, 220
Tuita, 171
Tumbez, 87, 91, 92, 102, 157
Tupac Amaru Amauta, 76
Tupac Amaru (Inca), 162–4
Tupac Amaru, Andres, 193–4
Tupac Amaru, Diego Cristobal, 192
Tupac Amaru, José Gabriel, 191–2, 194
Tupac Inca Yupanqui, Felipe Velasco, 194
Tupac Yupanqui (Inca), 56, 72, 84
Tupaj Catari, 191–5, 211 n.
Tupiza, 191, 193
tupu (or *topo*), 93 n., 222

Ugarte, Ruben Vargas, 252
Uhle, Max, 55
Ulloa, Antonio de and Jorge Juan y Santacilia, 173, 176, 183
urban architecture, 125–30
Urcon, 86
Urteaga, H. H., 20, 82, 83, 252
Uru, 11–12, 14, 47, 65, 66, 69, 186, 207
Urubamba, 50, 59, 86, 125, 127, 161, 162, 163, 164, 218

Valcarcel, Luis E., 19, 140
Valladolid, Congregation of, 16, 165
Valverde, Vicente de, 226
Velasco, Juan de, 186

Viacha, 191
Vicaquirao, 86
vicuña, 90, 161, 222
Vilcabamba, 86, 116, 162
Villamil de Rada, Emeterio, 2
Violich, Francis, 125, 230
Virajocha, 13, 41, 44, 45, 47–8, 68, 74, 76, 81, 131, 132, 139, 227
Viracocha Inca, 84, 85–6, 131, 132
Viscarra, Eufronio, 201
Vitcos, 161, 162, 163, 164, 180, see also Vilcabamba

Whitaker, A. P., 171 *n.*
Whitelocke, General, 198

Xeres, Francisco de, 20, 97

Yahuar Huacac (Inca), 84
yanacona, 173, 180–1
Yungas, 51, 164, 206, 217, 237, 238, 244, 245, 246, 250, 251

Zárate, Agustín de, 22, 27, 239

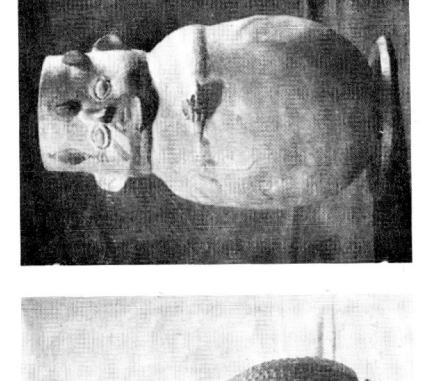
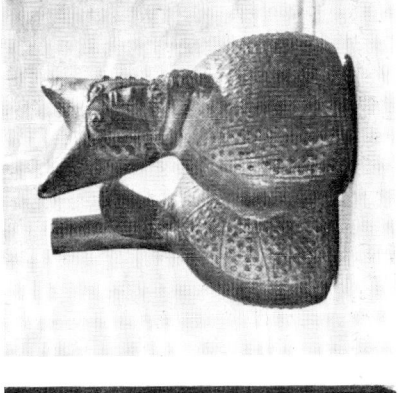

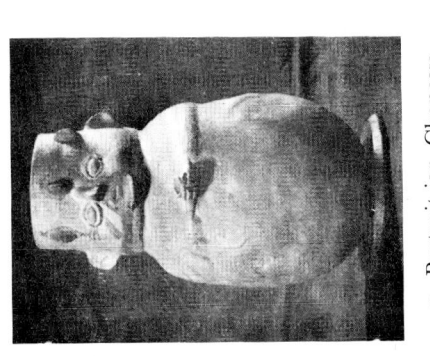
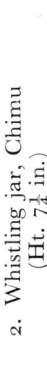

1. Portrait jar, Tihuanacu (Ht. 4¼ in.)
2. Whistling jar, Chimu (Ht. 7¼ in.)
3. Portrait jar, Chancay (Ht. 12½ in.)
4. Whistling jar, Chimu (Ht. 7¼ in.)
5. Zoomorphic jar, Chimu (Ht. 7 in.)

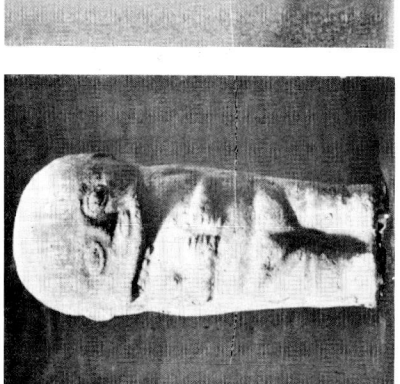
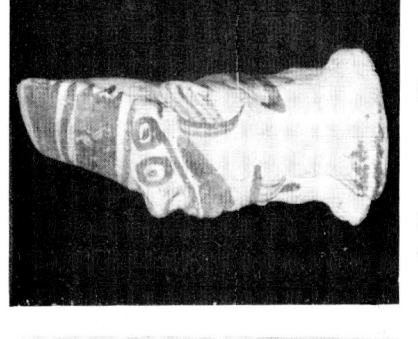

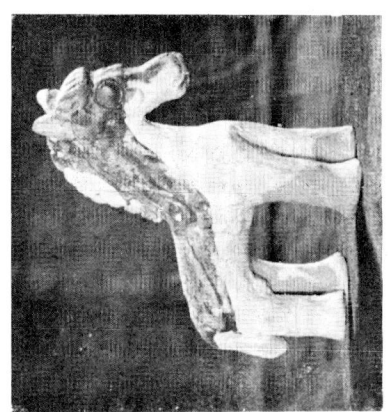

6. Terracotta, Chimu (Ht. 9½ in.)

7. Water jar, Chicama Valley (Mochica) (Ht. 10 in.)

8. Terracotta, Chancay (Ht. 8¼ in.)

9. Modern Indian terracotta figure (Ht. 4½ in.)

10. Modern Indian terracotta figure (Ht. 4¼ in.)

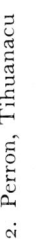

12. Perron, Tihuanacu

14. Machu Picchu

11. Sun Temple, Ollantaytambo

13. Quechuas

15. Tin Mine, Bolivia

16. Tihuanacu sculpture

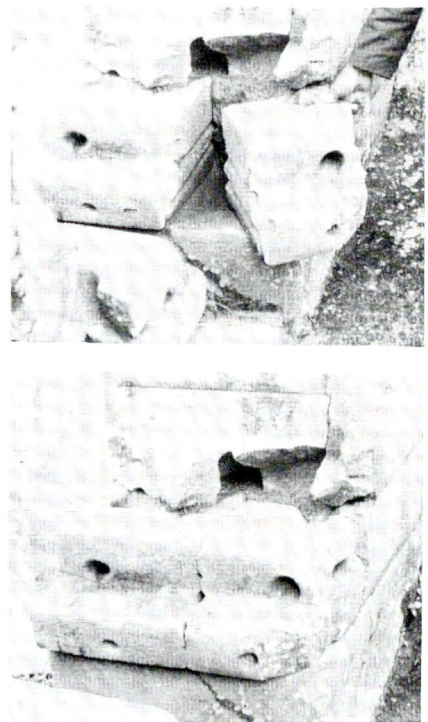

17. (*a*) and (*b*) Stone work, Machu Picchu

19. Tihuanacu village

18. Indians with Llamas

21. Coca drying-floor

20. Coca Plantations

22. Indian quarter, La Paz

23. Llamas, La Paz

24. Aymara types

25. Chola

26. Cholo children

27. Chola street-seller

28. Cholo

29. Aymara aguayo

30. Urubamba Valley